A LOT OF WATER

OVER THE B.

Book 4 in the Saul Trauer Series

by Keith Harris

www.keithharrisauthor.com

Some of the names of the characters
in this book have been changed
in order to avoid prosecution

All rights reserved.
No part of this book may be used or reproduced
without written permission from the author

Being on a boat that's moving through the water, it's so clear. Everything falls into place in terms of what's important and what's not.
James Taylor

If I could choose the life I pleased
Then I would be a boatman
Along the canals and the rivers free
No hasty words are spoken

Levellers - The Boatman, from the album Levelling the Land

CONTENTS

Chapter 1   Westward Ho

Before leaving Saul Trader for the winter at Ventenac, I took extra care to ensure that everything was shut down and weather-proofed. I didn't really expect the temperatures to get as low as freezing this far south but then with the sort of freak conditions that seemed to be affecting countries all around the world as a result, or so we were led to believe, of 'global warming' or 'climate change', anything could happen. The fact that Rob would be spending a fair bit of time on 'Pisgah' just a few boats away, also helped to lessen any anxiety .

After spending another couple of months back in England, sorting out the paperwork and bills that had piled up in my absence, I deployed my customary escape routine and disappeared to the Far East for the rest of the winter. When I returned in the April I had another mountain of admin to wade through and some work on my narrowboat at Stockton to sort out before I could finally get back to the south of France, and Saul Trader.

The reason that I have bored you with detail in the previous paragraph is merely to explain why it was that nearly ten months had elapsed before I set eyes on the boat again at the beginning of July.

And I paid the price - not for the mooring I hasten to add as I was never charged a bean for that probably due to the vagaries of the French system. They had my bank details and a signed direct debit but for reasons known only to them it was never activated.

No, the 'price' was two solid days spent cleaning up. The boat was absolutely covered with tree bark and sap that was stuck stubbornly to the paintwork. The beautiful yellow glossy finish that had cost a packet at Dordrecht had turned a dull sandy brown. It did eventually come off, after a lot of hard work and a liberal dollop of elbow grease, and the old shine gradually restored. The inside wasn't so bad, and an afternoon of dusting, polishing and hoovering soon returned the accommodation to its former glory.

My friends Pete and Kate were flying down to join me for a week but I had a few more days in hand before picking them up from the airport at Carcassonne.

By chance I had found out that a stage of the Tour de France would be passing relatively close by. I had recently splashed out on an iPad and with the help of a friendly assistant in the SFR shop in Béziers I had bought a dongle for 30 Euros which hung in the window and by some strange miracle gave me a month worth of Internet. It was all a new and rather vague technology for me but I somehow managed to grasp enough to be able to get Emails and access the net. That's how I found out that the Tour was due to pass through a town called Limoux, about 80 kilometres away, around noon the following day. It would be a new experience for both of us so Rob and I set off in the car to watch the spectacle. We arrived at Limoux at midday and although the streets were already getting crowded, we learned that the riders would not be passing through before 2.00pm. We had a bit of lunch and a beer before finding a vantage spot to await the action. I hadn't witnessed a Tour before and I have to say that I would probably not rush to see another. We stood in the crowd for two hours while various entourages came and went, with scantily clad girls throwing freebies to the excited spectators - balloons, sweets, and inflatable promotional cushions bearing sponsors' names: no condoms this time as far as I know, and the usual exhibitionist police motorcyclists swerving around, showing off and doing nothing remotely useful, and trucks with huge speakers on the back blaring out a deafening musac. This we discovered was what they call the "La Caravan." We stood at the side of a roundabout with several hundred others, eagerly awaiting the action. When it did finally happen, it happened in the blink of an eye. There was a rumble of expectation from the crowd and a flurry of excited anticipation and then the leading bunch flew past at breakneck speed without so much as a friendly wave. Then after a few more minutes the packed ranks of the Peloton followed: hundreds of bikes seemingly glued together as one then swept past with a whoosh of air and then - nothing.

"Was that it?" said Rob.

And that was it! The spectators trudged off and the street returned to normal. I'm sure that if you had the time and the local knowledge to find a remote spot on a narrow track half way up a mountain, the experience of watching the riders grind and sweat as they plodded their weary way to the summit, or even a steep downhill bit to watch them hitting stone walls and piling up one on top of another would be a far more satisfying experience, but a roundabout in the centre of Limoux did not offer a lot in the way of excitement. As usual, the best way to watch was on the dreaded gogglebox. See everything and keep up to date with commentary.

Following the crowds towards the centre of the town looking for a bar, we noticed a sign that announced "CANOE - KAYAK" in large illuminated letters. Limoux was on the River Aude. Seppe and Diwi, as well as Wilbur had often spoken about the fun they had riding the rapids, and we spontaneously decided to take a look, something which in retrospect was probably a bit foolhardy. You can always be wise after the event. We drove in the direction of the sign for three miles out of the town before coming to the hire base. It was getting on for 3.30pm but we spoke to the proprietor who assured us that the passage would take no more than a couple of hours. I think this advice was proffered more for commercial reasons than for anything to do with our proficiency, or lack of, in canoemanship.

Not wishing to appear frightened to death in the face of this challenge, we stood like lost sheep whilst we were shown a crude diagram of the route we should follow and given a printed sheet of A4 which was rudimentary to say the least. Something that sounded like a dire warning was mentioned - where to go and where not to go which I didn't understand. Rob, who spoke good French, muttered something like Christ, which I tried to ignore. Our adventurous spirit got the better of our judgement and we were relieved almost subliminally of 25 Euros each, bundled in a semi-daze into the back of a minivan, and seconds later we were heading upstream on a narrow twisting road, crash helmets and lifejackets in hand, and two battered sit-on-top kayaks bumping along behind on a trailer. As we got nearer to the launch site the butterflies were starting to gather momentum but there was no turning back now. We climbed out of the van and found ourselves on the top of a steep bank some 20 feet or so above the deceptively docile looking river with a crudely shaped corrugated shute leading into the water. Our driver gave us the last rites, sat us on the kayaks, and pushed us gently down the slope with a cheery shout of something that I didn't catch. For all I knew it might have been "See you at 5.30" or "God help you!"

Whatever, it was of no consequence now as we hit the water and the bows turned swiftly in the downstream direction. We were underway.

The first problem came at the first obstacle, just a few hundred yards away. We were rapidly approaching a lot of white foaming water which led off in at least three different directions. It suddenly hit me that we should have taken more notice of the instructions or at least tried to understand the route shown on the diagram. It was a bit late for that now as Rob's copy had been soaked on launch and all the ink had been obliterated and mine had blown away! We were approaching the danger zone at an unhealthy speed which as we got nearer revealed an awful lot of rocks and boulders sticking out of the water and I wondered about the strength of the bottom of these kayaks, when suddenly four more canoes appeared from the bank and headed for the foaming abyss. At that stage we didn't have a clue as to whether they knew any more about it than we did but instinct and fear kicked in simultaneously and we followed like lambs to the slaughter. We were immediately caught up in the swirling tumbling current, surging forward into the unknown. The last two things I remember seeing was Rob seemingly doing fine about twenty yards ahead, and the very large smooth - faced rock that my bow was about to mount. Then suddenly I was under the water and feeling rather like a pair of underpants in a washing machine. As I came to the surface my crash-helmet made contact with the top of the kayak that was now upside down and on top of me. I momentarily cursed myself for still not having made that Will I had been meaning to do for years. I could see raging water and rocks and the white of the kayak's bottom as I was swept relentlessly along two feet below the surface, and then from somewhere deep down I found the strength that comes with the thought of imminent death and managed to heave the boat out of the way and rise to the top for a gasp of air. I was still out of control and moving through the water but the kayak was now the right way up and I was clinging to the carrying handle at the back of it. Somehow I managed to steer it away from the strongest of the stream and guide it towards a shallower part of the river into more rocks. The kayak grounded with a crunch and I realised after my knees made contact with something hard that I could now stand up in the water which was waist deep, and take stock of my predicament. Rob had safely negotiated the rapids and was paddling in relatively still water about fifty yards downstream. I saw him grab something that was about to overtake him and realised what it was - my paddle! For some reason that I presume was connected to shock, I started to laugh. Rob, thank god, had managed to retrieve the paddle and started to come back upstream towards me. Once I had hold of that rather important piece of equipment I climbed back aboard and was quickly swept through the rocks and into the placid stream, coming to rest alongside Rob, who was resting on his boat with a smarmy look on his face.

"What the fuck you do that for?" he asked, as though I done it for some sort of personal satisfaction.

"Oh, I was getting bored just sitting on the thing and thought I'd practice my eskimo roll," I said, "what the hell did you think I did it for - the bloody thing capsized under me."

There was no time for protracted debate. We needed to catch up with the other crowd and hope they knew the way home. The rest of the trip went without too much incident. We caught up with the others, who had beached their boats and were actually lazing nonchalantly on the bank smoking. They turned out to be French, bloody poseurs, who we gathered had done the passage several times in the past. We decided to swallow any pride we still had and wait for them. There were a few other rapid passages that we managed to safely negotiate, following their lead as closely as we could. At one point we came to a solid wall, where the flow cascaded over the top of a ledge in a waterfall twenty feet high. One of the Frenchmen , who had obviously seen the need to look after these two ageing geriatrics, kindly got out of his boat and helped slide us over the ledge where the water was just inches deep. Once over the point of balance, the bow took a dive and we had to hang on for dear life as we were plunged into the depths below. We arrived back at the base at 6.30, a bit later than expected due to the unforeseen delays.

I hoped the owner wouldn't charge me for a dented crash hat but we managed to get our deposit returned without any awkward questions. We both agreed that it had been great fun and we wouldn't hesitate to have another go someday and we were both lying through our teeth.

I collected Pete and Kate from the airport at Carcassonne and settled them into their accommodation. We were heading to Carcassonne to watch the Bastille Day firework display, which was reputed to be the second best in France after Paris. Pete and Kate weren't quite Saul Trader virgins - the last time they had been on the boat was in 1998 on the River Severn. They lived in Stourport and came with us for a day trip when we ventured as far north as possible above the town before being warned over the VHF by a trip boat skipper that we were heading for the shallows.

I had known them for about 25 years - Pete worked with me as the manager of one of our depots in Cheltenham. He never seemed to age, still retained all his thick fair hair and his trim waist-line, and always dressed immaculately. He was one of those annoying people who could look like a million dollars wearing a potato sack and I teased him relentlessly about looking like a model from the C&A catalogue, although he assured me that he always bought his clothes from Primark!

Kate on the other hand, was a down to earth native of Dudley, in the heart of the Black Country canals, with an intelligent practical view of life and a no-nonsense attitude towards anyone who might upset her - ah, need to be on my best behaviour then! Unfortunately this resolution didn't last long, and it was only a matter of days before I faux-pas-ed somewhat embarrassingly. We spent a couple of days going in the opposite direction, back to Capestang and Sallèlles d'Aude before heading west. On the way to Homps, where we stopped for the night, we passed the large port at Argens-Minervois, home to a Locoboat fleet and watched over by the Church of St Roch, that stood haughtily high above the town. My indiscretion came as we approached the double lock staircase at Pechlaurier.

These locks appear quite suddenly around a very tight right-angled bend, which means that you don't see them until you are virtually on top of them. We rounded the bend to find four hire boats lined up waiting to go through. There was just enough room behind the last one to get alongside: at least I thought there was but soon realised that the gap was about a metre short. The guy on the boat ahead dithered and fannied about trying to push our bow away from his vulnerable plastic as I became more and more agitated. There was a hotel boat coming down through the bottom lock and I really needed to get out of his way. After at least five minutes of shouting at him it suddenly dawned on him that all he needed to do was to pull his little bathtub a couple of yards forward into the space to give me enough room to get alongside.

I muttered sarcastically to myself.

"Thank you very much you fucking twat!"

Just enough room to pass at Pechlaurier

Unfortunately my mutter was a bit too loud and I heard a quiet cough from behind me. I looked around and saw that Kate had appeared and was standing on the other side of the wheelhouse, just feet away.

I turned a whiter shade of pale as I realised my gaff and attempted an apology, which only served to make matters worse.

"Shit! I'm sorry Kate - heat of the moment and all that."

I don't really think it worked and she was understandably a bit on the cold side towards me for the rest of the day. Well if you don't like bargee slang you shouldn't mix with bargees. Coming from a Black Country background I'm sure she had heard worse. It was all soon forgotten I'm glad to say and I don't think it spoilt their week. (*Mind you they haven't been back since, have they eh? Ed*)

At Homps I called in to report to the Capitan in the tourist office, which is situated on the quay in the old port building. There is a display on the wall showing all the wines produced in the Occitaine, with handily accessible retail opportunities. We took advantage of the free first night which includes water and electricity which in my view is a great way to encourage boaters to spend a few Euros in the restaurants and shops to put a bit back into the local economy. English canalside local authorities take note.

A few hundred metres south of the town on the D610 there is a service station with an excellent grocery where we filled several baskets with provisions, to satisfy our needs and to ease our consciences. Remember to take your own carrier bags with you to supermarkets and stores as the French will charge if you don't have them, a practice that has been in force for many years in France, another example of our Gallic friends being light years ahead of us ancient Britons!

We had a lazy morning sleeping off the effects of a late night and post prandial vino and cribbage session and pottered a few kilometres further to the large lake at Jouarre. There are swimming facilities and sailing boats here and we took a lunchtime dip in the deep, clear, but not so warm waters. I was always a bit wary of swimming in rivers and lakes in France -

too many tales of cat-fish the size of sharks for my liking. Old waves tales they may have been, but the thought of suddenly coming face to face with one with its hideous whiskers and walrus-like fangs somewhat tempered my enthusiasm. Nevertheless it was cool and refreshing and set us up nicely for the rest of the day. Passing through the single lock at Jouarres and the small town of La Redorte we came to the double lock staircase at L'Aiguille, just past the town of Puchéric. These locks stick in my memory for two quite different reasons - the weird and wonderful contraptions that line the lock-sides like a rusting metallic army, and the lock-keeper who doesn't like boats disturbing his reverie.

The "army" is a collection of models that are made out of bits of scrap metal and iron and are ingeniously mobile with moving parts, some of which are connected to the lock mechanisms. Thus when a paddle is drawn, all hell breaks loose as a rusty figure on a bicycle pedals frantically as the paddle gear moves up and down, a moustachioed musician with the appearance of a Mexican Mariachi starts to strum his guitar, a jogger with a head made from a motorcycle seat stamps his feet and swings his arms, an array of farmyard animals clatter and rattle their feet, and a toff in a suit and tie turns his head and noisily head-butts the rusty metal floozy standing suggestively alongside him. Elephants, pigs, giant grass-hoppers, cockerels , rhinos and giraffes, all welded together from bits of old cars, tin boxes, drain pipes and bicycle spokes combine to add to the general cacophony.

This is all very exciting but can distract boaters from doing what they should essentially be doing, and tending their lines. The whole display was the brainchild of the encumbent éclusier, a Monsieur Joel Bärthe, and whether or not he is still working there I'm not sure. The present éclusier spends most of his time fraternising with his adoring public often to the detriment of the hard-pressed boater, who really just wants to get through his bloody locks and back to the peace of the canal. I have passed through these locks several times over the last few years and I have always been made to wait while Monsieur entertains his fans, regaling them no doubt with the amount of time he took fashioning some monstrosity or other. Once I was held above the top lock for forty minutes, getting blown around in the wind and totally ignored by the lockie, in spite of, or more probably because of, issuing several blasts of the horn. The man, in my humble opinion, is a bit of a menace, more interested in his sideshow than carrying out the job for which after all he is paid to do. (*finished now? Ed*).

We finally left the Symphonie L'Aiguille behind and sped off with a friendly wave.

One kilometre further on, just before the Aqueduc St-Martin, I spied the unmistakable stern of Johanna, tied to the tree roots, with the lovely Diwi dancing and waving and beckoning us like the Siren to tie alongside: and that was the end of our day's run. We had covered all of thirteen kilometres and passed through five locks! It didn't take Diwi very long to convince us that we had to stay for the night. She was cooking up some delight and Seppe was collecting the eccentric Wilbur, the Patrick Moore of the telescope world, who would be staying overnight before setting off for San Francisco to lecture at a conference where anyone who was anyone telescopic-wise would be in attendance. Diwi produced some excellent coffee and glasses of chilled rosé and we lounged on one of Seppe's creations on the deck soaking up the sun and catching up on the news.

Wilbur turned up on the back of Seppe's ancient Indian motorbike at about 4 o'clock in his favourite "holy" T shirt with a world travelled rucksack slung on his back.

Any ideas we may have had about a late afternoon siesta soon went out of the window as Seppe announced that he needed some help to "harvest" some bamboo canes he had just happened to notice growing near the canal a few hundred metres away.

So off we went, armed with machetes and a wheelbarrow to the chosen spot. We first had to clamber down a fairly steep overgrown bank of long grass before setting about cutting the canes, that stubbornly refused to be severed but eventually capitulated and were dragged up to the towpath and loaded onto the barrow. After an hour of sweated labour, Seppe decided he had enough for the project. He had rescued some one inch angled steel from a déchetterie somewhere and cut and welded them together to form the frame for a double bed. The bamboo canes were cut to length and served as the base onto which was placed the double mattress which he had rescued from another déchetterie somewhere else!

Such was the ingenuity and self-sufficiency that enabled the two of them to live this life that they had chosen on a very limited budget. And we weren't finished yet. We were going to earn our dinner. The Indian had developed a slow puncture in the back tyre which needed fixing. In the absence of a suitable jack and stands, the bike had to be lifted manually while Seppe set about removing the wheel. Pete and I took one side each and Wilbur did try to help but ended up being more of a hindrance. We did manage to find some wooden blocks which I told Wilbur to put underneath the frame to give us a bit of respite while the puncture was located by the age-old method of submersion in a bucket of water, and the offending hole sealed with a rubber solution and a patch. Repairs completed, the wheel was replaced, and Seppe went off along the towpath for a trial run.

"No more than ninety now," I shouted - "in first gear," but the irony was lost as he disappeared in a cloud of smoke.

Another friend turned up - just in time for dinner 'conveniently,' and announced himself as Dog. Diwi enthused that Dog was existing by cleverly defrauding the state using some little-known loophole that I couldn't get my head around.

Percy at Puchéric on another occasion, not taking much notice of the Mariachi ......or the boat

Over the years I had met many of these barrack-room lawyer socialists who abused the system to the detriment of honest tax-paying law-abiding citizens and to be honest I wasn't particularly comfortable with it. I always thought that if these people put their creative abilities to legal use they could probably benefit society and make a healthy living in the process. I kept my mouth firmly shut however, as I didn't want to upset our beautiful hosts or, more to the point, compromise the meal that was simmering away below and smelling delicious. After our fish curry and apple and raspberry (scrumped from the wild naturally) crumble ,we sat on the deck with Bob Marley and a couple of funny-smelling cigarettes that Seppe produced and chewed the cud until after midnight.

Wilbur spent the night out on the deck on the newly constructed bed before Seppe delivered him on the pillion to the airport at Carcassonne from where he was flying via London and a look in on his mother, who lived in Sidcup. I sincerely hoped she might persuade him to change into a half decent shirt, even possibly one with a collar for the trip, but I had my doubts.

He was flying business class on BA, courtesy of the organisation that he was due to address, and I tried to imagine the look on the faces of his fellow travellers as he took his seat in 5A. We bumped into Wilbur several times over the next few years - he seemed to follow Johanna around like a puppy dog. He was a bit of a latter day Robinson Crusoe and certainly made the most of his carefree life on the cut. He had an ancient Raleigh Stowaway folding bike and a rubber inflatable canoe, and one his favourite outings was to pack the canoe into the shopping basket on the bike, cycle fourteen or fifteen kilometres on the towpath to a spot where the River Aude ran parallel with the canal, blow up the canoe, fold up the bike and put it into the boat, then paddle back down the river to his starting point, probably stopping en route to gather some wild nuts and berries for his lunch - perfick! The last I heard he had set up a hippy commune high in the Pyrenees Mountains and had surrounded himself with a harem of like-minded ageing hippy women - no doubt spending the nights gazing into the heavens.

We had another lazy day - 9 kilometres and 8 locks, and spent the night on a convenient wooden jetty at Marseillettes, where the only restaurant was closed, the bar was not open, and the small épicerie had run out of bread and cakes! Pete did manage to climb the hill in the morning for fresh baguettes and pain au chocolats. At Trèbes we moored on the quay a bit too close to the row of restaurants for my liking, and had to weave our bow rope underneath one of the tables to secure it to a mooring ring. Opposite was a beautiful barge, the Berendina, immaculate in every detail, making Saul Trader look somewhat shabby in comparison. People were always admiring Saul Trader and commenting on the elegant sweep of the sheer and the gracefulness of the lines. It was often mistaken for a converted original Dutch vessel, even by Dutchmen themselves. Berendina was in another class I have to say and one reason for this was that she had a permanently employed skipper cum engineer cum maintenance man cum caretaker. We met him in a bar near to the boat and he told us that the owner was too busy running his empire to spend much time aboard. He was also afraid to drive it himself and left it to the skipper to bring it from Homps, where it was permanently moored, to Trèbes once a year, where the owner threw lavish parties for some of his best clients.

It was the 13th July, and Trèbes, in an attempt to wrong-foot Carcassonne's Bastille Day celebrations, held its own feu d'artifice, a brilliant display of pyrotechnics which we watched from the bridge over the Aude, the sky lit up with a thousand sparkling coloured leaves that reflected and then fell into the water. Even at 70, I could never resist the opportunity of a good firework display, and I think it is perhaps one example of the dreaded Health and Safety providing a benefit. In the old days growing up in Hastings, my father always made the effort to build a bonfire in the back garden and fork out from his meagre earnings for a couple of boxes of fireworks. The inevitable Catherine wheels that were nailed to a washing line prop and would never spin properly, penny bangers that would fizz and splutter before giving up the ghost for good, packets of sparklers that burned your fingers, and the odd five shilling rocket that would barely reach the height of the house before the stick came thudding down inches from your head. I fondly remember the morning after on the walk to school, picking up burned out rockets and banger carcasses that had landed in the streets. These days firework displays are grand events, albeit perhaps a bit sterile, where organisers pay thousands of pounds for the most exotic and expensive examples of the art of the pyrotechnician, all remotely controlled, safe and utterly spectacular - entry five pounds! Towns and villages across the world put on fantastic displays, vying with each other for supremacy - and its not confined to November 5th either. These events are spread over two bloody weeks. There is something about a firework display that has an undying appeal for young and old. They used to have a fantastic bonfire in Battle, a few miles from Hastings, and the site of the battle. The local bonfire society built a huge bonfire on the green in front of the Abbey and would parade down the narrow High Street with flaming torches, Satanic themed floats, bugle bands, and a massive effigy of the head of someone who had recently been in the news. Over the years I remember seeing Fidel Castro, Nigel Mansell, Maggie Thatcher and Dennis Healy go up in a plume of fire on the top of the huge pyre. All the pubs removed carpets and furniture and anything else that might be seen as fuel to add to the fire and stayed open late. I think it still happens, but it now takes place in the middle of a field and you have to pay to watch. All the atmosphere and excitement diluted in the name of health and safety.

Unbelievably , at the very moment that I was writing these few words about our time in Trébes, I was sitting in a remote Isaan village near the small market town of Buachet in Eastern Thailand, 20 kilometres or so from the Cambodian border, where peasant farmers tend their smallholdings of rice paddies and rubber trees and ferry their produce on ancient carts driven by petrol engines that sit high up in front of the driver who steers the contraption with a handlebar attached to a long prop shaft that propels the front wheels, and survive on a meagre income of two or three pounds a day. I was gazing out of the window overlooking this flat and remote peaceful landscape, dotted coconut palms swaying gently in the breeze, and pondering my next sentence. It was as far removed from the affluence of Western Europe as can be imagined. As I stood there absent-mindedly watching a group of workers covered from the heat in loose baggy trousers and smocks and large floppy coolie hats, lazily swatting bamboo cane with machetes, I became vaguely aware of the BBC World News bulletin that was playing quietly in the background. My attention was sparked alive as I thought I heard the word "Trébes" mentioned. Surely I must have misheard it. I went back into the room and stood aghast in front of the TV. As the story slowly unfolded it transpired that a gunman, thought to be an Islamic terrorist, had shot a policeman in Carcassonne and escaped to Trèbes where he had killed at least two people and taken hostages in a supermarket in the unassuming canal-side town. I stood transfixed watching the transmission with a hollow feeling in my stomach. It seemed so unreal, so futile and senseless. What could possibly drive anyone to carry out such an atrocity, an affront, on innocent people in the name of what - what bloody god has advocated such an outrage. I tried to continue with my writing but somehow everything seemed to pale into a pointless insignificance. I was just completely stunned by the events that had taken place in Trébes and it brought home to me just how close to home these things can happen. I had another glass of wine and went to bed but I couldn't sleep. Next morning I heard that a Gendarme who had bravely volunteered to take the place of one of the hostages, had died from his wounds and police had shot and killed the gunman. An illogical thought went through my mind. Which one would be getting the blonde virgins, the man who unselfishly sacrificed his life to save another, or the murderer who brutally took three innocent civilian lives?

Fast asleep in the dawn of ages
The soul of every child
Has waited to be born a stranger
Underneath the drum of his mothers heart

Lying deep in a dream of darkness
Where fear has never gone
Each spark of a life is started
Blind and pure to the world we come
Blind and pure to the world we come

Each of us a dancer to the drum
Each of us a dancer to the drum
Blind and pure we come

One is born to a life of hunger
One will be a king or a rich man's son
One will kill out of greed or anger
One will give his life for another one

There are smiles in the lies of innocence
There are blooms in the walls of stone
And we will see ourselves
In the eyes of everyone we have ever known
Everyone we have ever known

Beth Nielsen Chapman - Dancer to the Drum

We arrived at Carcassonne at 3.00pm on the following afternoon and found Rob on Pisgah tied to a tree again - I was starting to wonder about Rob. Pisgah was actually tied to tree roots and Rob had done a bit of the Dutch trick and managed to keep a space just big enough for Saul Trader astern. Tying to the roots is in itself a tricky business, involving some contorting of the body and delicate balancing on the steep banks to avoid tipping over into the cut. We were about five hundred metres from the basin in the centre of Carcassonne. The canal is built on a level above the town which gave us uninterrupted distant views of the Citadel, from whose battlements the fireworks would be set off. Rob's partner Wendy and his son Jules arrived with his wife Jess - Seppe and Diwi turned up, and it was decided that we would all dine together on Pisgah's stern deck. Diwi would take care of the hors d'ouevre, or horses' doovers, Rob would barbecue the prawns, and we would provide the dessert. Well, for "we" read Pete. He had been a chef in a former life and was keen to show off his culinary prowess with a strawberry meringue galette and if that wasn't enough, a Tarte Tatin for anyone who might still be hungry! My meagre contribution was to supply the Vin Rosé.

I would love to be able to describe what I am assured was a superb display of fireworks, but alas, I over- indulged in the food and more pointedly, the wine, fell into a sound and peaceful sleep, and didn't wake up until it was all over - and I hadn't even seen a bloody sparkler.

By mid-afternoon the next day most of the boats had left and spaces closer to the town began to materialise. I wanted somewhere reasonably secure to leave Saul Trader as I was going on a three week trip around Europe by train. Carcassonne was typical of tourist spots in that it did tend to attract more than its share of beggars and drop-outs, who spent a lot of their time on the grass banks beside the canal. The port itself was crowded and out of the question for that length of time. I spoke to the young lady Capitan who suggested the off-side of the canal on the Trèbes side of Carcassonne centre past the moorings that were reserved for the depot of a hire boat company. This was far enough away from the centre but I couldn't get the boat anywhere near the bank because of the depth. I tried several places, prodding about with the shaft, but there was nowhere with more than a couple of feet of water - and we had a draught of 1.1 metres. (*We know that now - ed*)

I spoke to an Englishman from Norwich on a peculiar craft with the cabin roof completely covered in solar panels. He suggested that there was about 20 metres of space at the Carcassonne end close to the railway bridge that was not used by the hire company. When I expressed doubts about the security there he came out with a theory that I had to admit did make sense.

"That a be no different to anywheres ellse," he said in his lilting singing postman accent, "you'd be jest as like broke into over there as over hare."

Well that was reassuring!

" An I'll tell er somethink ellse. Once you go away you be worrying fer ten minute then you forget all abowt it till you get back. So you just go an enjoy yerself."

He was quite right of course. The mooring by the bridge was just right, with plenty of water and bollards to secure the lines.

We had a free day before Pete and Kate were due to leave so we took the bus from the Place du Dôme (fare 1 Euro) to visit the ancient walled Cité, that sits in a commanding position on the top of a steep hill overlooking the new part of Carcassonne. The fortified town dates back to the Roman Empire (3rd and 4th Centuries AD). It fell into ruin after being used as a garrison and was restored in the 19th Century. It is quite an amazing place to visit, although inside the walls it has been somewhat vandalised by the development of rows of souvenir shops and cafés - another sign of the times in this tourist-dominated age. A walk around the top of the walls is well worth the entry price giving expansive views over the area, with the town to the North, and the Aude Valley and the distant Pyrenees to the South. It's a lively place with street musicians, mime artists and trips on one of those awful road trains and a horse-drawn bus. I suppose it's one of those places you just <u>have</u> to see before you die. Back in the town we wandered for an hour or so window-shopping in the Rue Pietonne (Walking Street) before returning to the boat.

I started to get things sorted out before I left the boat unattended for three weeks. I stowed any portable items down below in the belief that out of sight was out of mind - any ropes not being used went down into the forward locker, shafts and boat hooks went below as well as lifebelts, deck chairs, mops and brooms and the British red ensign, which I always worried, in a state of illogical paranoia, could provide the proverbial red flag to the proverbial bull. In the evening we ate in a nice little friendly Italian restaurant alongside the canal opposite our mooring and finished off with a couple of beers in a bar with live music, albeit French live music. They are still some way behind the rest of the World in their musical taste I feel. We chatted to a Welshman who I had spoken to at the boat in the morning. I assumed he was a tourist but as is often the case, one shouldn't make assumptions. I was intrigued to see him again in the bar with a French family, and speaking fluent French. It turned out that he was a rugby player who had played for Wigan and transferred codes and countries to play for Toulouse. He had retired after an injury and married a French girl. He still looked very fit to me, built like a brick outhouse, and I told him I wouldn't particularly fancy running flat out into him.

"Maybe a couple of years ago, " he said modestly, "nowadays you'd probably knock me flat."

With his sixteen or seventeen solid stones I somehow doubted it.

Another benefit of our new-found mooring was that the station was no more than five minutes walk away. Pete and Kate caught the airport shuttle bus to their morning Ryanair flight to Bournemouth, and I was on the 11.05 smart new Duplex TGV to Marseilles. As the train pulled slowly out of the station, I looked down from the bridge at Saul Trader sitting like a dog whose master has just abandoned him and uttered a silent prayer that the boat would be unmolested during my absence. Then I forgot all about it as I watched the landscape of Southern France flash past from my grandstand seat on the upper deck as we hurried through the Camargue countryside, catching occasional glimpses of the Mediterranean Sea and some familiar snapshots of the Canal du Midi.

Chapter 2   Midi to Toulouse

I returned three weeks later to find Saul Trader exactly as I had left it: no sign of any forced entry, no parish notices stuck in the window by the VNF, and no graffiti daubed by anti-British, anti capitalist vandals. As I began to get things ship-shape again, I had a visit from the singing postman.

"Ever think all right then? Told yer not to worry didn't I?"

Rob had moved Pisgah back to Ventenac and came up on the train to give a hand on the final leg of the Midi to Toulouse - all uphill now and not the easiest locks to operate single-handed. The first obstacle was the tiny Pont Marengo bridge below the Carcassonne lock. Du Breil showed it as being 3.33 metres at the highest point, 6 metres wide, and just 2.36 metres high at the sides. Not a lot to play with then. To make things more difficult, and worrying, the lock was in continuous use by the Bateaux Mouche that plied up and down crammed with photo-stick wielding grockels. They were given priority over pleasure craft which sometimes meant having to wait for the lock for fifteen or twenty minutes, drifting about in the wind and the wash. All this in front of hundreds more rubber-necking gongoozlers lining the lock sides hoping for a disaster. No pressure then!

We had taken the precaution of lowering the boiler chimney and closing the wheelhouse doors and we eventually got a green light to enter. Rob stood on the bow watching the clearance. It was essential to keep the boat exactly central and the only way to do this was by going very slowly and using the bow-thrusters to keep the boat straight. Too much speed, and trying to check it with reverse gear would end in trouble as the prop wash kicked the stern to one side, and into contact with the slope of the arch. Immediately past the bridge was the lock and we graciously, and slowly, edged forward. Once in the lock it was necessary to steer right or left to the wall but it was important not to start this until well clear of the bridge. All in all it was a fairly tricky job but I think we passed the audition.

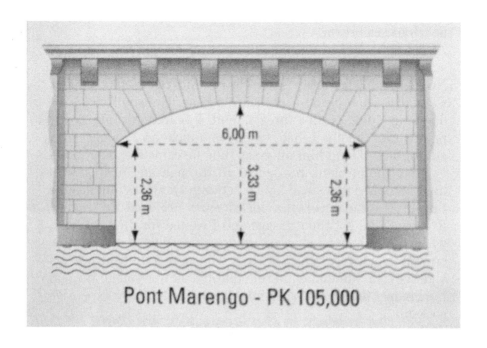

Pont Marengo - PK 105,000

Dimensions of the low bridge below the lock at Carcassonne. Du Breil warns ' to avoid accident, you should approach this bridge slowly and ask all your crew members to keep their heads down! '

Rob, after he had come back to earth from the sight of the young nubile lock-keeper who was showing as much sun-tanned leg as was morally possible below her miniscule patch of cut-off denim shorts, threw her a rope which she turned around a bollard and tossed back. We slowly ascended and motored out into a large basin with a Canalous hire base, several jetties for the trip boats, and a line of barges moored to the opposite wall. Rob coiled down the lines and came back to the wheelhouse.

"Fookin 'ell," was all he could manage, and I wasn't sure whether he was referring to the narrow squeeze under the bridge or the amount of flesh exposed by the éclusière - and I didn't like to ask!

The rest of the trip was fairly uneventful - well for us anyway. We stopped at Bram where we were entertained by the mother of storms, but luckily only had to dash a few feet from the boat into the L'Ile aux Oiseaux, (lucky on two counts as we only got in because of a late cancellation), where we enjoyed some delicious sea bream.

At the approach to Castelnaudary there are several flights of staircase locks and I got very pissed off with an Italian in a Noddy boat who drove standing up and ricocheted off lock walls like a marble in a pinball machine. He would not slow down in spite of my threats, and I feared for my costly paintwork. Finally I had taken as much as I could take, attempting to fend him off every time he came crashing into a lock and point-blank refused to go through any further with him. I stopped in a small lay-by between two locks and despite the protestations of the lock-keeper, refused to budge. Eventually he got the message and I waited for the next boat, which as it happened, was another hire boat but this time crewed by a lovely family of Scots who were long-time boaters and knew the fundamental rule that the slower you go the less the chance there is of an almighty and potentially expensive cock-up.

At the top of the four lock St-Roch staircase (9.42m rise) which is operated by an éclusier who sits half way up the flight in a tall lookout tower reminiscent of a concentration camp, we entered the large expanse of the Grande Bassin at Castelnaudary, largely devoid of any suitable visitor moorings surprisingly, and headed for the small bridged gap on the far side to enter Le Port. Castelnaudary is a popular mooring stop and boats lined both sides of the canal for about 500 metres. The friendly attractive Capitan found us just enough space after persuading a couple of hire boats to shift up together, we paid up for a two night stay and nestled alongside the quay where for the first time on this trip we had the luxury of electricity, water and wifi. The umbilical cord was retrieved from its locker and plugged in to the shoreside socket and we placed the magic magnetic card supplied by the Capitan on the top of the borne - and hey presto - we were connected. The speciality of the area is a dish known as Cassoulet, a sort of stew made with pork, duck and beans. We ordered one from the Capitanerie (we thought it rude not to) and it was delivered to the boat in a porcelain casserole dish which was included in the price!   We polished it off with a bottle of rosé - the cassoulet that is, not the dish .

The railway station is a five minute downhill fold-up bike ride away and I took the Brompton to La Gare (I know that it's "la" as I was told, by a lady incidentally, that the way to remember it is that trains go in and out of it so by inference it must be female), and caught the train to Lézignan, from where I cycled the ten kilometres or so to Ventenac to retrieve the car. The Brompton is a wonderful British invention, and the best of its type in the world (*imho* as they say in textspeak), but there's no way I would want to do much more than ten kilometres on one. Of necessity, they have very small wheels and it is difficult to sit high enough to be able to stretch out the legs whilst pedalling. Fortunately the route from Lézignan was fairly level and with the wind astern I completed the voyage in under 45 minutes.

Back at Castelnaudary, we found a nice little bar (cycling is thirsty work) not far from the quay, Le Grand, with an interior not unlike a typical London city pub with wood panelling, and refreshed ourselves with a couple of glasses of bière a la pression, before partaking of one of my favourite French dishes, porc filet mignon with potatoes au gratin, in a quayside restaurant, Le Cassoulet Gourmande.

At Le Ségala a kindly English gentleman who introduced himself as Ray, and who had retired to France some twenty years ago and whose house we moored alongside, gave us two bags of lettuces and tomatoes from his garden.

"Only me now and I'll never get through that lot," he told us sadly.

The only restaurant was fully booked but the propriétaire agreed to do a take-away cassoulet for us - dish not included this time. Between here and our next overnight stop at Gardouche, there is what I think must be a unique motorway service area at Port Lauragais. This particular Aire serves motorists on the A61 Autoroute des Deux Mers, that connects Narbonne and Toulouse. The rest area is situated beside a small lake next to the canal and tired drivers can relax from hours of travelling at 120 kilometres per hour on picnic benches beside the water and watch the boats cruising past at a leisurely 6 kph. There are moorings and a hire base on the lake and I nosed Saul Trader into the entrance intending to stop for lunch and then thought better of it. There wasn't a lot of space and I was worried about the depth. I didn't really fancy the idea of getting stuck on the mud in front of so many spectators. We were getting a bit lazy in the self-catering department but at Gardouche we did manage to use up some of our donated salad , the healthy aspect of which we balanced with some fried potatoes.

We had met an interesting couple on a hire boat while we were at Le Ségala. Tom told us he was still in the Royal Navy after 45 years of service and his wife Anne was a retired Wren. She had apparently left the service with a 'nice little earner of a pension' twenty years ago. They were regular hirers in France and had spent a number of holidays on the Midi. They went ahead of us and a couple of days later we came across them again at the lock at Montgiscard on their way back to their base at Castelnaudary. Tom was a large gregarious man with a thick Cockney accent. I joked about Pussers being the worst boat handlers I had ever seen and told him about the antics of the sailors on their sponsored narrowboats in England. As he left the lock I gave him a mock salute and off they went. Rob, who had walked ahead to the lock as they came through, showed me a calling card which Tom's wife had given him. I couldn't believe what I saw. Tom, according to his very official looking card, was no less than Lieutenant Commander (wait for it, you lucky people) Tommy Trinder! The card certainly looked genuine and my first thought was that his parents must have had a sense of humour. There was an Email address and I did contact him as I was interested to know more about him, but sadly never got a reply, so I still don't know whether it was a ruse or not. If you ever read this Tommy, doubtful as that is, please get in touch with me and we'll catch up over a pint or two.

Above the lock at Montgiscard there is a very nice off-side mooring on a small wharf with a pizza take-away restaurant just across the road. It didn't take much thought to pass up on the idea of another salad so we tied there for the night. The pizzas were excellent - and there was a bar next door with outside tables where we passed the time waiting for the food with a couple of demi-pressions. The French surpass the Italians when it comes to this variety of convenience food in my opinion, but please don't quote me as I am no authority on the subject. Strangely, Rob consumed his with relish. I say strangely, as several years earlier in Maubeuge, we almost starved to death when Robert threw his toys out of the pram and refused point-blank to even enter a MacDonalds. By the time we had toured the streets in vain, everywhere else had closed. Rob prided himself as a fully paid up member of the Society for those who have never been into a Tesco's - bloody snob!

"Wouldn't be seen dead eating a bloody big Mac," he insisted, obviously preferring to die on the pavement outside.

From here we had a fairly easy run of 20 kilometres and two locks to the port of St Sauveur, right in the heart of Toulouse. We passed through the lock we came to know as "Pizza Lock," where Rob inadvertently closed the gates on a small cruiser that had just cast off from the opposite bank, hoping to muscle into the lock with us. Once the magic button is pushed there is no turning back, and my attempt at an apologetic wave was met with an icy stare. Oh well you can't please all the people all the time. The last lock before the pound to Toulouse is Castanet. It is 5 metres deep and has a well patronised restaurant alongside which was packed with lunch-time trade. There were tables outside close to the edge of the lock - not the sort of location for a cock-up like hanging up the boat on a snagged rope or smashing into a gate, and we duly took all precautions to avoid an accident. We passed the Haute Nautique of Port Sud at Ramonville Ste Agne and the imposing dry docks at the VNF yard at Pont des Demoiselles, places I would get to know well over the next few years, and arrived at the more central Haute Nautique of Saint-Sauveur at midday, and tied on the towpath side just outside the port. The area around here bustles with activity day and night. Joggers and kamikaze lycra-clad buttock cyclists racing along the towpath, crash-hatted heads down, oblivious to any form of human life. There is a busy Pompiers depot here, the sound of their two tones blasting out every few minutes signifying another desperate emergency, or as Rob commented each time they sped off and motorists scattered in their wake, diving on to the pavements to let them pass.

"Another cat stuck up a tree then!"

The port itself was surrounded with high-security palisade fencing with castration-ready pointed spikes and gates protected by strong locks and in retrospect I suppose it should have told me something. The port looked full (well that was my excuse) and my misguided sense of economy prevented even asking the question about the overnight mooring charge. False economy Lesson number two. In a text book example of bolting horses and the closing of stable doors, saving, as I later discovered, a paltry 50 Euros for two nights mooring with electricity, water and security, cost me an alarming one thousand five hundred pounds sterling.

'How?' I hear you cry. Quite easily as it happens.

I had become increasingly nervous as darkness descended and the two-wheel murderers had returned to their apartments to admire their biceps and measure their ever-decreasing waistlines. The joggers had retired complacently to the bars to replace the 150 calories they had lost on their twenty minute run to recover from the exertion by adding several hundred more in alcoholic sustenance, and in their place shady characters who looked as though they had come straight from the pages of a Dickens novel, slowly and insidiously infiltrated the area. Two of them sat right outside the boat talking quietly to themselves. I wasn't over the moon about it but as Rob said, they would hardly make themselves so obvious if they had any harmful intent. Any sane intelligent person would have immediately taken precautions to safeguard their possessions, but this was Harris we're talking about here - the innocent abroad who never really saw any evil in anyone: a trusting and naive complete bloody idiot! The idiot who in spite of everything left two beautiful Brompton fold-up bicycles chained on the foredeck in the illogical belief that no-one, but no-one, would possibly be in possession of a pair of bolt croppers and would want to cut the chain and carry them off in the dead of night. Which of course is exactly what happened.

I checked outside before turning in at around 11.30. The two somewhat "iffy" looking characters were still talking quietly on the bench outside the boat but there was nothing I could do about it and as far as I knew they weren't breaking any laws. In the middle of the night I stirred at the sound of voices but in my comatose state dismissed it as people walking past on the towpath, and immediately went back to sleep.

In the morning I was in the wheelhouse having breakfast when I suddenly noticed a glaring space on the foredeck alongside the winch - the space where just yesterday my two lovely Bromptons sat side by side unmolested. At first I couldn't believe they had gone. I ran to the bow and there on the deck lay the severed chain - all that remained of the bicycles. I had owned one of them for over 20 years when the price of the standard model was just £425.00. I was soon to find out just what their popularity and inflation had done to their price. New replacements would cost a staggering £1000 each. Rob appeared and told me that he too had heard voices and he too had dismissed them and gone back to sleep. Once reality had sunk in I decided that the first thing to do was to contact the police. I hadn't a clue as to where the nearest Gendarmerie might be so I went to ask the Capitan at the port. Madame the Capitan wasn't very helpful to say the least. I had to contact her through the intercom on the gate as I didn't have access to the port and trying to get her to understand my plight was not easy. A little knowledge is a dangerous thing and that certainly applied to my limited knowledge of the French language. I could just about communicate my request in French but the "dangerous" bit came with the response. The French always rattled out the most obscure diatribe when they replied, even when the only answer you really needed could be conveyed with a simple yes or no, or oui ou non, as the case may be.

The first thing she asked was whether the boat had been moored inside the port which of course it had not. At the realisation of this Madame lost any interest she may have had in the first place. She shrugged and lifted her arms in a sign of resignation and it didn't take an interpreter to know that what she was telling me was 'well, what do you expect if you moor on the towpath. I cannot help you.'

I tried in vain to tell her that I wasn't looking for sympathy and I wasn't asking her to help me find the bikes, I just wanted to know where I could find the nearest Gendarmerie. Rob then arrived on his way back from the supermarché and used his considerable command of the lingo to discover that the nearest cop shop was about 2 kilometres away. So off we trudged dejectedly along the towpath towards the centre of Toulouse in a blistering 32°of midday heat. On the way I managed to contact Penny, the lovely clerk at my insurance broker who asked the question she always asked.

"So where are you sunning yourself now?'

Penny promised to check my policy small print and get back to me as soon as possible. The words small print did not fill me with a great deal of hope. The Gendarmerie, when we finally found it, was full of the usual suspects - small time crooks, pick-pockets and shoplifters, non-payers of fines and drunks all eager to make use of some obscure human rights act to prove their innocence. Needless to say we were not put at the top of the urgent priority list - thousands of velos were stolen every day of the week, fold- up and otherwise. I registered at the desk and was told to take a seat.

I thought about the time many years earlier that I had been caught speeding in Liverpool. Why I was in such a hurry to see the Reds beat my beloved Saints I can't really remember, but he who never lies, the radar gun, said that I had been doing 102 mph in a 70 limit. I had to appear at Huyton Magistrates Court for "sentencing" and I arrived at 10.00 am prompt. To my dismay there were about a hundred other offenders in the room and I seriously wondered whether I would ever be called to account. Then a clerk came hobbling into the room calling out.

"Non-payment of fines Court 2 - Non-payment of fines Court 2," and within seconds I was left completely alone, to be dealt with in Court 1.

In the event I was fined £100 and banned from driving for seven days. In my defence I told the Magistrate that I was very surprised at being clocked at 102 miles an hour as the handbook of my 1st Series Land Rover Discovery said that the top speed was 92, to which he replied, somewhat incredulously.

"Yes I was rather shocked - a Land Rover doing over 100 miles an hour?"

When I went to pay the fine the girl at the desk was similarly shocked.

"What - now ? You want to pay now?   What - the whole amount? You don't want time to pay? Nobody ever pays their fines here."

When I gave her the cheque for the full amount of £100 she gazed at it for fully five minutes in disbelief before finally issuing me with a receipt.

After an hour of watching half the down-trodden population of Toulouse and their dog come and go I was getting increasingly pissed off when my mobile rang. It was Penny from the broker with the joyful news that sorry but bicycles were not covered unless they were stowed inside the boat and secured with appropriately insurance company approved padlocks and chains. You know the sort - ones that couldn't be severed with a pair of Pound Shop bolt croppers. So that was it then. The might of the Toulouse police force seemed highly unlikely to be thrown at the investigation into the theft of a couple of little bikes, and they weren't covered by my extremely expensive comprehensive insurance policy. I thanked the desk Sergeant, or whatever the French equivalent, and walked out of the place, glad at least to be back out of the claustrophobic atmosphere of the Headquarters of the Toulouse Gendarmerie. On the way back to the boat we passed a little oasis of relief, the De Danu Irish bar, where Guinness was available chilled at 8 Euros a pint, and somehow we were pulled by some invisible force into the air-conditioned depths, where our request for two creamy topped pints was delivered by a cheery Irishman called Paddy, and the Levellers sang out from the rafters.

"If I could choose the life I please I would be a boatman
On the canals and rivers free no hasty words are spoken"

"One thing for sure then," I said to Rob, " the Levellers have obviously never done any boating!"
Things were starting to look up a bit.

Chapter 3.

Le Canal Lateral a la Garonne

We got to rather like De Danu, named after a mythical Goddess and at that time owned by a more recent Irish god, Trevor Brannan, the Irish flanker who was once banned for life for hitting an Ulster fan who had allegedly insulted his mother. He had also played for Toulouse and opened the bar in 2003. In my experience it was rare to find a "real" Irish bar abroad - every country in the world seemed to have them, usually recognisable by their signposts telling you how far they were from Dublin or Cork and decorated with large Irish flags and framed advertisements for Murphy's Irish Stout and Caffrey's Irish Ales, photos of proper Irish pubs and gaily painted doorways, but that's where any sort of likeness with the real thing ended. They were invariably Irish bars in name only, run by Italians, Australians, Poles, French and even Thais, serving flat bottled Guinness if you were lucky, and spaghetti, and playing anything but traditional Irish music. Most of them wouldn't know a jig from a reel! De Danu was an exception - a proper Irish bar, with proper friendly Irish bar staff from Derry and Galway, excellent Guinness and delicious Irish food - the burgers were the best I've ever had, and even Rob commented on how tasty they were. The place understandably extremely popular with ex-pat Irish and the local trendy youth alike, and got very busy most nights of the week but especially at weekends when there was rugger or football on the box.

We stayed in Toulouse for two more nights. I had closed the stable door and removed anything portable from the decks and we had no more trouble from the local itinerants.There were a couple of small supermarkets nearby and a very good boulangerie. We explored the city on foot and found a wonderful Sunday farmer's market at Saint Aubin, where book sellers and bric a brac stalls mingled happily alongside piled-high displays of fresh fruit and exotic vegetables. There was a magical atmosphere enlivened by a fantastic drum groupe and steel band which gave the whole place a Caribbean feel. We strolled through narrow streets past the church of Saint Aubin into the square Jean-Jaurès where a vintage fairground ride turned slowly to the jaunty music of a barrel organ. The sun shone and the world was at rest. It was difficult to equate with the seediness and squalor that descended on some areas of the city after dark. We eventually came to the banks of the River Garonne which bypasses the centre, canalised by the Canal du Midi. There is a short branch canal, the Brienne, which leads off from the Midi at its junction with the Canal Lateral Garonne and accesses the river through a single lock at Saint Pierre. There was a convenient bar close by with outside tables and we felt that we had earned our couple of glasses of seize soixante quatre, or "numbers" as it's known in Salisbury, that was served up in frosted glasses.

Rob returned to Ventenac and I collected the car from Castelnaudary and picked up the next shift in the shape of Dave and Becky, who were crewing with me to our final destination at Valence d'Agen, from La Gare Matabiau. Some friends from Salisbury who had lived in Toulouse for many years, Andy and Jeanette, met us and took us to a fish restaurant in a back street near the Saint Aubin. It was so hidden in fact that it took Andy half an hour to find it, even with the "help" of the GPS on his 'phone, but it was worth it in the end - the scallops were delicious and the vin rosé a compliment parfait to the food. Andy had served his apprenticeship at the renowned R.A.F. base at Boscombe Down, home of the acclaimed Test Pilot's School, and had worked for Airbus in Hamburg before transferring to the headquarters of the company in Toulouse. He had progressed to a position which took him around the world extolling the virtues of the product to airline Finance Directors and buyers in all corners of the globe. He was essentially a technician and I told him I was glad he wasn't a pilot if his sense of direction at finding the restaurant was anything to go by. Andy was a very laid back assured and capable sort of bloke, and it was reassuring in a strange sort of way when you heard weird noises coming from the aircraft minutes after take-off -

sometimes it sounded as though there was someone underneath sawing bits off with a hacksaw - that someone like Andy had probably made sure that all the nuts and bolts were in the right place and tightened to their correct tension and the oil had been topped up to the correct level.

We set off next morning with mixed feelings about leaving Toulouse. There were lots of good things - beautiful avenues and boulevards, a lively cosmopolitan feel, and of course De Danu. On the other hand Toulouse seemed to have more than its share of desperate looking people living on the streets, most of them harmless and pitiful but some with more insidious and anti social intentions. I certainly wouldn't miss the all-pervading stench of stale urine that invaded the senses in the back streets and alleyways of the city, rendered all the more pungent in the heat of the afternoon sun. This was no more apparent than alongside the canal that led to the first of the three downhill locks at Bayard, opposite the railway station. The lock dropped over six metres into a dark and dank abyss and was surrounded by railings. I wasn't sure whether these were to keep out potential muggers or vandals, or to stop drunks falling in. Perhaps I was being too cynical but I doubted it. The locks are controlled from a cabin at the bottom lock and you have to twist a pole on the approach to Bayard to set the operation in motion. Once in the lock there is nothing to do but wait and hope that the CCTV connection to the éclusier is working. The canal wends its way through the city, past the headquarters of the Gendarmes where I gave them a friendly wave, and continues straight for one kilometre from the bottom lock to the very tight turn to the right at the Port L'Embouchure, (liberal use of bow-thruster employed), into the Canal Lateral de Garonne - roughly translated as the canal that runs parallel to the river Garonne. It is with a sense of relief that you enter the long straight of the Garonne canal and gradually leave behind the dirt and noise and clamour of the big city.

Becky settled into her usual seat at the back of the wheelhouse as we passed the Stadt Ernest-Wallon on our left, home of the Toulouse rugby union side. There is a movable footbridge here which is drawn across the canal on match days and effectively closes the navigation for several hours. Luckily there were no games scheduled for today. Becky took out her knitting and began earnestly tapping away with her needles creating a woolly something or other for one of her five grandchildren. She reminded me of "Nursie", Queenie's nanny, played so brilliantly by Patsy Byrne in the Blackadder series. Between St Jory and Grisolles we passed a huge storage yard with thousands of new vehicles parked awaiting shipment to dealerships across the south of France. The complex stretched for a kilometre alongside the canal, with brand new cars and vans lined up as far as the eye could see. There were railway sidings where car transporter trains were unloading and car transporters queueing to be discharged of their loads. Amongst the Renaults and Citroens and Toyotas I noticed a couple of rows of Jaguar Land Rovers looking aloof alongside their more down-at-heel neighbours. There was even a British liveried EWS Class 66 diesel locomotive which I assume had arrived with its train from Tyseley via the Channel Tunnel.

Grisolles provided a nice convenient overnight mooring stop but not much else. There was a Relais café and restaurant on the far side of the railway line but we were pleased that we had stocked up in Toulouse and could concentrate on the wine and the crib without the need to leave the boat, while "Nursie" took care of the dinner.

We had a short run the next day, sixteen kilometres of more or less dead straight canal and just one lock and arrived at Montech at midday. It then took us over an hour to find a suitable mooring and get tied up. There was very little available space and most of it was much too shallow to be able to get anywhere near the side. Eventually we managed to get within a metre or so from a rickety wharf opposite the entrance to the branch canal to Montauban. There is another intriguing installation here, the Montech water slope, fed by a separate channel which stretches for several kilometres alongside the Canal de Garonne and was designed to replace five locks. The slope itself is 440 metres long and can raise boats of up to 38 metres long and 250 tons a height of 13 metres. I use the word "can" advisedly as unfortunately the lift has been out of service following a mechanical breakdown in 2009. It is a great shame as if it was operational it would create a fascinating tourist attraction whilst helping boats save the time taken for the passage through the five locks. The basic principle is that a sealed tank of water is pushed up and down the slope by two rubber-tyred diesel locomotives that run on the roadways either side of the channel. Boats enter the chamber when a guillotine gate is raised at the entrance which is then lowered to seal the boat inside. This chamber is then pushed upwards (or of course downwards?) with the boat still afloat at a speed of 4 kilometres per hour. The operation takes about six minutes. We walked the length of the slope and wondered when, if ever, we would get the chance to see it in operation, or indeed be able to use it ourselves. There was very little information and nobody around to ask and I wasn't particularly optimistic. The two locomotives look very similar to standard railway diesels and apparently the problem was that one of these had failed. On the face of it you wouldn't think it a major task to repair, and in Britain it would probably have been adopted by a gang of volunteers and put right in months with a little help from a public appeal for donations. Let's hope that one day soon the VNF will see the light and get things moving - literally.

We had a couple of days to spare and decided to explore the branch canal that led to the basin at Montauban and the River Tarn, a distance of 10 kilometres with 9 locks. Dave and Becky were active participants in the life of the village of Winterbourne. Dave's father had run the local Post Office and Dave succeeded him and carried on the business for many years. At the time he was Chairman of the Parish Council and Becky was a churchwarden at the church of St Michael & All Angels, and was also instrumental in organising the annual village fete. They were friendly with the local vicar, the Rev'd Peter, who happened to be a bit of a Francophile and a keen advocate of the peculiar game of boules. He also happened to be visiting France for some international competition or other and arranged to meet up with us at Montauban. When we arrived in the port there was only one vacant mooring with a notice adjacent that read "réservé aux bateaux de passagers."

The redundant and forlorn locomotives at the bottom of the Montech waterslope

Now I had seen this notice before and understood it to mean that the mooring was reserved for hotel boats - boats with passengers. John of the Tressnish insisted that it actually meant "reserved for <u>passing</u> boats" but somehow I knew this wasn't right and it was confirmed moments later as we attempted to move into the space. The Capitan appeared from nowhere waving his arms and shouting. I pleaded with him that there was nowhere else to go and it transpired that there weren't any hotel boats due to arrive for the next two days anyway and we were welcome to stay for the period. It must have been something to do with the hand of God. The port was a few kilometres from the town and we amused ourselves with a stroll after lunch to see the two staircase locks that led into the River Tarn. The river was navigable for about 10 kilometres but we had to stay where we were so that the Rev'd Peter could find us, and I made a mental note to explore this short stretch of the Tarn sometime in the future. Like a lot of the rivers in this part of the world, it was liable to flood dangerously and quickly, so any passage needed careful planning to avoid getting stranded.

41

Peter arrived with a toot on the horn of his Citroen Pissarro in mid-afternoon with a tent, a battered rucksack, two sets of boules balls, and a daughter, Suzy. That did pose a bit of a dilemma. We only had one vacant bed - a double, and I wondered where exactly the vicar and his daughter were going to sleep. As it was the situation was easily resolved as Peter dragged a large bag from the boot and erected a bright orange tent, Suzy dumped her gear inside, and Peter took the bed. He also presented us with a bottle of whiskey and a packet of some delicious Breton buttered biscuits - this was the sort of vicar I could get to like! There was a restaurant within the Haute Nautique and that's where we ate. Large steaks in various forms and frites were the mainstay of the menu which we washed down with several large beers and although the steaks were very good and cooked to (Anglais) perfection, they defeated most of us. All of us in fact except the Reverend, who shovelled everyone else's left-overs on to his plate, polished off the lot, and then ordered another round of pressions grande. We left the restaurant, or to be exact, were politely asked to leave, at half past midnight, long after all the other clientele had retired. Peter excitedly proclaimed that the pathway that led back to the boat provided an ideal piste (boules for the tossing variety) and immediately extricated a Jack from his bag and chucked it into the dust. Rather than settle nicely in place several metres away, the little ball bounced, paused, and then started to gently roll down the bank towards the water. Peter ran after it and dived headlong into the grass before stretching out an arm to stop its progress in a move that would have graced a Lord's Test. I declined the invitation to participate - boules to me came under the same sub-heading as golf and snooker, too difficult, too boring and requiring far too much concentration. Nevertheless Peter and Dave spent the next hour tossing their balls happily into the dirt. Ah well, whatever turns on a vicar !

Peter was up with the lark practising his pitching and tossing before breakfast in preparation for the big event. It had been a whirlwind visit in more senses than one, and I think we all took a deep breath as we waved them away to do battle for Britain at the annual Limoges Festival of Boules, the little Union Jack that was tied to the aerial flapping in the breeze.

We set off to tackle the climb back to the top of the canal and the junction at Montech. The light-hearted mood on board was rudely brought down to earth as we approached the top lock of the Montauban Canal. There was a hotel boat moored in the wide pound between the last two locks which we passed and motored slowly into the lock. As we ascended I noticed Dave talking to someone who was standing watching us from the lockside.

"Gentleman just admiring the boat," said Dave, nodding towards our gongoozler, who was dressed somewhat incongruously in slacks and loafers with a V-necked pullover and tie. It was apparent that he wanted to talk and I moved across to the wheelhouse door as we waited for the gates to open. People were often interested in the history of Saul Trader, the usual opening gambit asking incredulously whether we had sailed across La Manche.

"Yes, indeed, lovely lines," he added, speaking quietly with what I deduced was a sort of soft Scottish Lowland lilt.

Before I had a chance to say anything else, the tone of the conversation changed as Mr Jekyll quickly turned into Mr Hyde!

"So which way are you heading?" he asked, still with the same inflection.

"We're going to Valence d"Agen, "I told him, still believing him to be an interested onlooker, 'so we'll be turning right at the junction."

"Aha, I see," he replied with the air of a prosecution lawyer who had suddenly seen a flaw in the evidence of the accused, "so you'll be passing through Castelsarrassin then?"

"Yes, that's right," I said. He obviously had a bit more knowledge of the canal than I had thought. Then came the damning blow, and I couldn't help but notice a hint of triumph that almost said aloud - Gotcha!

"Well in that case," he went on with a sneering grin, speaking slowly and deliberately, obviously enjoying the moment, "I think I ought to warn you that there are a lot of boats moored there and if you go past them at the speed you came past me they get very upset and throw rotten eggs."

I was completely lost for words. This smarmy supercilious bastard had caught me with an obviously tried and tested speech and it had caught me completely off-guard. He was the owner of the hotel barge and unbelievably was accusing me of speeding past his boat. In the fifteen years that I had owned Saul Trader, during which time I had negotiated three thousand locks and navigated fifteen thousand kilometres, passing countless thousands of moored boats, I had NEVER been spoken to about my speed. I always without fail slowed down past boats so as not to cause an undue wash - and this was in the fairly short pound between the two top locks. What is more, the hotel boat was three times the size of Saul Trader and hardly likely to be disturbed by our little bit of wash.

Where the hell was this bloke coming from? I was so taken aback that I could only stand and gape as he went on about the speed limit being three kilometres per hour passing boats and it was the law punishable by fines and public flogging etc etc. My biggest regret was that I was so tongue-tied and flabbergasted that I couldn't respond with any of the verbal vitriol that I could usually dredge up on these occasions. As we motored out of the lock I did ask him whether his precious boat had actually moved as we passed it. When he nodded at this I managed to reply with a fairly innocuous retort.

"In that case sir, I would suggest that you take a look at your lines and make sure they are properly adjusted."

So there - that told him!

On the canals and rivers free no hasty words and never a harsh word spoken - hey ho!

How about self-righteous sanctimonious little pricks then for starters. It was obviously a well-rehearsed speech which he thought was cunningly clever. Montauban a popular destination for hire boats most of whom knew only two speeds - stopped and flat out, so I imagine he must have plenty of opportunity to practice. I did have a quiet chuckle as I remembered a story that Rob told about an altercation that Joe Parfitt had with a hire boat that had sped past his yard with two feet of wash in his wake. Joe cupped his hands and bellowed at the offending steerer.

"Ralenter votre vitesse s'il vous plait."

"Fuck off yer French twat," came the immediate reply, flavoured with an unmistakable Scouse accent.

I seethed and swore under my breath for most of the way to Castelsarrassin, where rather than being met with any sort of farm produce flying through the air towards us, fresh or otherwise, we were greeted with friendly waves of welcome from the line of moored vessels. In fact some of them went far beyond the call of duty as we edged sideways into a mooring alongside the quay. At least half a dozen boaters lined the wharf offering advice and beckoning for us to throw them our lines, and even applauding as we nestled gently alongside with inches to spare at either end. Eat your heart out Mr Hyde. The next time we encountered him the boat was being steered by someone I didn't recognise and Mr Hyde was standing at the bow looking smugly Napoleonic. I gave him a Benny Hill salute and fired a broadside jibe, calling out as he passed.

"Sorry Captain - didn't see you in time to be able to dip the ensign."

A bit childish I suppose but it amused me anyway.

At Castelsarrassin I paid the very sexy Capitan for the night (for the mooring I hasten to add) and we enjoyed a free concert of music and dance in the packed Salle Jean Moulin hall on the opposite side of the canal. There were very few visitor moorings for barges at Castelsarrassin and unfortunately, due to a recent "modernisation" of the port, these have now been replaced with short pontoon moorings set at right angles to the quay thereby excluding mooring for anything longer than about 15 metres. It seems to be a trend that barges are not welcome in some places - presumably as six or eight 10 metre boats paying say 20 Euros for an overnight stay make more profit than one or two barges of 20 metres or more paying 25 Euros. It's a shame, particularly in places like Castel, where there are excellent facilities, safe deep water moorings, and a railway station close by.

At Moissac there are no such problems, as yet, but the port here is extremely popular and we were lucky to find one space. The port was run by an English couple, Iain and Caz, who were always helpful and a useful source of local knowledge. Moissac is a perfect town with very good restaurants, a wonderful 11th Century Abbey complete with cloisters, and fine riverside walks along the banks of the Tarn. There are additional moorings on the river, accessed through a double lock

45

staircase. We stayed for one night as we were running out of time and spent the afternoon on a stroll around the town. We were drawn to the Abbey by the sound of Bach being played on the big organ and were treated to an impromptu hour of the most beautiful music. We noticed a poster advertising an evening of choral music that was being held in the Abbey that same evening. We enjoyed a seafood meal ashore followed by the evening concert which was performed by a brilliant visiting Parisian youth choir. Moissac was definitely a place we had to visit again when we had more time to spend.

Chapter 4. Valence d'Agen Spectacle

The following day we made the final run of the trip to Valence d'Agen, where we were going to watch a show that John had told me about which the town put on each year on the side of the canal, 'Au fils de l'eau - une histoire,' which translates literally as ' over the course of the water - a story.' It was billed as a 'Spectacle", and spectacular it certainly was. When we motored into the small port of Valence it was as though we were entering a Medieval village. The backdrop of the set stretched for 250 metres along the offside bank of the canal, depicting a school, a church, a bank and shops. A grandstand had been erected opposite with seating for 2000. This was directly behind the wharf that John and Judy occupied with Tressnish and part of their agreement stated that they had to vacate the mooring for the whole of August, while the show was being set up. In fact John and Tressnish had now been seconded into the cast and played the role of a gunship that cruised slowly on to the scene just before the finale of the show, emerging from a smoke screen with all guns blazing. For this reason, John had moved Tressnish a few hundred yards from the port and we joined them tying astern to a sign post on the bank.

In the town we found an excellent laverie where the lady agreed to do a service wash and iron on our two bags of boatman's laundry for a very reasonable 8 Euros. There was a bar nearby with seats outside and cold pressions where we wiled away a couple of hours. We noted a restaurant, the Café Indus, just off the market place that showed scallops and frites on the menu, which I for one could never resist. We went in the evening and were not disappointed. The joint proprietor was lovely and attentive although she did look as though she could do with a good meal herself, and the food was par excellence. We nicknamed it "Skinny's" and it became a firm favourite of ours which we patronised frequently over the next

47

few years. Our tickets for the show cost 18 Euros each, for which we were given grandstand seats with a fantastic view of the proceedings. There were varying grades of ticket, ranging from a top of the range package that included a full five course pre-show meal with wine and silver service in a fancy silk lined marquee to the 'economy' package of mayonnaise laden hot dog and chips on wooden benches in the open.

We settled for the Noix St Jacques and frites at Skinny's.

The show started at 10.00 pm and finished at midnight. It was non-stop action all the way and difficult sometimes to see everything as there was so much going on. The 'cast' involved 450 folk from the town and surrounding villages, all dressed in colourful period costumes. The vast stage, with the 250 metre backdrop provided action from young and old together with a large menagerie of live animals - horses, dogs, rabbits, chickens, cows, ducks and pigs. The action began with three young lads, the sons of the village, embarking on a voyage into the unknown - actually the far side of the canal basin, in a small open boat, their passage illuminated by a flickering candle. The actin was non-stop. Bustling markets, a 1920's Tour de France, a dramatic fire and a wedding all cleverly lit with delicate laser lighting, giant images projected on to the scene and the subtle use of pyrotechnics. There was always something happening, and often several scenarios all happening at the same time. There were some hilarious moments, combined with sensitively acted scenes of reunions and romance.

The Tour de France (a la 1920's), passed in front of the grandstands before crossing the bridge over the canal. Spectators were coerced from the audience to line the route. The local 'Bobby', complete with whistle and cap borrowed from the English policeman in Allo Allo, struggled in vain to contain the crowd. They were constrained behind a rope barrier, and the hard-pressed Bobby had everyone in hysterics as he first pushed one end of the surging crowd back from the road, whereupon those at the opposite end surged forward and he spent the next ten minutes rushing back and forth in a vain attempt, whistling frantically, to push them back into line, only for the first lot to surge forward again, until the 'Tour' finally appeared from behind the stand. Riders in flat caps and singlets on ancient bicycles with buckled wheels, shepherded by a small fleet of vintage cars, one with a badly buckled bicycle wheel strapped to its roof.

At one point the church caught fire and a horse-drawn fire engine clattered across the bridge followed by several fire-fighters running behind with buckets of water to throw on the flames.

A bustling street market was quickly set up in the area in front of the stands, where vendors noisily carried on their trade amid the general pandemonium. A vagabond stole a live chicken from one of the traders and was chased up and down the stairs by the overworked policeman with his whistle, brandishing a truncheon. Crowds of people crowded the stalls and an old lady strolled around towing a pig in a basket behind her on a trolley before the scene disappeared as quickly as it had begun. The two hours passed in the blink of an eye and then in the final scene, Tressnish emerged through a thick fog of smoke from under the bridge to dock on the far side and disembark its passengers - the three lads who had originally set sail from the shore seemingly many decades earlier. John had recruited the services of his friend, a Dutchman called Dik, to stand at the side of the wheelhouse and direct him through the fog to the mooring. It is difficult describe all this frenetic activity in words and I have borrowed some of the publicity photographs which will hopefully give a better idea of the event.

The extravaganza had been taking place annually in August for more than twenty years but sadly it has now finally run its course and the difficult decision to call it a day was made in 2017, after an incredible run of 23 years. It is going to be replaced with another show, to be called 'Cana en Scéne, details of which are still to be finalised. Whatever the outcome. I am sure that the Spectacle 'Au fils de l'eau' will be sadly missed by participants and audiences alike.

Backdrops in position ready for the show

Allez Allez allez

Scene from the finale

Chapter 5
Expensive Air Fares and Leaky Glands

I had hoped to be able to find somewhere to leave the boat for the winter. John and Judith on the Tressnish had rather landed on their feet with the very nice residential mooring on the town wharf and John seemed to think I would be able to find a spot on the bank opposite them. Obviously this wasn't possible during August but the disused wharf looked ideal. There was plenty of water and an easy step up on to the bank. What's more there was a small roadway that meant that we could get the car right alongside the boat. I had hoped it would be available for the winter. I spoke to the Maire and also to the VNF but for some reason I got an implicit -impossible.

On the morning after the show I went to the station to catch a train from Valence to Toulouse and retrieve the car - except that there was no 11.35 train to Matabiau. An illuminated sign told me that a replacement bus service was running which would stop outside in the station approach. When it finally arrived, 35 minutes late, it was packed to standing room only. I did manage to get a seat halfway though the journey after some others had got off, but then more got on and it was back to standing. We finally arrived at the Gare Matabiau 45 minutes late. There was no apology whatsoever about the late arrival or the overcrowding and I was very glad that I hadn't been relying on it to connect with a flight. I thought it was a pretty shoddy turnout to be honest. There were probably a lot of other people who were relying on the train to catch flights or keep appointments but typically the French bore the inconvenience with a passive shrug.

They were a strange race the French in may ways and it was difficult to understand how they could be so utterly different from us Brits, who after all are only 22 miles away at the nearest point and have had more than a few historical minglings. I read somewhere that this difference in our psyches could be summed up quite simply - the French do not have a word for excited. "Je suis excité" does not exist in French. The English live in the faire (to do) and the avoir (to have) whilst the French live in the être (to be). That is why the French close their shops for three days a week. They do not have the same materialistic ambition that we have and are largely content with their lot.

My friend Andy who works for Airbus and who has lived in Toulouse for nearly twenty years told me that the French do not live their lives in blind pursuit of wealth and the culture of 'more', but enjoy the simpler things in life - time with their families, long lingering lunches and as many days off from work to indulge these pleasures as possible. Hence the fact that shops are closed for half of the day half of the week, something that is difficult for the Brits to get used to, having the convenience of stores that are open, as they say, 24/7. Personally I think it's a much more civilised and cultured way of life, and I would love to return to the peaceful Sundays of the past. *(and banning bloody lorries from the outside lane of dual-carriageways - Ed).*

Mind you, when they do have a grievance, they certainly know how to make their feelings known, as M. Macron is finding out. His proposed increase in fuel tax was met with rioting in the towns and cities across the country which forced him to back down. Not content with that, students joined the fight against tuition fees, and the labour movement soon added their weight behind plans to reform long-established employment law. In Britain we're too ready to 'sit back and take it' and then complain when it's too late, a complacency that hasn't done us much good over the years. News coverage of the French riots is very limited in the UK and I think Mrs May must be getting very worried for fear of the protests spreading across the Channel.

I drove Dave and Becky to Carcassonne the following morning for their flight back to Bournemouth, courtesy of Mr O'Leary.

Dave paid dearly for omitting to print out the return boarding passes. He was charged a ridiculously exorbitant fee of 75 Euros <u>each</u> for the priviledge of watching the check-in girl spend two minutes at the most to do do this for them. Dave was naturally distraught and it soured the whole trip. This sort of thing is akin to air piracy in my opinion but rules, as they were quick to point out, is rules. The no-frills airlines did exactly what they said on the tin: fine if you wanted a cheap way of getting from A to B, especially on short haul flights, as long as you didn't want any luxuries like hold baggage, on board food or free coffee, or a landing at an airport anywhere near the centre of a city. If they could get away with it I'm sure they would be charging extra to have the luxury of a seat or to use the toilet. I suppose one way to look at it is that the people who do avail themselves of these 'extras' are unwittingly subsidising those that don't and are at least keeping the cheapo airlines in business. Ryanair has expanded rapidly through Europe, through some pretty nefarious business practice it has to be said, and now operates a fleet of over 450 Boeing 737 aircraft flying to 35 European countries. There's an excellent video on You Tube of a group of ladies calling themselves Fascinating Aida singing a song called 'Cheap Flights' which sums up the no-frills airlines very nicely. If you haven't seen it be sure to look it up.

Before leaving for the long drive home, I noticed that something had settled on the boat which was like spots of orange peel, which we could not shift. It was a sort of sap and had really penetrated the paintwork. There were several theories as to the cause which ranged from tree sap to a fallout from a nearby nuclear power station. Whatever it was I didn't like the idea of leaving it over the winter and arranged to return a couple of weeks later with my friend Jerry - big strong Jerry of Polish parents who was phased by nothing. Scragg had christened him several years earlier as "that Rambo bloke."

So it was that two weeks later I flew down to Carcassonne with Rambo bloke, hired a car at the airport, and arrived at the boat prepared for some serious work to clean up and polish all the topsides. When we arrived at the boat I could not believe my eyes. Somehow, and nobody has ever really been able to explain how, there was no trace whatsoever of the offending blobs - it had all disappeared and I felt a bit silly having brought Jerry all this way for nothing. We weren't booked to return for a couple of days but Jerry did make himself useful sealing off some of the deck lights with mastic where they had started to leak water. I also took the opportunity to top up with

400 litres of diesel. There was no tanker delivery available so I borrowed some extra 5 gallon drums from John and made four round trips to the local filling station with five plastic drums in the boot of the hire car bringing back 100 litres per trip. It was hard work but actually worked out cheaper than the last tanker load that I bought from Salelle d'Aude.

It was 2013, twelve years since we first ventured across the Channel. Since then we had explored the Benelux countries and most of France and covered a distance of fifteen thousand kilometres and three thousand five hundred locks. I liked the Canal Lateral Garonne for many reasons. It was quiet and laid back with relatively few locks and none of the queues of hire boats that had frequently held us up on the ever popular Midi. All the locks were automated with the hanging pole on the approaches and control bornes on the lock-sides. There were lots of interesting places to stop off at and of course the climate during the summer months was kind to the joints. Valence was an ideal base with all facilities in the town and plenty of secure parking, and all these factors combined to keep us in the south for the next five years. From time to time I thought about returning to St Jean de Losne and putting the boat on the market and each time put off the idea 'for another year'. It would mean a long slog upstream on the Rhone which was something best undertaken in the Autumn so it became a case of 'this time next year!' Over the course of the next few years we had frequent visits from various friends which always gave us a valid excuse to go back over familiar ground.

One obvious disadvantage of being based so far south was the time it took to drive from the channel ports. It was possible to fly but not very practical with half a dozen 12 volt batteries, four large fenders, gas bottles,(I still hadn't got round to adapting to the French ones), folding bikes, boxes of clean linen, spare parts, and even on one occasion a 12 foot long wooden shaft. British Airways economy class was somewhat backward when it came to accommodating such necessities on their aeroplanes.

We were fortunate in that an old friend from Salisbury, erstwhile British Touring Car star Alan Curnow, had recently given up driving punters around Thruxton circuit at 150 mph on BMW track days and bought a Linssen steel motor cruiser in which he was cruising the canals around St Jean de Losne at a much more leisurely 4 mph. This usually meant that I could break up the drive south half way down France for a convivial evening with Alan and his wife Dawn aboard their boat, the 'Animo.'

During the winter I'd spent hours trawling the listings on Evilbay looking for secondhand Bromptons. I eventually managed winning bids for two bikes, a lovely almost new 5 speed model in bright luminous lemon yellow and a rather more mundane 3 speed version in black which I collected from a lady in Tonbridge who assured me that it had only done a few miles as she had used it solely to commute between Charing Cross station and her workplace in the Strand. The yellow model was delivered by Hermes. It was so well packed up in hundreds of yards of bubble wrap and corrugated card, all held together with several miles of parcel tape, that it took the best part of half an hour to extricate it. The cost of neglecting to secure the bikes below and sleeping too soundly in Toulouse - fourteen hundred and fifty pounds - less about fifteen quid's worth of bubble-wrap!

Alan and Dawn were moored at Pouilley on the Canal de Bourgogne which made for a very convenient and convivial overnight stop.

I had brought a couple of starter batteries with me as I had noticed on our last trip that the engine had seemed a bit sluggish to turn over. Returning to the boat I replaced the batteries and topped up the hydraulic steering fluid. This was a bit like bleeding brakes and I enlisted John's help to turn the wheel while I tweaked the nipples on the steering ram to release any trapped air. This had the desired affect and firmed up the pressure on the wheel. Then I noticed that the bucket that I always left under the stern gland had half filled with water. This meant that we had a leak through the stern gear which would need some attention. The stern gland is the connection between the prop shaft on the inside of the boat, and the propellor itself on the other side of the hull. It is sealed with a packing wedged between two flanges and wrapped around the shaft. It is filled with water-proof grease, which is topped up via a cylindrical tube with a handle on the top that pushes the grease behind a disc and transfers the gooey grease into the packing. As usual in this day and age there are several different types and sizes of packing and various internet forums providing advice on the subject. They would invariably offer a dozen or more different opinions on which was best. I always maintained that if you asked enough "experts" for advice you would eventually find one that you liked. I would normally give a half turn on the greaser at the end of each days' run at the same time as I topped up the diesel day tank. Once a week or so I would lift the floor boards in the after cabin to check for leaks. Periodically the tube would need replenishing and I got an early lesson in the correct way to do this from Keith, the large, and larger-than-life fitter at Saul. He nearly wet himself watching me scoop the grease from the tin with a wooden spatula and try to push it into the brass tube, rather like Mr Stop-Me-and-Buy-One filling an ice-cream cone.

"You prat," he said kindly, after recovering his composure, "Give it here and I'll show you how to do it properly."

They really knew how to treat their customers at Saul. Well I suppose it should have been obvious, and to anyone with the most elementary engineering bent it probably would have been, but the likes of me, a failed accountant with absolutely no training in anything remotely practical, it required a patient demonstration. The trick was to push the empty tube into the grease in the tin - I had always wondered what the little hole in the plastic cover was for, and then slowly wind it anti-clockwise so that the metal disc returned to the top of the tube. The result of inertia, or gravity, or vacuum, or some such weird and wonderful magical theory, then took over and the grease was sucked out of the tin thus filling the tube. It was easy when you knew how as they say, and I did have a few pangs of regret that I had never really taken any interest when my mates took apart their motorcycles or did complicated things under the bonnets of their Minis.

Over the years with Saul Trader however, I had learned quite a bit through necessity, and though I say it myself, managed to accomplish a few running repairs. The stern gland on this particular occasion was unfortunately not one of them. I hated the idea of water inside the boat, although God knows it had had more than its fair share at Migennes not so long ago, but nevertheless I hung a bucket underneath the drip which seemed to take in more water each day. I tried tightening the nuts that gradually nipped the flanges together - Joe Parfitt had told me that the method of ensuring it was not too tight was to check that the prop shaft could still be turned by hand, but the dripping persisted.

Before setting off from Valence I thought it best to try solving the problem and decided to replace the packing. Two reasons particularly influenced my decision. John had some spare graphite gland packing which I "borrowed" and as he was just across the canal I would be able to call on him for advice if I contrived to bugger up the operation - a not so unlikely outcome. I was worried about doing the job while the boat was in the water, as the whole object of the packing was to stop any ingress through the shaft and I imagined that once this was removed there would be nothing to stop the water gushing into the boat. John assured me that it shouldn't be a problem and that there may be a trickle of water dripping through but no more. He talked me through the operation and volunteered to come over to help but I declined his offer as I didn't want him clambering into the engine-room. He had difficulty enough getting on and off Tressnish and his condition had got so bad that Judith was having to crane him ashore in a cradle they had set up on the hand winch.

So I donned my boiler-suit - well I would look the part at least, and armed with spanners, mole grips (always a good fall back), hammer (if you can't fit it, hit it) and a crochet needle borrowed from Judith. This was not to make a woolly hat - John said it was the best tool for extracting the old packing, and I took up position, legs akimbo, astride the prop shaft. He also lent me a set of feeler gauges to ensure that the shaft was tightened up with an equal space on each side.

And there I sat, staring at the flange, the one thing that was stopping a cascade of water crashing in, with fear and dread. I couldn't back down now. I was at the point of no return and after a few minutes I began to gingerly undo the nuts that held the whole thing in place, first the locking nuts, and then with gathering trepidation, the final connection between me and millions of gallons of canal water. So far so good. The next thing was to gently pull back the flange and expose the offending coils of packing. The stuff that John had given me was of the graphite variety which he recommended and which he used himself, and first needed to be cut into lengths that fitted snugly around the shaft. Four or five lengths were required, placed in such a way that the joins were in different positions i.e the first at 12 o clock, the second at a quarter past etc etc. The first problem was that when I tried cutting the packing with my somewhat blunt Stanley knife, the ends tended to fray making it difficult to make a tight join. I solved this problem by using a large pair of cutters and soon had six lengths laid out and ready. Surprisingly, when I pulled back the flange and removed the first two coils of the old packing there was no sign of any water at all - not even a drip - apart from the one who was doing the job of course. Gradually, with the help of the crochet needle, I managed to extract the old packing. I checked with the torch as best I could to make sure that all the old stuffing had been removed and at that point a slow trickle of water started to emerge. It was hardly a deluge and I soon had the first of the new coils in place. John had recommended that I put the first piece in at 12 o'clock but it was actually 1.45 by the time I had it wedged in place! I then gently rammed the next piece home at a quarter past, or 90° from the first one, using the square end of a punch to push it home, until I had five pieces firmly in place. I then replaced the flange and tightened the two nuts with equal turns, checking the clearance on the prop shaft with the feeler gauge, then checked that the prop was free to turn by hand. It had worked - I had successfully renewed the stern gland packing and   felt quite smug. My self-satisfaction was a bit premature however. I was about to replace the floorboards when I heard the tell-tale sound of a drip. I held my breath. Was I imagining it? Then it was followed a few seconds later by another one. The job had failed. The bloody thing was still leaking.

There was really nothing more I could do at that time apart from keep an eye on the situation and regularly empty the bucket. It wasn't as though the water was pouring in and as it happened there was only about one inch more in the bucket when I checked each evening. We were heading for Castets en Dorthe at the western end of the canal. This is where it enters the tidal River Garonne that leads to Bordeaux and the Atlantic

Ocean. We would spend the next five years to-ing and fro-ing between here and Toulouse on the Garonne, with an occasional detour back to the Rhone at Beaucaire.

The next town of any significance from Valence is Agen, 26 kilometres and three locks away. The approach to Agen is through a long tree lined avenue with towpath moorings, which looked rather too similar to those at Toulouse where the bikes were nicked. This was a totally illogical assumption as there was no evidence whatsoever of any suspicious looking people anywhere - paranoia setting in again!   After passing though a narrow bridge, positioned at such an angle that makes it impossible to see whether there is anything coming the other way until it's more or less too late, the canal opens into a large expanse with a hire base immediately to the left, and some moorings on the far side from the town, which were all occupied. The basin here is on an embankment above the railway station and although there were places to tie up on that side they were adjacent to a busy road and a bit too exposed and noisy for my liking. While we were dithering around in the middle of the pond wondering what to do, a barge that was moored on the opposite bank obligingly cast off leaving us a space just the right length which we filled with irreverent haste. Access to the town was by means of a rickety steel footbridge that spanned a dozen of more railway sidings alongside La Gare. As we walked across a long freight train of grain hoppers rushed through the station heading west and two sets of Duplex (double-deck) TGVs - eighteen coaches long, came to a halt on its way to Marseilles. The centre of the town was a short walk from the station. We passed an Indian Restaurant which advertised prawn Rogan Josh on its menu which we earmarked for the evening's repast. Close by in a quiet square we took a look inside the 12th Century Cathédral of Saint Caprais, once a staging post on the pilgrim's trail to Santiago de Compostella, enjoying a few minutes of calm in the cool peaceful ambience of this beautiful building, now listed as a Unesco Heritage site. The town has a lot to offer: a busy indoor market and a pleasant river frontage on to the Garonne, which the canal crosses on a magnificent 23 arch stone aqueduct subtly illuminated at night and was, among other far less important things, the inspiration for the title of this book. There are plenty of interesting individual shops along a pleasant pedestrianised street - not an M&S, Next, SpecSavers or Argos anywhere in sight. Some of the lamp-posts had been fitted with fountains that sprayed a welcome cooling mist over passers-by and delighted the children that danced around them. The Indian food did not disappoint and we finished off with a local favourite dessert of prunes in Armagnac. Agen is famous for its prunes - there is even a Museum dedicated to these healthy little fruits, the Musée des Pruneaux unsurprisingly,, and a prune festival is held each year in August - a regular event if you'll pardon the inference.

Leaving Agen, the canal winds its way past the sorting office of La Poste with the ubiquitous little yellow vans buzzing busily in and out. Dave, ex postmaster general of the Winterbourne branch and one-time postman himself, was enthralled by the activity and looked on wistfully as he recalled his past and the fun and camaraderie of his days at the GPO.

"All gone now," he sighed, "Just another job these days."

"Post postal depression? " I suggested.

The canal takes a sharp turn to the left and suddenly we were confronted with a traffic light that was showing red. This was the approach to the single-file channel across the 539 metre aqueduct over the River Garonne. At the far downstream end there was the first of four downhill locks, the entire length under the control of a single éclusier. There were no other boats approaching as far as I could tell through the binoculars and the lights soon changed to show a red and a green to indicate that the lock was being filled for us. Five minutes later we got a green and started across the amazing structure that carried us high above the river with a tow path on either side and wonderful views over the town. Once through the top lock, the others are set automatically and the éclusier disappeared into the VNF workshop, presumably for a smoke and a glass of wine!

As we neared the bottom lock I noticed a gang of youths jumping from the footbridge that spanned the lock into the water. There was a small boat leaving the lock and two or three of these idiots leapt from the lock-side on to the boat. There was no sign of the VNF man and I was starting to get a bit worried about the situation. As we entered the lock I made it quite plain that I didn't want anyone jumping on to the boat and gave a long blast on the horn to warn those swimming in the lock. Anybody that came between the 50 odd tons of Saul Trader and the lock wall would not live to tell the tale. They eventually got the message and scrambled quickly up the ladder on to the lock-side. I waved away pleas of "give us a ride mister" but on leaving I did condescend to placate a particularly simple sort of lad who had asked me to sound the horn. I asked him how old he was.

"Seize ans," he said with a grin..

"Seize ans,!" I repeated in genuine disbelief, "so why do you act like a six year old?"

I'm not sure whether he understood but he yelped with glee and jumped up and down as I gave two loud blasts on the klaxon. Then they climbed onto the footbridge ready for another suicidal dive into the lock.

Ten kilometres further on through a thickly wooded cutting that resembled an Amazon backwater we came to the delightful and charming village of Sérignac sur Garonne. There was a line of pontoon moorings with plenty of depth alongside, electricity bornes and water taps and just one other boat. It was just too good to miss, and even though we'd only done a few hours boating, decided to tie up for the day. The other boat happened to be a friend of John and Judith's, the Dutchman Dik who piloted John at the Specatcle in Valence. Dic lived aboard and shared his little vintage wooden boat with his lovely border terrier, Jimmy. I think these dogs are ideal on boats: they're small, don't shed a lot of hair, and make wonderful companions, full of mischief and character. They are also good vermin hunters, quite a useful quality for the French waterways, that had more than their share of mice and rats. We had been relatively lucky in this respect, only finding the odd stowaway beneath the sofa on a couple of occasions, but we tried not to do anything to encourage their presence by leaving out food or piling up bags of rubbish.

Phil at Saul had a terrier, Sid, named after the enigmatic member of Pink Floyd, the late Sid Barrett. At one of the Saul Boat Gatherings, or Goat Botherings as they had become known, the local Sea Cadets had set up a stall selling hot dogs and burgers. I noticed Sid running away with a large sausage in his mouth. When I mentioned this to Phil he said.

"Greedy little sod. I told him to get two."

We got to like Sérignac very much and stayed here several times over the next few years. The village was a few hundred metres from the canal where there were a couple of restaurants, a very good épicerie with a small bakery, where you had to be up with the lark to get your pains chocolats as they were snapped up very early in the morning. I couldn't work out whether this was because they were so good or whether the baker never quite got to grips with the potential demand and didn't bake enough of them. There was also a tabac alongside which usually had one or two day-old English newspapers, so that you could make yourself miserable catching up with the political antics and social shenanigans that were making the headlines in our green and pleasant land, with a pain chocolat and a cup of proper coffee.

The moorings were controlled by a lady from the tourist office who we nicknamed Madame Cholet on account of her rather pointed nose and her penchant for necklaces of coloured beads. She only seemed to work four or five days a week which meant that anyone in the know could arrive during her absence and get away with a couple of free days. We could get a Wifi reception at the office but it didn't stretch as far as the moorings, which were about 600 metres from the town. This meant that I had to take the iPad with me when I went for the bread, in order to get my daily "ether fix" sitting on the wall outside. The other little gem in Sérignac was the restaurant L'Escale, a lively and friendly place in the corner of the square opposite the Mairie. At the time it was run by a crazy character called Jean-Luc and his wife Francine, although I understand it has since changed hands. It was always busy with a lively atmosphere and a healthy crowd of locals. The food was excellent - omelettes and pizzas a speciality, and we became quite well-known and always welcomed with open arms. Open arms and hugs and kisses too - a most welcome bonus from the lovely bouncy waitress, Claudine. Sérignac had everything you could want, and we always enjoyed our time there.

One evening, Sepp and Diwi arrived on "Johanna" followed shortly afterwards by the hotel boat "Rosa" which was piloted at the time by Rob's son Julian. We spent the evening with them and Mike, the chef from the "Rosa" accompanied with a few bottles aboard Johanna, catching up with the gossip. The "Rosa" was the barge used in a TV series by Gordon Ramsay.

The "Rosa" had now changed hands and the new owner apparently travelled with the boat on every trip but never ate with, or even spoke to, any of the two and a half grand a week paying guests, or "bloods" as they were known on P&O, the word presumably being derived from the expression 'blood money'. We had a very pleasant evening with them all enhanced with some of the superb food cooked by Mike left over from the passenger meal.

On the approach to the popular port of Buzet the canal drops down through two closely spaced locks and crosses the River Baise on a small aqueduct over the single arch river bridge. At Buzet there is a junction with two river navigations, the Baise and the Lot which are accessed through a double lock staircase at the eastern end of the port. Opposite the junction we found Dutch Dik and his friend Jimmy, and managed to tie up on the bank just ahead of them. Jimmy was delighted to see us and leapt into the wheelhouse before we had fully stopped. His little tail was wagging furiously, whether in anticipation of the belly tickle or the biscuit wasn't clear but I suspected it was the latter. Dik told us that we would probably be able to get a Wifi signal from the port for free: Dik was rather careful with his cash, or as they say in the Forest of Dean - "he was so close with his money that he'd skin a fart and sell it to a Nun if he thought he could get away with it" - and anything he could get on the cheap was always welcome.

He told us he had been on the rivers in the past and got stranded by floods on the Lot for an entire winter but luckily managed to find a mooring for which nobody had requested any payment. It seemed that the Lot was definitely out of the question for us because of the depth but the Baise, where the navigable section terminated in the charmingly named town of Condom (did the ice cream trikes have signs on the side saying "buy me and stop one," I wondered). did seem to be a possibility and I made a mental note to have a look at it in the future. Another decision that I would come to regret. There was a large Nicols hire base here which had excellent facilities

- showers, washing machines, a small shop with a good selection of Buzet wines, and a maintenance workshop, something we would be making use of more frequently than I would have liked in the not too distant future. There were several good restaurants, an épicerie, newsagents and tabac, and a salon de coiffure, where I took advantage of a twenty minute gap in the appointments schedule of the attractive lady barber to have the barnet tidied up.

It was Bastille time again and we moved on to Mas d'Agenais where there was a good mooring with electricity that you paid for with a credit card in an automatic machine. 2 Euros bought you 4 hours of power. There was a somewhat rare sight here of a DIY operated toilet pump-out although I couldn't see any instructions on its use, and a shower room which was also accessed with a jeton - plastic token. I thought it was an excellent idea and wondered why some of the so-called "honey-pot" moorings on the English canals had not installed similar facilities. It might help to get the selfish tight-fisted overstayers to move on. In France the local Mairie seems to control moorings and provide facilities to encourage boaters to stop and spend money in the community. Too sensible for England I suppose. There were a couple of small stores in the town on the hill, a cafe and a lavoir, but I couldn't find a bar.

At Villeton there is an excellent Pizza Restaurant with a lively friendly atmosphere but unfortunately no July 14th fireworks.You may well think that eating pizza in France is sacrilegious, but there is something about the ones they produce here - they leave the Italians in the shade in my humble opinion.

We stopped for a couple of nights in Meilhan, where the port was run by an English couple, Mike and Cath. Mike managed to squeeze us into the last available space alongside the quay. He worked for the English company, Napton Narrowboats, who operated a few narrowboats under the name of Minervios Cruisers. They also had a base at Le Somail and we had met a guy called Scouse (no idea where he was from!) who worked at Napton and spent his holidays ferrying boats between the two bases. Mike had a look at the stern gland for me, which was still dripping, but couldn't suggest any remedy, other than getting the boat out of the water in order to have a proper look at it. The nearest place that this could happen was probably Toulouse so the job would have to wait for the time-being. It was July 16th, two days after Bastille Day, but by a stroke of luck for us the local fireworks had been postponed because of heavy rain on the 14th and were being held that very night. The small town of Meilhan, population about 1500 souls, is some 50 metres above the canal which involved a steep climb but well worth it for the view down over the treetops to the canal and the valley floor. There was a very good boucherie and a small store and tabac. There was also a weekly night market with live music and food stalls. The entire population of the village turned out for this and there were lines of tables where everyone sat outside to eat and plentiful quantities of Rosé and the air was filled with chattering and laughter. An added bonus for us was the firework display, which we watched from the grounds of the Chteaudu Sillac, high above the canal.

I had another somewhat surreal experience while we were in Meilhan. Just a few days earlier I had received an Email from Sheila, the wife of Duncan, who had piloted us across the Channel fourteen years ago. I had known them since the early 1990's when my narrowboat was being built at Saul. Duncan had been with us several times on the English canals and helped me bring the former 1936 built working narrowboat, a large Woolwich Town class, the "Birmingham ," from Rugby to the boatyard at Saul Junction for renovation by Phil Trotter. He had also accompanied us on Saul Trader when we negotiated the tricky passage from Sharpness to Bristol on the Severn Estuary at the start of this whole adventure back in 2000. They lived on the banks of the River Severn in Epney and he had once taken me out on the river to ride the Severn bore in an inflatable dinghy. We didn't get to meet up very often because we were both busy in different parts of the world, but I always got an invite to his birthday pig roast. When I replied to Sheila to tell her that I regrettably wouldn't be able to make it to the party, I had explained that we were on the Canal Garonne and heading for Meilhan. When she replied she told me that she had stopped at Meilhan 25 years earlier. Before they were married, she and Duncan had spent four or five years on a yacht in the Mediterranean and she had been moving the boat through the canal to Bordeaux with her friend

Bobby when they stopped overnight at Meilhan. Now that was coincidence enough but nothing compared to what was about to evolve. There was a nice little wooden motor launch that had arrived earlier and moored a few boats from us. As I walked past I nodded to a guy who was sitting in the wheelhouse with a beer.

"Mr Saul Trader," he said in a thick Gloucester accent, "don't remember me do you?"

I had to admit that I didn't recognise him.

"Dave Johnson," he said, coming over and offering his hand, "friend of Duncan Milne. Came down the Severn with you when we took all those boats to the Bristol Festival of the Sea - about '96 I suppose it was.

Bloody hell! I was almost lost for words as I shook his hand.

"You won't believe this," I said, "but I was only talking to Sheila a couple of days ago and she was telling me that she's been here with Bobby on the yacht."

"Yeah, that's right, - she's here look. Bobby," and he called down below as a tanned and weather beaten face appeared in the hatchway.

I could feel the hairs on the back of my neck stand up and shivered.

"Bloody hell - I don't believe it," what a crazy coincidence. Bobby told us how she and Sheila had crewed the yacht from Narbonne to Bordeaux, before Duncan had arrived to take it back to England.

There were a few tables and chairs outside Mike's office and in the evening some of the boaters gathered for 6 o'clock beer. We reminisced about the trip when we took three working boats and my narrowboat down the Severn to Bristol - Dave had steered the "Birmingham" and there was Glynn Phillips on the "Aquarius", Duncan Pottinger with the "Petrel" ?, and Wat Tyler. It was the first ever International Festival of the Sea and "Birmingham" was seconded to take demonstration loads of palletted newspapers from the Feeder Road into the festival site where it was unloaded by the steam crane. There were street performers and music and I particularly remember seeing the inimitable Sid Kipper who sung a song he had written about the crab fishermen of Cromer.

"They always had six men to row the boats - two short men at the front, two middle-sized men in the middle and two tall men at the back. And if you happen to go to Cromer today, or Sheringham, or tomorrow, you'll see tall men, short men and middle-sized men still walking the streets, which just goes to show that this story is true". Brilliant stuff.

Dave (the other one) and Becks were going back to England and the nearest station was at Marmande, some 14 kilometres away. There was a local bus that ran twice a day - fare 50 Eurocents .

We caught the 10.15, which arrived in a cloud of dust bang on time. There was an excellent L'Eclerc which the bus stopped outside and I took the opportunity to stock up the pantry - and the fridge.

Crew replacements came in the shape of Phil, who I had got to know in Thailand, and his Thai wife Bee. Bee turned out to be a brilliant crew, and immediately took over the fore-deck. She could fling a rope around a lock bollard from fifteen yards and soon mastered the trick of easing the boat to a halt with a spring, before whipping it securely round the bits. What is more she was up most morning swabbing the decks in her short shorts and psychedelic purple polka-dot wellingtons, and her green Thai curry was delicious. I said goodbyes to Dave and Bobby still mumbling and shaking heads about the circumstances of our meeting, and we headed for the last port on the canal, before the staircase locks that led into the river at Castets en Dorthe.

At Fontets the going got increasingly difficult as we picked up more and more thick weed around the prop. Eventually it got so bad that we were making very little headway and I decided that we needed to do something about it. Unlike the narrowboat, Saul Trader did not have the luxury of a weed hatch which allowed access to the prop from inside the boat.

The only way to get at it properly was by getting into the water. We launched the inflatable and I tried to get to the problem by leaning over the sides but the curvature of the stern made it virtually impossible to get close enough to the problem.

The large Woolwich motor - the "Birmingham"

After several attempts at clearing the debris with a boathook to no avail, the time came to bite the bullet and get into the water. I always checked to make sure I had no open wounds about my person before going into the water - Wiles disease was something I could definitely do without and I didn't take any unnecessary risks. We had a swimming ladder which at least meant that you could ease in gently and I also donned a life-jacket which allowed me to stay buoyant and keep my head above the water leaving my hands free to work on the job in hand, rather than fighting to keep afloat. I pushed myself around the stern and managed to get my feet on to the skeg. I had a sharp knife and soon felt the source of the trouble. Apart from the weed, which came away relatively easily with a tug, a lot of other less savoury material had taken the opportunity to wind itself inextricably around the shaft - rags and old clothes, tangled up with bits of fishing tackle - and lots of rope. Another thing that I was always aware of was clothing that still contained the body part that it had once protected, but luckily the water was fairly clear (and warmish) and I checked to make sure their were no arms or legs apparent. The knife was pretty ineffective against the soggy material that had tightened and knotted itself together and I was beginning to think hacksaw when I saw that Bee had climbed into the dinghy and was wielding a boathook.

"You won't be able to get it off with that," I said, "it's too tightly stuck."

Still she persisted saying something I couldn't understand and prodding about with the hook and I started to get a bit impatient.

"That no good, - Mei dee" I repeated using some of my limited knowledge of the Thai language to try to get the message across, but she was determined to make her point.

"No no, not that one - do like this one," she was starting to get frustrated, making signs and jabbing the boat hook around.

Then it suddenly dawned on me.

What she was trying to tell me to do, aided and abetted with some frenzied sign language, was to attach the hook to a piece of the rag so that she could pull it taught. Of course! This made the cutting much easier and it parted like butter: after a few more minutes we had managed to free the lot. This girl was amazing. Years of harvesting rice and living off the land in the north of Thailand had obviously taught her some very useful and practical knowledge. I could do with a crew like her - she was a real gem.

Phil, meanwhile, wasn't particularly interested in the boating and was happy to enjoy his holiday sitting on the fore deck with a book and a beer.

As we approached the last lock into the basin at Castets I noticed a small boatyard on the left which had a mobile crane parked alongside a rusting steel shell. It didn't look very active but it crossed my mind to maybe have a chat with someone about my leaky gland! (*don't you need a doctor for that....Ed*)

There was a notice in the lock with a VHF channel for contacting the Capitan which I tried calling but didn't get a reply. We left the lock and motored slowly past a line of moored boats - most of them retired commercials. I could see the next lock ahead and there didn't seem to be a lot of spare room. Beyond the barges were a few rows of pontoons at right angles to the quay which were too short and fully occupied. Bee stood ready with her bow-line, legs akimbo, while we moved slowly forward. Then I saw a bicycle cruising up the towpath, a large flag on a mast fluttering behind in the breeze, and the rider waving and pointing. This, it turned out, was the Capitan, Bruno, who we had met at Briare some years earlier. He indicated to me to breast up alongside another barge of similar length to Saul Trader.

Bruno turned out to be another wonder of the waterways - nothing it seemed was too much trouble for him, and nothing seemingly impossible. There was something about the mooring, with a nice view across the basin, and the welcome from Bruno, that seduced us into staying in Castets for a whole week. Bruno brought a baguette and fresh croissants in a canvas bag to the boat every morning and left them hanging on the door handle of the wheelhouse. There wasn't very much in Castets itself to be honest - an excellent gourmet restaurant beside Lock 52, strangely enough called L'Écluse 52, a small bakery and a Post Office. Bruno took me in his car to Saint Macaire to extract some much needed cash from the ATM and on the way back screeched to a halt alongside a vast field of sunflowers. He jumped out of the car, brazenly walked into the field, took out his pocket knife, and cut half a dozen or more large yellow blooms which he presented to Bee with a flourish when we got back to the boat. She returned the gesture with a wide Thai smile and a kiss on the cheek which caused Bruno to glow red, and then found a vase to put them on display beneath the mast on the cabin top.

We took the Bromptons and cycled across the wonderfully elaborate girder bridge over the Garonne and followed the back roads for 10 kilometres to the large Super U supermarket at Langon, where we stocked up with stores. Ten kilometres is a long way on a Brompton, especially with two heavy carrier bags balanced on the handle bars, and a pit stop was found on the return leg at a small cafe on a hillside overlooking the river. I also paid a visit to the boatyard above the lock and met the two owners, a tall Frenchman who introduced himself as Fred, and his English oppo Adam Townsend, who had been based in France for many years and knew Joe Parfitt and Rob. He came and had a look at the offending leak and pronounced it an out-of-the-water job, so after a lengthy consultation with Fred, in French, it was decided that the weight on that end of the boat

71

was probably about 25 tons and their mobile crane was man enough to be able to lift Saul Trader's stern far enough out of the water to enable the work to be carried out in the dry. In the excitement I completely forgot to ask them for an idea of how much this exercise would cost me, while they stood excitedly adding up the Euros in their heads. No matter - it was a job that needed doing, and I was getting increasingly worried about the amount of water infiltrating the boat. I really couldn't leave it in this state over an entire winter.

The following day we took Saul Trader back up through the lock and gently nudged into a space that they had made for us alongside the crane. The bow was secured to a rusty ring set into a large lump of concrete on the bank and Phil held the stern on a line while Adam passed a six inch wide strop under the stern and attached the two ends over the hook of the crane. I had envisaged things sliding around inside as we were lifted skyward and had taken the precaution of moving any vulnerable bits that I thought likely to be affected and placed them on the floor. Fred started up the crane and gradually the strain was taken up and we were ready for the lift. I was a bit apprehensive to say the least but slowly and surely the stern rose up until the point where at about an angle of about 25° the offending prop shaft was clear of the water. At one point I thought the crane was going to lose the battle and topple into the cut - and then with a loud bang and a thud, the boat fell back and crashed into the water, sending a tidal wave across the canal. The crane had given up the fight and the fail-safe mechanism had kicked in and we were back to square one. It was just about time for lunch and so it was decided to have a break and review the situation.

Adam and Fred returned at 2.30pm and told me that they had come to the conclusion that it was too risky to attempt another lift and that they thought they would be able to do the job with the boat in the water. I wasn't particularly enamoured with the idea but faced with no real alternative decided to put my trust in their professional expertise. They brought a heavy duty pump on board, the sight of which didn't do a great deal to ease my concern. They would have to remove all the packing and pull the flange out so that they could pack some sort of waterproof mastic in behind the joint. Adam assured me that there would not be a vast amount of ingress and I could only take him at his word.

In the event a serious gush of water rushed in but they managed to contain it with the pump and quickly finished the job before pushing the flange back into place. When they had everything secured they replaced the packing and tightened the nuts on to the flange, before spending another half an hour drying out the bilge. I was thankful to have got the job done and parted with five hundred Euros for the priviledge. Five hundred bloody Euros. I did think that was a bit steep for three hours work and a failed lift but paid up with clenched teeth. The exchange rate in those days was slightly more favourable but it still equated to about £370 - quite enough I thought.

I must have thought that I hadn't spent enough money for one week, so on the Friday evening we indulged ourselves in L'Écluse Cinquante Deux where I had a superb mouth-watering steak au poivre, cooked to perfection, with sauteed potatoes and fresh crispy vegetables, followed by the Café Gourmand and as I had suggested it as my treat, another eye-watering bill. In fact as I checked through it to make sure they hadn't added and extra nought, the thought occurred to me that it was about three times more than the cost of my first car. Mind you, that was in 1963 and as the little trio playing live in the corner sang, "the times had certainly been a-changing." The band consisted of guitar and keyboards with a lady vocalist and their music ranged from Pink Floyd to Joni Mitchell.

We had a glass of wine and a chat with a couple of members of the band. The main man who played guitar went by the name of Orville, (I refrained from trying to explain any connection between me, Keith Harris and Orville), and the singer was his wife Erica. I asked them whether they knew any of Sandy Denny's songs and it transpired that they were both big fans of hers and knew all about the history of Fairport Convention. Erica sang Sandy's beautiful haunting song, Écoute Écoute and later in the set they performed a version of Fairport's Matty Groves.

After the gig they came over for another glass and Orville told us about a private concert they were playing at a farmhouse on the outskirts of Langon on the following evening with his group, the OCB Band. They invited us to the party and when I said it would be difficult as we had no transport, Orville insisted on arranging for us to be picked up from the boat. It was agreed that we would take the boat to Fontets and be collected from there at 6.30 the following evening. It was to be a sort of fancy dress party and if possible could we come in hillbilly style.

Chapter 6
Hillbilly Party and Trouble on the Baize

When we turned into the little port at Fontets, the first thing we saw was John and Judith's boat, Tressnish, moored on the quay. John beckoned to us to come alongside. There was a bit of mild hostility from some of the other boaters who were trying to say that barges were too big for the port, so as soon as we had secured our ropes I went to the Capitan's office and paid up for two nights. The Halte Nautique here is situated in a small sheltered harbour off the main line surrounded by trees with a small lake for swimming and pretty landscaped grounds. There was a good bar and the staff, unlike some of the resident boaters, were friendly and welcoming.

We did struggle a bit to find any clothes that could pass as hillbilly. I had a rather loud red checked shirt which I dug out and some brown boots. John leant me a pair of braces and a leather cowboy hat and Bee wore a pair of high-heeled calf-length boots, a white cotton blouse and a wide-brimmed straw hat. Phil said bugger that for a game of hillbillies and came exactly as he was, although thinking about it he could have easily passed for a hillbilly in his normal clothes anyway, with his lanky frame, laid-back gait and unkempt appearance.

We were duly picked up as promised on the dot of 6.30 by two ladies that we hadn't met and driven to the venue which turned out to be a splendid restored ranch, complete with corral fencing, outdoor swimming pool and a huge beautifully renovated barn which was set up with straw bales for seating and a stage where the group would be performing. The scene was completed with several vintage cars parked in the drive including a replica red Jed Clampett style Ford pick up with "Red Baron" painted on the tailboard, a '52 Chevvy convertible and somewhat incongruously, an immaculate left-hand drive 2.4 litre Jaguar with wire wheels. Most of the locals had really gone to town over the dress, and some of the costumes left ours looking a bit on the have-to-do side. Many of the ladies wore long flowing cotton skirts and colourful blouses with short puffy sleeves and bonnets, while the men sported dungarees and ten gallon hats. There were probably 100 people there and the first thing we were told was that the music would not be starting until 9.30. That gave us two and half hours to sample the well-stocked (and free) bar, and engage as best we could with the rest of the crowd. What was the French for "howdee pardner ?"Actually I found out later on that it seemed to be 'howdee partner' with a French accent!

The music from the OCB Band, when they eventually took to the stage, was fantastic - a sort of country-blues sound. There were eight in the band including two backing vocalists -four guitars, a banjo and a drummer who managed to get an incredible sound out of what looked like a packing crate and three cymbals. He explained afterwards that the "box"had cost £1000 from Sweden and it was called a gig-pig! He played a fantastic solo on it and I don't know how he did it, but he got a sound that was as good as that from a complete drum kit. He did let me have a go after the show and I have to admit I made a complete hash of it. Luckily everybody had left the barn by then. The guitars too were a revelation. They were all made from old wooden cigar boxes and gave a wonderful blues sound. Erica and another woman sang the backing vocals and harmonies and Orville and most of the other band members took the lead on different songs. I particularly remember Orville doing the classic Canned Heat song, "Goin' Up The Country." They played to a packed barn for two solid hours - it was quite brilliant. I assumed that the name O.C.B. stood for Old Cigar Box, but Orville said that it was actually the name of a well-known brand of hand rolling cigarette papers that had been made in France since the early nineteenth century.

They finally finished the set after three encores at 11.45 and I thought that was the end of the evening's entertainment but there was more to come. The next stage of the entertainment came in the form of a fantastic barbecue with steaks and sausages, corn on the cob and apple tart and more beer. The festivities went on into the small hours and we obviously had to stay as we had no way of getting home - not that we really needed an excuse to stay. Everyone was very friendly and made us feel at home. Several people jumped into the pool, some of the ladies removing their skirts and leaping into the water in their frilly pantaloons, and the owner of the ranch who apparently ran the local tabac, appeared in an Ali G swimming costume that looked at least two sizes too big for him - the one that looks like an elongated letter "X" and brought the house down when he started the routine of pulling it up from the shoulders before leaping into the pool.

We were finally driven back to the boat by another couple, Martine and her husband Roy, and got to bed at 3 o'clock in the morning. It was a fabulous evening - everyone was friendly and interested in our travels with the boat. These people certainly knew how to enjoy themselves. We invited Orville and Erica, Martine and Roy and a few others to come to us the following evening, and joined by John and Judith, who had made the pudding, we returned their hospitality with a huge pot of Thai prawn green curry and rice thanks to Bee which we ate al fresco alongside the boat, with some accompaniment from Sandy Denny on the iPod.

It was time to start heading back towards Valence but there was one other place in Fontets that we had heard about - the Matchstick Museum.

We were greeted at the door by a large red-faced jovial-looking man who was sitting behind a cash desk. The entrance fee of 2 Euros seemed almost incidental to his obvious joy and enthusiasm at having people experience his amazing collection. It wasn't till he swung himself out from the desk that we saw that he was in a wheelchair, an electric wheel chair in which he scooted off into the first of the two exhibition barns, beckoning us to follow. The first part was a motley disconnected collection of various bits of art and bric a brac which he pointed at with a stick and insisted on describing in French. I wondered where matchsticks came into the equation but all was revealed as we were eventually guided into the second room which was filled with a huge display of intricately built matchstick models. Monsieur Gergeres proudly took us around and told us the history of each piece - the Notre Dame, the Palace of Versailles, and the piéce de resistance, a truly wonderful scale model of Reims Cathedral that had taken over 350,000 matchsticks, and God alone knows how many hours, to construct. At the end of the tour, our guide flicked off the lights with a theatrical flourish which revealed all the models subtly illuminated, the light reflecting the stained glass of the cathedral windows as the bells started to peal their calling to the faithful. On our way out, Monsieur Gergeres produced two matchsticks which he heated and bent into shape before fusing them together and presenting Bee with a perfectly formed heart. Bee was delighted and returned the gesture by planting a kiss on his cheek.

We returned to Castets where Phil and Bee were leaving by train from Bordeaux in a couple of days before Alan and Dawn, with Andy and Jeanette, were joining me for a week. We spent the next few days in Castets cleaning up the boat, while Bee set about the laundry. That was another plus with Bee. She did all the washing by hand in the shower tray, squatting down and scrubbing furiously and carefully rinsing out the soap. I strung up lines fore and aft and before long the boat was dressed overall with drying clothes and took on the appearance of a thriving Thai Laundry. The following day Phil and Bee left by taxi to the station at Bordeaux and the relief crew turned up in Alan's car, having left Andy's in Valence, our destination - oh the logistics of it all! The plan was to get to Valence for another dose of the Spectacle. I had told everybody about it - the new crew were keen to see it, and I really didn't need too much persuasion to witness it all again.

We stopped for the first night back in Meilhan where we got into conversation at the bar with an interesting sort of Jack-the-lad from Bristol, who was taking his wife on his newly acquired 30 ft Benetton, not an entirely appropriate vessel for the canals, through to the Mediterranean, where it would be much more at home. This was Chris, a somewhat larger than life character who was obviously relishing his voyage of discovery. Chris was a bit of a petrolhead who owned a secondhand car dealership and remembered Alan from his racing days. He told us all about his latest venture. He had recently acquired a well-known company from the Receiver, that specialised in motorhome conversions, and had apparently turned the business around to the point where they were 'shifting' several hundred units each year.

Orville and the OCB Band in full swing

Some mighty fine gals dressed for the occasion

We spent a pleasant hour or so reminiscing about Alan's glory days in British Touring Cars in the 70's and 80's and Chris even remembered that Alan had finished as runner-up in the 1980 Saloon Car Championship driving a Ford Fiesta.

"Nice to know someone remembers it," said Alan somewhat modestly.

I also spoke with Mike, the port Captain, and an English couple who were discussing the dreaded T.R.I.W.V. certificate, or to give it it's full title, The Technical Requirements for Inland Waterway Vessels! This was introduced in a European Union Directive in 2006 and applied to all boats over 20 metres in length by a bunch of cardboard cut-out bureaucrats who obviously thought that anyone swanning around the canals of Europe on a barge didn't have enough to worry about: and this sneaky bit of legislation certainly did get a lot of people very worried. It was basically a certificate of worthiness. A similar scheme had been introduced on the English canals for all craft several years ago, the Boat Safety Certificate, which was renewable every four years and without which you could not get a licence. At the time of its introduction it was derided for being far too strict and potentially costly. The examination was more stringent than a vehicle MOT - and this for a narrowboat travelling at a maximum speed of 4 mph! A whole new mini industry came into being with courses for technicians to qualify as 'Boat Examiners' who could then charge up to £150 for the test. A bit of a sledge hammer to crack a nut, and condemned by boating organisations as purely a licence to print money.

The TRIWV was an even more stringent examination and involved a hull thickness test, something that could only done with the vessel out of the water. As is usually the case with such things, a confusing amount of speculation and fake news surrounded the test and it was difficult to sort out the wheat from the chaff. The examination was phased in over a number of years with older boats required to comply first. Saul Trader was only 24 years old at this time and I found out eventually that I did not need to get the certificate until 2017 which meant that I had another 3 years before I needed to get something organised. It was conceded by most that there were some checks that did make sense - carbon dioxide leakage monitoring for one thing, currently certificated fire extinguishers too, although other more obtuse requirements, like the posting of a "Man Overboard Procedure" notice or "No Smoking" signs in the engine room, seemed a bit more fastidious. One of the stipulations that frightened a lot of people with older boats was the need for a watertight bulkhead. At least ST had one of those.

The people I spoke to in Meilhan had a 1920's Spitz and they had just returned from the dry dock at Toulouse. Their boat had passed most of the test but there were a few things that they needed to put right before the certificate could be issued. Saul Trader, as I have said, was too deep drafted for some of the smaller docks, and apparently Toulouse offered the nearest viable option. It was something that had to be done sooner or later and I resolved to look into it more closely. There were a lot of older retired commercial boats coming on to the market without a certificate, most of which had little or no chance of finding a buyer. I tried to cast these problems from my mind believing the theory that there was little point in fretting about anything until the time arrived for action.

We stopped at Villeton the next afternoon having decided that we would slum it and dine on the pizza again.

There were several boat lengths of empty mooring and I opted for the furthest, behind a small steel cruiser, but found that it was too shallow to get more that a metre from the quay. There was a woman sitting on a bench who asked me whether I could move back as her hotel boat was due to arrive and this was their usual mooring. I was about to move anyway to try and find a bit more water and shunted astern three or four boat lengths where we nestled beautifully alongside. I was a bit surprised that a hotel boat was apparently drawing less than us, but sure enough, half an hour later the 28 metre hotel "St Louis" arrived and nudged gently on to the pontoon. Later that afternoon, Andy returned from a stroll into the village clutching a bottle of wine and grinning like the proverbial cat.

"Present from the skipper of the 'St Louis'," he said, "as a thank you for being nice and moving to leave him room to moor!"

Since then, whenever we met up with the St Louis we were always greeted with a friendly wave. The beautifully appointed boat was run by an Irish couple, Wendy and Peter, and the pilot, a large amicable Irishman with the unlikely name of Minnis. The irony of course was that it was the very same boat that had belonged to the supercilious Scotsman at Montauban.

We chatted with another couple of 'grey pound' adventurers in the shape of Tony, a squeeze-box playing Welsh folkie who was touring Europe with his wife in a sort of garden shed that he had built himself and secured to the back of a Ford Ranger with ratchet straps! They gave us 'the tour', which actually simply involved standing at the back door and peering into the small box that made up the accomodation. There was no room for more than 1½ people.

Another barge, 'Bluegum' arrived and tied up behind us, and the wife told us she was a keen runner and jogged back each day to where they had left their car to drive it back to the boat in readiness for the next days move. This could sometimes mean a run of over 20 kilometres - a strange sort of way to keep fit, but it did mean that you always had the car handy for excursions to the supermarket!

I even managed to sell one of my books - well, to be honest it was Jeanette who sold it. I had a poster stuck in the window of the wheelhouse but whenever I saw anyone taking an interest, I shrunk shamefully into the background with embarrassment. Whether our latest punter enjoyed the book or threw it away after the first chapter I never found out.

We stopped briefly for a lunch break at the ancient village of Mas d'Agenais, which sits at the top of a steep hill on a limestone ridge above the canal. We stocked up with a few stores and took a look inside the church with its well-kept secret - an original painting by Rembrandt of Christ on the Cross which hangs in the nave. At first glance it looked a bit vulnerable hanging there but on closer inspection I noticed a hidden security camera and what looked like the wiring for an alarm. Not that I was thinking about trying to get away with it tucked under my shirt, but I'm sure others had thought about it. There is another ornate castellated bridge here that crosses the Garonne, a quaint market hall and a superbly restored laverie, or wash-house, that is fed by a spring said to have been flowing continuously for 2000 years.

Back at Buzet sur Baise we tied up on the quay outside the office where the Wifi reception was much better and there was water and electricity bornes alongside - and paid the price for such luxury - 40 Euros for a two night stay. The electricity was extra - 2 Euros for a token that gave about four hours of the magic volts. Before slotting the token into the machine I noticed that the meter was still showing a fairly large balance of power so to speak, so I plugged in and was rewarded with eight hours charging free, gratis and for nothing. Little results that make life a bit more bearable. I wondered whether the meter had been over-fed by the 'St Louis' which would have made it doubly ironic. We had a few days to spare so I decided to bite the bullet and venture on to the River Baise. At the lock I was asked for the draft which I gave as 1.0 metre. This had always been something of an unknown. The original markings on the side of the wheelhouse that had been there since the boat was built showed the draft as 3 feet, but I knew from experience that this couldn't be right. As far as I knew the estimated 1.0 metre was nearer the mark, and what was an inch or two between friends. It was something I would come to regret and which almost lost me some friends.

Below the bottom lock of the staircase boats can go straight on downstream to access the Lot, where a special tug is stationed to tow lower powered craft against the stream to the first lock , or make a 180° turn to the right to continue on the Baise. This was the route we took as the Lot would definitely not be deep enough for us and we soon passed under the canal on a 10 kilometre stretch to the first lock below the village of Vianne. All went smoothly enough and after an hour and a half we approached the lock, protected from the weir stream by a low wall. Andy leapt off and climbed the steps to set the lock in motion, the gates opened and I motored slowly inside.

Or at least that was the plan. Halfway into the lock we grounded, hard and fast half way in and half way out. I opened the throttle gently in an attempt to coax us over the cill but it wasn't having any of it.

One of the drawbacks with automatic locks is that you can't open paddles manually to let in water unless all gates are

83

closed, which may have helped us just enough to ease into the lock. After a lot more revving and clouds of smoke I did manage to get the boat to go backwards very slowly and threw a rope to Andy who had come back down to the wall. It was four o'clock in the afternoon and there wasn't a soul about. A hire boat did come down through the lock a bit later on and I thought momentarily that the extra water and the wash as he passed us might help give us a bit more flotation but nothing doing. We were stuck good and proper with no immediate prospect of getting help. Andy leapt back aboard across the gap on to the 2" wide gunwhale lip. He was fit and lithe for a forty five year old but it still frightened me to death every time he did it and I always shouted automatically to him to be careful, to which I just got a cheeky grin in return.

At least we had a cook and Jeanette took control of the galley and suggested some garlic prawns, something that was unanimously approved. I telephoned the lock at Baise to tell them about our predicament and they promised to send somebody out the following morning. So there was nothing for it but to sit out the night, stuck embarrassingly in mid channel. We could have got ashore by crossing the lock and following a footpath to a road bridge in order to get across the river into the village but there seemed little point. We had enough on board for the night and so we decided to sit it out. We opened a bottle of Vin Buzet and set up the crib board.

At nine o'clock the next morning we heard a shout and looked up to find a lock-keeper standing on the gate. He had already started to empty the lock and I wound up the engine and waited apprehensively. We had been hard aground on the mud overnight about 4 feet from the wall but the sudden rush of water from the emptying lock put just enough water under the bottom to lift the boat long enough for us to be able to push off from the wall. The gates opened invitingly and I motored tentatively towards the lock, more in hope than expectation. The level hadn't changed overnight and I knew we would get the same result trying to get over the immovable object that was the lock cill, and as expected half way in we came to a grinding halt. I gave it a bit more revs to no avail and the keeper, who now had control of the paddles manually, lifted them half way up and the flow of water surged underneath us and lifted the boat a few more inches so that with a bit more power and the rev counter showing 1500 we very slowly passed over the offending ledge into the lock. At the top I expected the éclusier to tell me that that was our lot, make us turn around and go back from whence we had come, but instead he waved an arm in the direction of the moorings beside the village, indicating that there was plenty of water there for us. I was amazed to find that we could get alongside with ease and we tied up for the day. I had a chat with the lock-keeper who told me his name was Patrice after we had secured and he seemed to think we would be OK to carry on to Condom but with an unusual reserve I told him that I didn't want to risk putting them to any more trouble and would rather return to Buzet. He agreed to leave us where we were for the day and come back to get us back through the lock next morning.

We had a very pleasant day in Vianne. We strolled around the village and visited a small workshop where we watched fascinated as a traditional glass-blower fashioned his beautifully coloured and shaped wares with an expertise that was quite astonishing. There were shelves of finished products for sale and Dawn splashed out on a set of beautiful violet tinted fluted champagne glasses. In the evening we ate outside a very nice restaurant - to be more exact Alan, Dawn and I while Jeanette seemed to be getting eaten and Andy spent half the time smearing Tiger Balm ointment on her rash of mosquito bites.

Our personal éclusier Patrice turned up as promised at 10 o'clock and we motored across to get in position to reluctantly enter the lock as soon as the gates opened. I thought I had caused enough trouble and didn't want to hold him up any longer than necessary as I was sure he had better things to be doing with his time. So the lock emptied, the gates opened and we motored out, over the nasty cill, only to stop dead more or less exactly in the same place where we had stuck two days earlier. Patrice opened the top paddles as far as they would go and a minor tidal wave of water came tumbling down the lock towards us. After about ten minutes of this, with the stern lifting and then the bow sticking, and then when I had moved the bow with the aid of a bit of stern gear and both bow-thruster, the stern slewed stubbornly back on to the mud.

Eventually we both realised that we were going nowhere and Patrice made a call on his mobile and came down to tell us that they were sending out a tug to rescue us - from Buzet, and it would be with us in an hour. I have to admit that my first thought was oh my god, how much was this going to cost me.

Just over an hour later the tug came blasting around the bend in the river, dropped a couple of men on the wall who shook hands with Patrice, and then spun impressively around to reverse up to Saul Trader's bow. Two more men climbed onto our bow and took a couple of large hawsers from the tug which they attached to our port and starboard bollards. They all seemed a bit over excited and agitated and it was obvious that they weren't used to doing a job like this. After a lot of shouting and gesticulating someone gave the signal to the tug driver, the strain took up on the hawsers and Saul Trader, after a few seconds of obstinacy, began to slowly slide forward. It only took a few yards before we floated free and the men in the bows, with more excited shouting, cast off the ropes. I slowed Saul Trader with the engine, we dropped off the supernumeraries on to the wall, and we were free again. Having regained their full compliment, the tug sped off leaving us to make our own way back to the locks at Buzet, wondering all the while just what sort of reception we would be getting. In the event, as we floated to the top of the upper chamber, the éclusier that we had spoken to when we left, strolled over to the boat and said nonchalantly,

"You tell me one metre. I don't think so!"

I thought the same to be honest but shrugged sheepishly and made a mental note to have the draft checked properly as soon as I could. I would like to explore the Baise, and for that matter the Lot, but it would have to be done in a smaller boat, one of these days! We stayed in Buzet for another night. John and Judith had arrived and we all ate in what was suggested to be the best restaurant, beside the canal. It was certainly the most expensive, and it was obviously popular as we had to book to secure the very last available table, but I have to say it didn't do much for me. The food took an age and was in my opinion almost average - the sort of trendy stuff that concentrates more on making the food look pretty and artistic on the plate, and less on the actual quality. Shades of Buzzard and his gourmet experience.

Back at Sérignac we met another English couple, Dave, who his wife Karen told me, liked to be called David, on their wide beam narrowboat, 'Oxymoron' - no sorry, 'Élegance'. They were a very nice couple, easy to like, and we quickly made friends with them. They had a residential berth at the far end of the pontoon and had developed a little garden outside the boat with swinging sun chairs and solar-powered lights hanging in the trees. We all ate that evening in the restaurant L'Escale. Surprising everyone, including me, Claudine rushed out to greet us and gave me a long lingering hug accompanied with a French kiss - well not that sort of French kiss, the one that the French do on each cheek. I couldn't quite remember but wondered whether this was anything to do with the size of the tip I'd left the last time we were here.

At Agen we found another space beside the grass on the far side of the basin and went into town for an afternoon stroll. While the girls were window shopping and Alan and Andy went off to find a bar, and I decided to go back to the boat. I stopped for a few minutes on the footbridge over La Gare to watch the trains. A TGV called at the station and I overheard on the tannoy that it would be calling at Bordeaux and Paris and my ears pricked up. I was going off on another railway jaunt around Europe in a couple of weeks time, amongst other things to visit a favourite narrow gauge system in the Harz Mountains in the former East German Republic and the unique and fascinating 100 year old overhead suspended railway that ran for 15 kilometres above the streets of Wuppertal. I had booked the first leg of my journey by TGV from Bordeaux to Paris Montparnasse. At the time of booking my intention was to leave the boat at Castets for the duration but at 25 Euros per day, a three week stay was going to be a little bit too expensive. I had arranged with Madame Cholet to leave Saul Trader in Sérignac for the same period for just 25 Euros per week. So putting two and two together and making five, I decided to re-book my trip and start out from Agen instead - much closer, much easier to park, and altogether a brilliant idea. I went back into the station and made some enquiries at the booking office. It was a simple matter to book the train from Agen and so I duly extended my ticket for a few extra Euros. I thought I was being very clever. It would mean changing carriages at Bordeaux but that should pose no problem as there was a good ten minute stop. Pride comes before a fall as they say. As it turned out, it would hardly have made the top one hundred in the Billboard cleverness charts.

Well the idea in itself was fine, it was the execution that left a bit to be desired.

The Spectacle was as good as ever and I likened it to watching a film for a second time when you notice lots of things that you missed first time around. Our allotted seats were situated at the opposite end of the grandstand which gave a completely different perspective and I noticed several street performers in the market scene that I hadn't noticed before - a unicyclist, a Dellboy character with a battered suitcase full of dodgy watches, and a conjuror who produced a live rabbit from a hat, which promptly did a runner and escaped into the crowds, before being caught (red-handed) by the overworked policeman. Half an hour before the end of the show it started to drizzle and Alan was particularly upset to see that quite a lot of people had to started to leave.

"That's terrible," he moaned, " all the effort all these actors have put into this and these wimps can't sit it out worried that they might get a bit damp. What would they say if all the participants disappeared?"

We stoically sat it out to the bitter end - and sod the rain.

My friends departed the following morning - Alan and Dawn to 'Animo' and Andy and Jeanette to Toulouse. Andy was flying to Texas the following week to give a talk to some executives from American Airlines, and Jeanette was off to her part-time job as a tour guide taking a party to Scotland and the Edinburgh Tattoo. For me, a day in Valenece before a single-handed run back to Sérignac to leave the boat with Madame Cholet while I galavanted around Eastern Europe. When I turned the key to start the engine there was an ominous clunk and it took several attempts before the motor finally burst into life. I thought it was probably a loose connection to the starter motor and forgot about it. I did the trip to Sérignac in a single day.

Then two days before I was due to leave, by train to Paris and beyond, Madame Cholet asked me to move Saul Trader alongside Élegance in order to free up space on the pontoon. I turned the key to start the engine which produced another obstinate thud. I tried again - and again, and several more times before coming to the conclusion that something was definitely not right. *"I didn't get where I am today without realising when something was not right,Reggie"*.

Dave(id) suggested the starter motor and it suddenly occurred to me that this had all started at the end of last year, when I had mistakenly diagnosed the problem as batteries. Shit! I was about to go off for three weeks and Dave and Becky were coming down a couple of days after my return. What to do now? There was a garage in the village and I went to see whether they could help. They suggested the mechanic at the Nicols hire base at Buzet and I telephoned the Capitan to explain my problem. There were two girls in the Aquitaine office, both of whom spoke excellent English and were always very helpful. Suzanna was actually Australian and she told me that their engineer was out on a call but could probably come over in the afternoon to assess the situation.

Alain arrived in his little van at 3.30pm and immediately went below, re-emerging half an hour later shaking his head. The starter motor was definitely en panne but he could take it to an auto-electrical workshop that he knew to see whether it could be reconditioned. That seemed a good plan so Alain took the offending part and told me to call him at the boatyard the following morning. There was good news and bad news. Yes it could be repaired but not for two weeks and at a cost of 1300 Euros!! Even with my limited knowledge of such things I realised that this was ridiculously over the top. I could imagine the conversation.

"Yes Algie. It's a huge boat. Guy's obviously loaded. And in the shit. Haha. Yeah. Think of a number and treble it. I'll take the usual 10% OK. Yeah no probleme."

Call me a cynic if you like. The only thing was to talk to another confirmed cynic, Mr Trotter at Saul. Phil was his useful "helpful" self.

"Can't remember what we put in there now. Long time ago. Obviously a good'un as it's lasted all this time. Try a bloke called Bob. Manchester I think - firm's called Middleton or something like that. He's pretty helpful. I haven't got the number. Be in the book. Good luck. I didn't get the chance to tell him that I didn't carry the complete telephone directory for Manchester in my back pocket before he'd put down the 'phone, but thanks to the old faithful Ipad, I found a firm that I thought must be the one - and after a listing for a Middleton Auto Electrical in Happy Valley South Australia, I found it - G.E. Middleton (*best Auto Electric place in North West, always get what you need here*) , City Road, Manchester.

"Hello. Is that Bob?"

"No it's his brother Jim. Is it Bob you're after?"

"Er - yes please."

"OK - right you are. 'ang on a tick."

Bob was very helpful. I gave him the part number that I had thought to keep a note of, and he said he would check in the stores and could I call back after dinner. They obviously still had dinner at midday in Manchester. When I spoke to him later he confirmed that he did indeed have a re-con starter motor on the shelf, ready to go.

"I can let it go for 250 quid," he told me, sounding almost reluctant to part with it. Well that was certainly better than Pierre's price.

"OK great," I said, " the only thing is I need it delivered to France."

From the tone of his reply you'd have thought I'd asked him to personally deliver it to Guadeloupe.

"Oh no, sorry, we can only deliver to the United Kingdom."

By now I was starting to get a bit frustrated - I was due to leave the next day.

"It's only France," I pleaded. "Don't you use DHL or Fedex or people like that?" I could tell I was talking to a brick wall.

"No no nowt like that - never 'eard of 'em. You'd 'ave to arrange sommat like that yourself like."

"OK," I said, trying not to add that this was after all 2014 and there were thousands of satellites orbiting the Earth at this very second.

"Leave it with me Bob. I'll call you back. Oh, and please don't sell it to anyone else," I added as an afterthought. I arranged a collection and delivery to France on-line with DHL and paid by credit card, in under ten minutes. It cost £55 for a next-day service, tracked.

Then I called Bob and paid him by credit card.

"They're going to pick it up between ten and eleven tomorrow morning," I told him, "You'll need to print off the label that they are sending direct to you by Email to fix on to the package."

I felt as though I was speaking to my 95 year old grandmother.

"Ah - OK righto then. We'll need to fire up t'internet then - haven't run it for a couple of days - takes a while to warm it up, specially this weather.

There was nothing more I could do about it except keep my fingers crossed. I drove to Aquitaine to explain what was happening. The part was going to be delivered to them so that Alain could get it fitted into the boat while I was away. I would leave the keys to the boat with Dave(id).

The next day I drove to the station at Agen. I parked in the station car park without checking the cost. Ten minutes later the TGV bound for Paris Montparnasse glided into Platform 2. I climbed into my seat beside the window and actually relaxed. I would have to change carriages in Bordeaux as I had two separate tickets. - For the first leg I was allocated a seat in coach No 3, whereas from Bordeaux to Paris I would be sitting in Coach no 13. I would have about five minutes in Bordeaux to make the move.

When we arrived I could tell immediately that I was going to need all of those precious five minutes. The station was undergoing a massive refurbishment and the narrow platform was made even smaller with scaffolding covered in green mesh netting. There were hundreds of people getting off and hundreds more clamouring to get on and I had to barge my way through the crowds in the sweltering heat, rucksack hanging on my back and my little wheelie bin suitcase dragging along behind. TGV coaches are very long, and I had ten of them to negotiate to find my place in Coach 13. I started to get worried and jumped into coach 12 in a panic, seconds before the train started to move. I squeezed myself through the train and eventually found my seat - 29, only to find it occupied by a young husband with wife and child alongside.

91

"Excuse me," I said, "but this is my seat, proffering my ticket. Coach 13 Seat 29".

"No no you are mistaken monsieur, this is our seats."

The young man started to look for his tickets as the conductor approached to see what the fuss was about. OK I thought, now we'll sort it out - damned imposters. Why can't people read the seat numbers properly? The conductor took a quick look at my ticket before telling me.

"You are quite right. This is the correct seat for you".

I had to try hard not to look too smug at this news, which as it turned out was just as well.

"But, monsieur, this is not your train. This is train 8202 and this ticket is for train 8504. Your train leave Bordeaux later by ten minutes."

It didn't seem possible that there were two separate TGV's leaving Bordeaux for Paris ten minutes apart. The conductor informed me that this train was "complet" - in other words there were no spare seats. I asked him where the next stop was so that I could get off and wait for the correct train.

"Paris," he said triumphantly, as though he was boasting proudly about the fine express trains in France that don't bother to stop just any old where. "Paris - it is the only stop."

He then mentioned that as I was on the wrong train I was in effect travelling illegally and would have to buy another ticket, but after conferring with his mate decided to let me off that small imposition, presumably as I wasn't going to be occupying a seat and he thought that I was a complete idiot.

So that was it then - my best laid plan had fallen flat on it's arse and I was destined to stand up for the next three hours. I cursed myself for not checking the number of the train - and me, a dyed-in-the wool trainspotter at that. I knew that I had to change carriages but it never dawned on me that I would have to change bloody trains. In the event the kindly conductor, who I think found it all rather amusing and a welcome relief from the monotonous task of finding everybody with exactly the right ticket in exactly the right seat, led me to the Buffet Car where I propped my bum on a bright red plastic tractor seat with a beer and a slice of pizza and watched the world speed past as we headed north at 180 miles an hour - heaven!

A train leaving one of the stations on the Wuppertal Overhead Railway.......... and another swinging along high above the street

I had an enjoyable few weeks travelling by train through Eastern Europe and returned to Agen three weeks later on the newly inaugurated Strasbourg - Bordeaux TGV, having visited France, Germany, Poland, the Czech Republic, and Austria and travelled on 25 trains, including those on the Harz Railway, and never getting onto the wrong train once.

Suzanne from Aquitaine Marine had emailed me to say that the starter motor had arrived and that Alain had fitted it successfully so thankfully we were able to carry on. I collected Dave and Becky from Agen station, the engine fired into life on the first flick of the key, and we pottered off west back to Buzet, where I settled up the balance with Aquitaine Marine. There was no room in the port itself and we tied a few hundred metres away in a small haven alongside the beautiful Dutch Luxemotor 'Spes.' While there I took the opportunity to have a chat with Mike, the owner of the boat, and a long-standing member of the Barge Association. Mike had done a lot research into the mysteries of the TRIWV and kindly gave me some information that he had printed out. Several DBA members had been trying to organise a group inspection by a surveyor from Holland, but he had been ill and it wasn't at all certain when he would be available. There were a couple of other names on the list that I contacted, a Frenchman who would have to travel 100 kilometres and quoted 3250 Euros, and another Dutchman, Rob van Dijk, whose company were based in Steenwijk in the Friesland region of Holland, over 1250 kilometres away, who quoted me 2000 Euros. Of course this didn't cover the cost of any remedial work that may need to be done, or the cost of the dry-docking. I started to study the various requirements that would be needed to get the certificate and soon gave up. As to be expected the DBA forums were buzzing with the opinions of amateur "experts", eager to shove in their five eggs. It was the stuff of sleepless nights and nightmares and I came to the conclusion that nothing, or certainly very little, was actually set in stone. Reports from some barge owners that there was a certain latitude in the interpretation of the rules by different surveyors was borne out when I compared notes with Rob who had used another company for the survey on "Pisgah" and had a completely different list of "essential" work to do to satisfy the examiner.

I had been giving all this some thought. and I had spoken to Balliol Foden, an English marine surveyor based at Braunston, who told me that he was not authorised to do the work, and suggested asking around for a French equivalent. I did not have to get the certificate until 2017, but as Balliol pointed out, the nearer the time came to the deadline, the likelihood of all qualified surveyors being over-run with work could make things difficult. It would mean a dry-docking and then at least we would be able to accurately measure the draft. The only answer, I concluded, was to suck it and see.

I had decided that the dry-dock at Toulouse was the best bet for us and the first thing I had to do was book the docking. The manager was a guy called Eric who I learned did not speak English and the waiting list was over 6 months. I didn't relish the idea of attempting to negotiate a deal on the 'phone so I drove to Toulouse to seek out Eric and find out the lie of the land so to speak. My GPS faithfully led me to the somewhat seedy-sounding Allées des Demoiselles and the entrance to the boatyard where I was met by an electrically operated gate that was firmly shut. An intercom set into the wall brought no response to my cheery Bonjour and I was beginning to think I had come all that way on a fruitless mission.

As I was pondering what to do a little white van, the ubiquitous VNF wagon arrived, the gates parted obediently and I took the chance to dart in quickly behind before getting trapped forever in their steely grasp as they slowly swung shut. I found Eric hunched over a desk with a serious frown, peering over the top of his spectacles at a large ledger. He didn't look overly excited by my arrival and muttered something in French which I took to mean well what do <u>you</u> want?

The first suitable free date that was convenient for me was in June the following year. He asked me for Saul Trader's draft and to be on the safe side I gave it as 1.1 metre - once bitten etc. I didn't want to be caught out again if I could help it. There were actually three dry docks - one large open-air space large enough for two vessels side by side, and a beautiful historic covered dock, with open arched sides. This, Eric told me emphatically, was where Saul Trader would have to go. The basin into the dock was accessed through a low footbridge over the towpath which was only opened twice a week. One week would not be enough to get all the work completed so I had to reserve two.The cost of the actual docking was ridiculously cheap - five Euros a day, plus a bit extra for "luxuries" such as a ladder to be able to climb on and off once we were settled on the blocks. Eric proceeded to fill out the application form which I signed - he didn't want any money at the time, and presented me with three pages of do's and don'ts while in the dock, which thankfully, was in English. One of the stipulations was that any work had to be carried out by a French certificated contractor, which put paid to any ideas I had of getting Dog up from Ventenac to black the hull. I thanked him for his time and we shook hands.

While I was standing admiring the craftsmanship of the empty cavernous dock wit its intricate brickwork and cathedralesque sweeping rafters and wishing I had a tape measure with me so that I could measure the depth over the cill, I was approached by a young man who had arrived in a battered Renault Master with a tail-lift and who walked towards me offering me a hand in which he was clutching a well-worn calling card.

"Hi. My name is Serge, and I do most of the work on the boats here. If you need anything at all I can do very good work for you. Welding, electrical, blasting, hull painting. Anything we can do it."

I have to say that my first impression was that he looked a bit dodgy - maybe it was the battered van or the fact that his face and arms were covered in dirt.

"Come here - look at this one," he said, leading me across the top gate to the open-air dock. There was a nice little Luxemotor flying a red ensign, it' s freshly blacked hull gleaming.

"This is Englishman - Frank. You know him? We finish this yesterday - good work you think? You can send me Email for price for anything. Always I give a good price. We do much work for English."

I had to agree that it looked like a very good job and I promised to contact him once I knew what we would need to do. The hull would need power-washing anyway for the surveyor to be able to do the ultra-sound thickness test so it would obviously need re-blacking. We shook hands and I left.

"Serge Ribes - Chaudronnerie du Canal du Midi," said the card.

I had already started to warm to him. He seemed a conscientious sort of bloke who was interested in his work and who spoke excellent English. He could prove a very useful find. I left the boat at Ventenac that winter, on the wharf opposite John on Tressnish. As I drove away the usual doubts and worries went through my head, but at least John and Judy would be there to keep an eye on it. I thought of the words of the old boy at Carcassonne.

" An I'll tell er somethink ellse. Once you go away you be worrying fer ten minute then you forget all abowt it till you get back". Well , not exactly forget all about it - but I took his point.

Chapter 7   2015 and the T.R.I.W.V

Over the winter I had several Email conversations and various quotes from Serge for the docking at Toulouse, preparing the hull for the TRIWV inspection and subsequent blacking. I had booked the dock from the 23rd June until the 9th July and had set up an appointment with Rob van Dyke to come from Holland for the survey on the 26th which would give Serge enough time to get the hull ready for the ultrasound check. I flew from Heathrow to Toulouse, took the bus to Matabiau station and caught the 19.25 train to Valence. I had bought my ticket online from the excellent SNCF website for 16 Euros for the journey of one hour. The route closely follows the cut and stopped at several familiar places - Montauban, Castelsarrassin and Moissac before reaching Valence on time at 20.30.

I am always surprised by the number of people, usually French, that travel on these trains without a ticket. The inspectors move through the train quite regularly and when they find someone with no ticket, and who then pleads poverty by throwing up arms or giving the guard a desultory look of defiance, they are asked for an address which is then recorded with no proof of identity required, and it is left at that. I imagine that most get away scot free and it is left to the honest traveller to subsidise the scroungers. I have even seen this scenario with people sitting in the 1st Class areas with their feet on the seats! Not my problem I know but it quietly infuriates me.

I wheeled my little case noisily through the streets of Valence, nodding a greeting to Skinny as I passed, and found Saul Trader exactly as I had left it. John and Judy were aboard Tressnish and Judith kindly provided me with a welcome meal. In the morning I set off with renewed vigour and headed for Toulouse. I successfully passed through the first lock - not an easy exercise single-handed, particularly when going uphill. First there was the ubiquitous pole that needed to be twisted to set the lock in motion, simple enough, and then when the water had emptied and the gates opened, driving into the lock. I then had to stop the boat against the wall with just enough forward movement, then walk forward to the bow and attempt to throw a bight of line over the lock-side bollard allowing enough rope to be able to secure it to the bits on the boat in such a way as to lead with enough angle to be able to motor gently against it. I then had to go back to the wheelhouse, reverse far enough to be able to reach the ladder, usually between six and ten feet astern, stop the boat, climb the ladder and push the button to start the filling operation, run back to the ladder and shimmy down to the boat, and shove the gear into forward again to take up the slack - all hopefully in the time it took for the gates to close and the paddles to raise. After this I could relax a little and let the lock do the work: gates closed, paddles lifted and the lock slowly filling while I adjusted the power to keep the boat alongside the wall, then gates open, let go the ropes, and away. Voila! All cushty until halfway along the next pound I suddenly noticed that the red alternator light was glowing and the rev counter had stopped working and worse the temperature gauge was slowly but surely rising. It could only mean one thing - a broken alternator belt. I scurried below to find that in this case my diagnosis had been spot on - little consolation. I coaxed the boat through the next lock, keeping the revs to a minimum. I knew that there was a possibility to tie up at the small Haute Nautique at Pommevic and luckily there were no other boats there. I glided Saul Trader slowly alongside, secured the ropes, and wondered what the hell to do next.

I did have a spare belt but when I offered it up it looked a few centimetres short. I phoned John and he told me he had loads of them and suggested I come back and have a look. I obviously couldn't take the boat so the Brompton was called into action and I cycled back the two and a half kilometres to Valence, clutching the fragmented belt. John was a marvel. He pulled open a drawer to reveal enough alternator belts to service a fleet of warships. There were over 20 of varying lengths and widths but unfortunately not being a bloody warship, none that actually matched mine. I took half a dozen that were a fairly close match and pedalled off back to Pommevic, not that hopeful that any of them would do the job.

Back on the boat I immediately went into action - made a coffee and rolled a cigarette. Time for composure and thought. Then I ventured into that unknown confusion called the engine room and peered at the offending alternator. One of the belts I had brought from John said it was exactly the same length (1150 inches) as the old one, but for some obstinate reason refused to tighten sufficiently on the adjuster. This I realised was because there was a nut on the alternator stopping any extra movement. You know - the sort of nut that is put there just to annoy and frustrate amateur pretenders who think they can do the work of the proper professional. After several more attempts and thoughts of resorting to the hammer, I returned to the wheelhouse for more procrastinating. Half way through completing the job (in my mind, that is) I became aware of a small black Scottie dog wagging its tail at me on the pontoon outside the wheelhouse. Scottie was then joined by Jock, an amiable native of that country who had, he told me, lived in Pommevic for the past twenty years - far from his home town of Dumbarton on the banks of the Clyde. Jock listened patiently as I explained my plight before suggesting I contact a Monsieur Lanniard, who ran a local Ford garage and who, according to Jock, could fix any problem you cared to throw at him. Scottie and Jock continued on their way and with a nothing ventured nothing gained mindset, I unfolded the Brompton again and pointed it in the direction of M Lanniard - or Denis, according to Jock. I found the garage easily enough. It was on the main road between Valence and Moissac. My first sight of Denis was a pair of booted feet that stuck out from beneath a rusty Fiesta, its back-end precariously propped up on equally rusty ramps. A muffled grunt from the depths accompanied by a kick of a boot told me that I should speak to the woman in the office next door. This was Mrs Denis, who was obviously the brains behind the organisation. I explained my predicament as best I could with the aid of the severed belt and she looked sympathetic. M. Lanniard however was very very busy and would not be able to do anything today. He would do his best to come to see me in the morning. Well it was better than nothing. In the meantime I would go back to the boat and have another try - I wasn't going to be beaten by a bloody belt. After several more failed attempts I concluded that I had been beaten by a bloody belt, opened a bottle of beer, and hoped M. Denis would find the time to come and have a look. Later that afternoon another boat arrived at the mooring - Frank and Penny on a very smart peniche - one of those irritatingly immaculate boats that looks as though it has never been through a lock in its life.

"Think Logic," advised Frank on hearing of my plight, "that's my motto."

I think he had remembered it from a night school diesel maintenance course for beginners.

As good as Mrs Denis' word, Mr Denis arrived in a little van at 10.00 am the next morning, carrying a toolbox and with half a dozen belts dangling from his arm. Praise the Lord. I had been saved ! After shaking my hand and declining my offer of a coffee, probably thinking, correctly as it happened, that it would be an English mug of weakly flavoured hot water, and settled himself in front of the patient. As is normal in these situations I made myself scarce and retired to the galley to make myself a mug of weakly flavoured hot water. I looked in on him after half an hour and he was humming away contentedly, a sure sign that progress was being made. After another half an hour Denis emerged into the daylight with a grin and indicated that I should fire up the motor. With a whoosh the engine burst into life, the red warning light disappeared and the rev counter needle flew up to its correct position. Simple - when you know how. I settled Denis' very reasonable bill which included a spare belt (of the correct size this time). I bade farewell to Frank, promising him that I would not forget his motto, cast off and set fair towards Moissac, where I intended to stop for the night. The approach into Moissac from the west follows a narrow walled channel that is reminiscent of some towns in Holland. After a blind turn you are confronted a hundred metres or so later with a very low swing bridge that is controlled by traffic lights and a bridgeman who sits alongside in a small cabin. Anxious not to hold up traffic any longer than necessary I crept through the gap before the light had changed to green and got a telling off for my trouble.

It was a Friday when I arrived in Moissac, the night when traditionally the sleepy headed boating community gather up their loins and present themselves at the "Sunbeam", a small inn close to the river, for pizza and pints and some jolly hilarity on the Karaoke mic. As it happened this particular Friday also marked the auspicious occasion of the birthday of the port Capitan, Iain. I must confess that I did rather have to have my arm twisted to join the merry throng but in the event I was glad I did. I sat with Jim and his wife Sandra and a lady called Jane who had a boat called Seawolf and knew the boys at Saul Junction, and we had a most convivial evening, marred only mildly by the intrusion of a number of tuneless performances from some of the more gregarious of the boating fraternity. Jim, who was born in Kent but wisely didn't stay long, had fetched up at Moissac some years earlier in his small wooden cruiser and dropped the proverbial anchor. He had spent many years in the States of Alaska and California, spoke fluent French and was apparently a trained chef and had a forceful opinion about most things. He had a pretty good singing voice too and gave a very good rendering of the Jimmy Buffett song "Margaretaville."

Narrow cut approaches to Moissac

It was a great evening with great company. I got to know Jim a little better over the next few years. He has now taken over as the Port Capitan after Iain and Caz departed for foreign shores - the Dominican Republic I think, but not by boat. I left the party fairly early as I needed to be away in the morning, but not before leaving a pint behind the bar for the birthday boy. One thing that did intrigue me was the demeanour of the owner of the bar, a sour miserable looking Frenchman, who looked as though it was as much as he could do to serve anyone with a drink. Less understandably as the bar was packed with people drinking freely and spending money. Would he have been happier if the place had been deserted I wondered.

I set off the next morning as soon as the locks were open at 9.00 am, and cracked on to Grisolles in order to make up some of the time I had lost over the alternator belt. The first three locks are quite tricky, especially for the single-hander. They are quite deep, 2.6 metres and the influx of water when ascending is a bit turbulent. The other problem is that the bollards are not particularly conveniently spaced for a boat of 21 metres and they change from side to side through the flight. I managed to navigate them without undue problems and turned from the top lock to cross the impressive aqueduct over the River Tarn. I passed Castelsarrassin, dodging all the rotten eggs and moored for the night at Grisolles. Once again there was nothing much on offer and I made do with a quiet evening aboard with a couple of glasses of red and a healthy salad.

At St Jory a somewhat intense boules competition seemed to be in progress. Most of the town had turned out, as had what looked like the entire Pompiers contingent. There was a full compliment of fire engines, emergency tenders, ambulances and vans. I dread to think what would have happened had there been some catastrophic incident.

"Hold on a minute Madame - just finishing a round of boules. What's that ? Well your cat will just have to stay up there for half an hour."

The approach to the centre of Toulouse from the Garonne is pretty seedy to say the least - not a great introduction to what after all is a beautiful and vibrant city. Apparently there are 95000 students in Toulouse and I would venture to suggest that there are almost as many drunks, thieves and ne'er-do-wells. Lock up your daughters and your bicycles. There are three locks that take you up to the centre of the city. The first and lowest is operated by a lock-keeper and the following two are automatic - or that is the theory. Having negotiated lock number two (4.43 metres deep) I approached the top one that rises from the depths over 6 metres into the sunlight opposite the Gare Matabiau and waited for the light - the light that never flickered from the red for STOP. I assumed that another boat must be coming down but after half an hour dismissed this in favour of a breakdown, or just as likely, the controller at the bottom lock had forgotten all about me.

I tied the boat to the one available bollard at the bottom of a foreboding set of stone steps that led up through dark passageway to the lock. I thought there might be a telephone alongside the lock that would connect with the éclusier but I was wrong. I risked my credentials clambering over the iron safety railings that surround the lock at waist level, and wandered around looking for the intercom but there wasn't one. Back to the boat to scratch the head and ponder my next move. I could be stuck there in this dungeon for the night. It was getting a bit too close to closing time for comfort. Luckily I had the number of the Capitan at Ste Sauveur, courtesy of a very useful little book that lists all the ports in the whole of France and managed to speak to Arathella who said she couldn't understand what had happened and promised to contact the lock-keeper straight away. Ten minutes later the red changed to red and green and the tell-tale sign of water flowing past the boat told me that the lock was finally getting readied. Once inside the next problem was to find a suitable place to secure. There were poles set into the walls in these deeper locks and I managed to position Saul Trader such that I could tie up forward and aft. I held on to the one behind the wheelhouse and watched carefully as the boat began to rise. These poles were all well and good but I was always wary of them and tried to make sure that there was nothing in the way that could jamb. Some of them were loose and wobbled about with the strain caused as the water surged in and I thought it must make life quite difficult for smaller craft. Eventually, after a very slow and gentle ascent, the facade of the elegant Matabiau Station gradually appeared over the top of the wall and we were once more in the land of the living, just a few kilometres from the haven that was the Port of Ste Sauveur. Arathella had reserved a space for me alongside the diesel berth and I reversed in and tied up, before checking in, paying for three nights stay (67 Euros inc Electricity) and receiving the all-important Wifi code and the key for the gate to the outside world. The internet reception wasn't brilliant but I found that if I rested the iPad on the deck outside I could listen to Radio 4 through a cunning little device that I had recently acquired, a bluetooth Bose Mini ll Sound Link speaker. Need to know anything about IT? Just ask!

Well to tell the truth I had been told about these devices by Percy, the tech savvy grandson.

It was a Sunday and the Pompiers were holding an open day. All the various appliances and specialist equipment had been dragged out on display, firemen in helmets splayed jets of water into the canal from the top of turntable ladders and kids were hoisted screaming aloft while their parents filmed the imminent disaster on their Iphones, and sat in the cabs playing with horns and flashing lights. A small roundabout had been set up and a stall sold candy floss and ice cream. It seemed that the Pompiers were far too busy these days to do mundane jobs like putting out fires. I tore myself away and headed for De Danu and a traditional French meal of Mexican chilli burger and chips with a cool pint of Guinness.

I took the fold-up to ride to the entrance of the dry-dock in order to familiarise myself with the procedure. The small entrance - it hardly looked wide enough, was closed by a narrow steel bridge on the towpath. The towpaths in Toulouse are death traps for walkers and you really have to have eyes in the back of your head to avoid being mowed down by these speeding velocipedes, manned by Japanese sniper pilots, helmeted heads staring into the void behind menacingly darkened goggles that obscure all before them.

The Rules and Regulations for Craft entering the cale-seche - Section 3 Paragraph 3(b) subsection (iv) stated clearly that the bridge would open at 7.00am, so like a good boy I cast off from Ste Sauveur at 06.30 on the Tuesday morning and arrived at the entrance at 06.45. There was one other small boat already in position but France being France nobody appeared until ten past nine and then spent another ten minutes shaking hands with each other, smoking cigarettes and scrutinising the bottoms of the lady cyclists as they bumped across the bridge on their way to work. Consequently it was nearly half past nine when they started the intricate operation of opening the bridge - two at either side to manually slide the four foot gate across the towpath and a fifth, obviously the technical one, to press the button on his hand held remote controller to slide the bridge away and open the access. The small boat went in first and I followed. At this point Serge arrived and pointed in the direction I needed to go towards the covered dry dock, telling me to throw him a rope from the bow at a point just outside and then cut the engine. This was because of the profusion of herbes mauvaises, weed to you and me, which we didn't want fouling the prop. Once he had the line I threw another one from the stern to his oppo Ahmed, and left the rest to them. They soon had the boat centrally placed, two more ropes were sent ashore and we were secured at all four corners of the vast dock. Half an hour later, after some tweaking and a bit more shouting, we were sitting comfortably on the blocks.

Next morning, work on the preparation of the hull started in earnest at 7.30am. It was noisy, dusty and hot, the noise exacerbated by the continual rattle of passing trains. Ahmed did most of the hard work and at times I feared for his health. I offered him sustenance - coffee, water, a sandwich- regularly throughout the day but all my offerings were declined with a polite shake of the head. I later found out from Serge that it was Ramadhan, when Muslims observe fasting during the hours between sunrise and sunset, to which Ahmed was religiously adhering. Rob van Dyke, the surveyor, was flying to Toulouse from Amsterdam and he was due to arrive at 10.15. Serge went off to collect him from the airport, but didn't return until 1.00pm. Apparently there was a taxi-drivers' strike and they had blocked the Periphique (they don't do things by halves in France), and it had taken them an hour and a half to do the fifteen minute journey. Once everyone had been introduced, Rob had a quick coffee before stripping down to shorts and Doc Martens and getting down to work with his measuring device, tapping the steel here and there with Maxwell's Silver Hammer. By 5.30pm he had finished the work - hull sound-tested for thickness, and the interior thoroughly surveyed. He then appeared with what looked like a long list of things that needed to be done and my heart sank.

The hull itself was fine - no signs of corrosion or pitting, but there were some things that needed sorting out inside the boat. The main concerns were the wooden engine room doors which would need to be lined with steel sheet on the insides, a means of shutting off the fuel supply to the engine from outside the wheelhouse needed to be fitted, and the plastic diesel filler pipes replaced with steel. Apart from these jobs, which Serge seemed confident he would be able to do, there were a number of minor things like labels at various points - diesel inlets, battery isolator, fuel shut off etc and warning notices about smoking, hard hats, water inlets and toilet outlets, and a list of Man Overboard procedures placed in a visible position in the wheelhouse. We also needed to replace the out-of-date fire extinguishers and acquire a proper lifebuoy with heaving line attached. Rob explained that we had two years to complete the outstanding work and that he would issue the certificate when we had sent him photographic evidence that the jobs had been done. The certificate would then be valid for seven years after the date of the inspection i.e. the 24th of June 2022. Mysteriously, the Dutch certificate was valid for seven years, while the French only covered you for five years and the Belgians for ten years. Rob had booked a hotel overnight in Toulouse but I persuaded him to stay on board and provided him with a dinner and a bed, thinking he might perhaps knock off a few quid by way of thanks but he still charged the full 2000 Euros. Well he was a Dutchman, so what could you expect. I remembered Rob Whitaker's advice and carefully counted my fingers after we had shaken hands.

Being singularly squeamish about living on a boat out of its natural habitat, I buggered off to Portugal for a week while Serge finished the hull blacking and took care of a few more small jobs that had been on my bucket list for a few years. The for'd steaming light was fixed against the mast which was all well and good when the mast was up, but on the canals this was rarely the case as it had to be lowered to clear the bridges. This left it at an angle of about fifteen degrees above the deck which meant that the light was useless as a warning to oncoming shipping but did warn low-flying aircraft of our presence. One of the jobs I asked Serge to do therefore was to put a hinge under the base such that when the mast was down the light would still shine forward. Another niggling problem was the guard on one of the bow thruster tunnels which the lovely Otto had failed to fit several moons ago in Dordrecht and that was another thing that Serge put right. He had also discovered that there was no grease actually coming through the stern bearing and between us we managed to sort out that little problem too. I arranged with Serge to return to the port of Ramonville for the winter so that he could finish the other work required for the TRIWV certificate. We also took the opportunity to properly measure the draft and Serge had painted on a pucker 'Plimsole Line' - at the bow we drew 0.9 metres and aft, at the lowest point below the engine room, the depth was 1.1 metres! We now had the definitive measurement and there could be no more guesswork.

When I got back from Portugal Serge still had a couple of jobs outstanding. Even though he had had two weeks to finish all the work, Ahmed finally fixed the forward light fifteen minutes before we got the call to prepare for filling the dock. We were towed out of the dock with all the available hands on the ropes and promptly grounded on the lock cill. Serge recruited as many people as he could from around the yard - people working on their boats in the open docks, wives, girlfriends, mistresses, cleaners and passing travelling salesmen, to jump on the foredeck of Saul Trader to lower the bow and tilt the balance to raise the stern just enough to get us clear. Free of the herbes mauvaise, I started the engine and turned left to head back to Ste Sauveur. As we left the basin with a shiny new paint job on the hull, Serge had the last word when he shouted to me from the bank.

"Now I hope you will drive the boat more carefully." This did made me think a bit. I wasn't exactly care-less but it was difficult sometimes to avoid the bows hitting the sides of locks. The rubbing strakes on Saul Trader were made from hollow "D" bar and tended to yield easily under the slightest bump. Serge's observation prompted me to buy two large round Polyform buoys which were delivered to my home in a deflated state during the winter. My friend Jerry, Scragg's 'Rambo bloke', helped me struggle for an hour to get them pumped up to the required level. While we were in the process, Jerry's son called his Dad, looking for a lift somewhere or other. After a few minutes conversation, Jerry said,

"Got to go now son. Me and Keith are just giving a blowjob to a couple of buoys!"

Luckily his son's comments were not recorded.

Inside the 'Cathedral'.   ...... stripped down ready for the hull inspection

Chapter 8
Carcassonne and Narbonne

And so it was that I returned to Ste Sauveur, Arathella and the bar of Danu, ancient Goddess and mother of the earth, the gods, fertility, wisdom, wind and of all the Celtic people, where I was due to pick up Andy and Jeanette and Alan and Dawn for the voyage to Carcassonne for Bastille Day, where I vowed to stay awake and compos mentis to actually watch the firework display.

After duly paying our respects to the mystical one - six Euros a pint for protection against storm, pestilence, famine and Frenchmen, we set a course for the Far East and headed off into the unknown, after careful study of Du Breil's Canal Guide. Our first day's voyage brought us to Gardouche, a pleasant enough little town, where we moored, ignoring the Interdit notice forbidding mooring on the lock pontoon, at 18.45 hours. The VNF, presumably after consultation with the equivalent authority in England, the Canal and River (Can't) Trust who had advised them on the best way to frustrate and annoy the innocent boater, had put-up signs banning mooring other than for lock use. The fact that the locks closed anyway at 1900 and there were absolutely no alternative spaces to moor presumably not their problem. Du Breil warned that the few spaces there were had been bagged long since by live-aboards and trip boats. Gardouche, according to the guide, boasted a Thai Restaurant, although enquiries in the area as to its whereabouts produced a blank and a Gallic shrug. However there was a very pleasant little eatery adjacent to the lock where we enjoyed some al fresco salads, with a couple of pichers of Vin Rosé. There are two bakers within 50 yards of each other, both closing on the same day - the very day that we were there in need of pain!

We left Gardouche on the dot at nine o'clock but got little reward for our early departure. At Renneville we passed a trip boat that was loading passengers and thought little of it. We

111

passed through the lock and headed for the next, a double staircase at Encassan. The light was showing a red and we waited patiently for a green which never came. The reason for this became clear when the tripper, full of pensioners on their annual 10 Euro a head jolly (lunch included) appeared and the light changed immediately to let him pass. I was not overly surprised by this as it was common practice to allow bateaux a passagers priority over the likes of us. It was the sequence of events that followed that really got up my nose. Once the trip boat had eventually passed through the two locks, an operation that in itself frustrated us as it seemed to take an eternity, we waited for the bottom chamber to empty so that we could follow.

After fifteen minutes during which time nothing had happened, it became obvious that there was some sort of problem. I could not work out what could be causing this delay - it wasn't lunchtime and the éclusier was still there beside the lock, so we tied up the boat and I went to investigate. As I reached the middle gate I noticed that the top ones were still open. I asked the lock-keeper what was going on and he explained brusquely that we had to wait for the trip to return and then pass back down the lock before we could progress. To say I was perturbed by this is an understatement. I was bloody furious. The nearest turning point was another kilometre and a half away and with the rate that the trip boat was going this was going to take an age. And completely unnecessary. All he had to do was to empty the bottom chamber, let us through, and we would pass Mr day-tripper half way down the next pound, and nobody need to be held up or inconvenienced. Try explaining that to a thick headed Frenchman or walk over to the nearest wall and smash your head against it. It was at least an hour and a half before the boat returned and passed down through the lock. When he finally left, the minion of a deckhand on the bow had the effrontery to wave at me to move to the left to let him pass. My answer to that was a long loud single blast on the horn and a positive move to the right. I was seething by this time - if he wasn't capable of passing me in the usual way, port to port, he shouldn't be steering the thing at all. As he sped past I managed the most evil stare I could muster - silly really, but bloody annoying all the same. It wasn't the last time we were to confront him either. We had virtually the same trouble some weeks later on our return trip.

We tied for the night at Segala and Andy and I took the Bromptons for a ride across the bridge and down a narrow lane to see the monument that had been erected to commemorate the work of the builder of the Canal du Midi, Paul Riquet. We were now on the summit pound of the canal, the highest point between the Atlantic Ocean and Mediterranean Sea, a modest 190 metres above sea level. The perimeter walls of a silted-up basin that once served as a feeder reservoir for the canal survive surrounded by a small forest of cedar trees. We took advantage of another cassoulet at the restaurant at La Segala - a large pot for six including beer for 65 Euros. According to Du Breil there is a local family that have been producing the bowls in which the dish is presented, along with garden pottery in their vast brick oven since 1820.

I had begun to weaken in my old age and actually telephoned the Capitanerie at Carcassonne to reserve a mooring in advance - 3 nights, 61 Euros. It did seem a bit defeatist and wimpish but I couldn't face the prospect of floating around aimlessly looking for a space with friends on board. Carcassonne was always very busy with boats and we were due to arrive on the afternoon of Bastille Day when demand was sure to be at its height.

However I failed to take the same precautions before we arrived the next day at Castelnaudary unannounced, another town where mooring was always at a premium, but luckily after a bit of diplomatic negotiation by the Capitan it was arranged for us to tie alongside another barge, the Heliox ,with the kind permission of the owners, Martin and his American wife Robin.

Old habits die hard and with the premise that if it ain't broken don't fix it, we dined alongside the harbour on porc filet Mignon at the restaurant Gourmet de Cassoulet. An early start next morning - towels on the lock gate at 08.45, and we were through the four lock staircase by half past nine. We spent that night on the lock pontoon at Lalande , with authorisation from the éclusier I might add, and wiled away a few hours before dinner watching the trains from a bridge over the busy Marseilles - Bordeaux mainline - call us sad if you like!

It was just a short run from here to Carcassonne and we arrived at half past one and descended the lock with the very low narrow bridge before tying up on our reserved mooring. There is something quietly satisfying about gliding importantly into your designated space, the only available space in the port and seeing the board hanging over the side which the Capitan has put out announcing,

"Emplacement reservée - 21 metres - SAUL TRADER."

We ate in the small Italian restaurant close to the boat before a short stroll along the towpath where we found an ideal spot to watch the feu d'artifice. We had a perfect view of the battlements of the ancient cité and sat on the bank with a bottle of rosé as the available space around us gradually filled with the expectant crowds. Apparently the event attracts some 700,000 spectators, although most of them choose the banks of the River Aude as their vantage point. The show began at ten thirty and lasted for about half an hour. There was a subtle display of light and colour, blues and yellows, white and green, red and gold that artistically provided back light to the ancient city, culminating in a spectacular finale of thousands of bursts of fire that filled the sky in the space of a matter of seconds. An ingenious profusion of light at the end of the performance gave the impression that the citadel was on fire, a feature that has taken place since 1898, when 'to conclude the festivities, they used Bengal lights to simulate a fire and transform the Cité into an enormous shimmering stone'.

It was such a success that they decided to keep this tradition of fire going, and to do the same thing again every year on 14th July at 22h30. I had been told that the Carcassonne display was regarded as second in France only to that held in Paris. I suppose it was artistic rather than explosive - subtle colours shimmering against the walls of the fort, creating mystical patterns that reflected in the night sky, delicate shades of light and shadow that beautifully illuminated the ancient battlements, and this time I had managed to stay fully awake during the entire performance.

The following morning, Andy took Alan to fetch his car while the girls went on a shopping expedition in the town. I would be on my own for a couple of days before Dave and Becks arrived by Easy Jet from Bournemouth for our little adventure to

114

Narbonne. I spent the next morning cleaning up the boat, and getting the bedding washed at the local Laverie, where I paid the extra few Euros to have it dried and ironed by the femme laveuse. I went to the Capitan's office to pay my dues and noticed a large stage set up in the square André Chénier, and a billboard advertising a free concert on the following evening. Our mooring was adjacent to a grassy bank close to the centre of the town and a short walk to the square. In the afternoon I sat in the wheelhouse watching the world go by when an elderly gentleman approached. He introduced himself and told me that he lived in Tewkesbury and had worked at the Avon Marina. He knew Saul Trader very well from the early days of trial cruises on the Severn and had been on the team that had rescued Darrell after he had been stuck on the rocks for three weeks at Marcliffe on the River Avon. Small world: Ivan told me that he and his wife regularly visited the canal du Midi - he had a son who lived nearby, and loved to watch the boats and reminisce about the times when the Avon was busy with commercial traffic carrying grain to Healing's Mill. He even recalled the days when Rob's barge 'Pisgah' had worked the river as far as Pershore. It was a real pleasure to talk to Ivan and hear about the days when the river was alive, not with pleasure boats and grockels, but with hard-working boatmen, bustling porters and stevedores pushing sack trucks piled with bags of flour . I could picture the scenes described so graphically. I often said that if ever I helped a wizened old lady across a busy road and she granted me one wish, I would ask to be transported back to 1950.

Dave and Becky arrived the following afternoon, dropped off by the airport shuttle bus just across the canal outside the station, some fifty metres or so from the boat. After they had settled themselves into the aft cabin and unpacked, we adjourned to the wheelhouse with a beer, catching up on the news from Salisbury, when I was surprised to see another familiar figure running down the bank towards us. It was David Gourlay, a tour guide who had accompanied me on a rail tour of Sri Lanka a couple of years earlier. He appeared a bit out of breath and explained that he was with a tour party of 29 punters and they had passed the boat on a sight-seeing cruise. He had remembered me telling him about Saul Trader and rushed over to say hello. The party were leaving by train in five minutes so it was a very brief reunion but it was great to meet up again. David worked for a company called PTG Tours, who organise both rail and cultural tours around the world. He was an excellent guide, totally unflappable and capable, with the temperament to cope with the most difficult situations and problematic guests. That was amazing - two encounters with people with whom we had some connection in the past two days. I wondered whether there would be a third.

In the evening we wandered across to the square and enjoyed the free concert with a couple of plastic beakers of cold beer. A large crowd gathered and filled the square, but there was still enough space for comfort. The support band of young musicians played a soulful funky set which got the crowd swaying and they were followed by the headline act, a Cuban band Group Compay Segundo, an internationally renowned orchestra with connections to the acclaimed Buena Vista Social Club. There were nine musicians who filled the stage and played a vibrant mix of both modern day and classical Cuban tunes. I was particularly fascinated by the energetic drumming and intricate rhythms. Carcassonne puts on on a vast programme of music during the summer months - over 120 concerts - 80 or more of which are free, covering all musical genres.

Over the next four days we travelled east retracing our steps to Ventenac en Minervois, stopping overnight at Marseilette and Homps, where we indulged ourselves with some haute cuisine at a vastly inflated price. There was much evidence of tree re-planting along this section where the diseased plane trees had been cut down. The VNF had orchestrated a massive campaign to attract donations from canal lovers towards the cost of this enormous project and it seemed to have been a success. We slipped into a space by the bank at Ventenac just a few boats from 'Pisgah'. The VNF had installed some conveniently spaced sturdy mooring posts in place of the trees and we nestled gently alongside. When I went below to top up the day tank I noticed the unmistakable whiff of burning rubber: it could mean only one thing, a slipping fan belt. I gave it a tweak and found a bit of slack. Rob knew a local lad, a mechanic called Cyril, and we arranged for him to come and have a look at it. I use the word mechanic advisedly. Sad - (Freudian slip there) - Cyril turned up next morning with a large hammer! I probably should have known better but left him to it to do his worst. Quite what he did I'm not sure but the result was a much tighter fit and, for the moment at least, another problem put to the back of the problem queue - all for the ten Euros that Cyril asked me for. It wasn't to be the last time that our paths crossed. In the evening we ate with Rob and Wendy in La Grillade du Chateau and I plumped for the Noix St Jacques. Wendy could be a bit of a trial, especially after a few gin and tonics - she was a retired left-wing lawyer, quite capable of arguing that black was white defending the indefensible, but luckily on this occasion she was on her best behaviour. Maybe Rob had had a word with her, although I secretly doubted that as it would more likely have been like a red rag to a bull and made matters worse. Wendy hated boats and boaters came a close second.

The branch canal that led to Salelle d'Aude, the Canal de Jonction, continued via a short river crossing to the centre of Narbonne on the Canal de la Robine and thence to the Mediterranean Port la Nouvelle. I had wanted to explore this last section to Narbonne and possibly beyond for some time and now seemed as good a time as any. On the first day we passed the little settlement of La Somail and bought some bread and croissants from the floating épicerie, crossed the aqueduct over the Cesse, and turned right on to the Canal de Jonction, and descended the six locks down to Salelle d'Aude.

I cycled to the staircase locks that led to the Aude crossing to have another look and it all looked straightforward enough. I asked the lock-keeper at Salelle about the depth of water and he said he didn't know what it was but assured me that I would be OK. I knew Rob had done the trip with 'Pisgah' but his draft was quite a bit less than mine.

So next morning we set off blithely into the unknown. There was no lock-keeper present at the Gailhousty staircase but the top chamber was full and we passed through without any problem. There was a boat on the blocks of the dry-dock alongside the bottom chamber where a cheery Englishman busily scraping his bottom gave us an encouraging wave. According to my admittedly somewhat outdated Merlot Guide,

117

there were buoys indicating the passage across the river, but in the event these had been removed. On leaving the lock channel you had to turn sharp right and then follow the bank a short distance to a rope barrier (that at least was still there) and then sweep around 180° to the left keeping close to the right bank underneath the bridge carrying the disused railway and passing a line of green buoys (they were there too !) before veering right under another bridge into the Canal de la Robine. I have since replaced my old Merlot Guide with the much clearer and up to date version of Du Breil No 7 which has an inset map showing the route in detail. Stable doors and horses again as we found to our cost on the way back. The rest of the journey, ten kilometres and two locks into Narbonne passed without too much problem, apart from the very shallow sections where we struggled a bit through the silted up channel, and a hold-up at the first lock where some interfering busybody had pushed the wrong button while we were in the lock and fouled up the mechanism, preventing the bottom gates from opening to let us out. This was soon put right after a call to the éclusier on the lock-side intercom, and a flea in the ear of the perpetrator. We passed a hydraulically operated dredger which didn't look as though it had done any work in the recent past.

Once into the centre of Narbonne there were very few vacant spaces, and none that were anywhere near long enough for us. We eventually had to succumb to a couple of nights mooring at the hire base of Le Boat for 20 Euros per night, but at least it was relatively secure. Parts of Narbonne reminded me of Toulouse - with more than its fair share of petty crooks and down and outs. I watched horrified as a black guy on the opposite side of the canal blatantly stole an ice-cream from a little girl outside the Carrefour supermarket. It was a callous act of bullying carried out in broad daylight. This guy just strolled up to the child as if he owned the place demanding 'for me for me - give me' and cockily waltzed off with his 'prize' leaving the poor girl in a state of shock and bewilderment. I shouted at him but he either didn't, or more likely wouldn't, hear me. I am no social do-gooder but I try to help those in genuine need when I can.

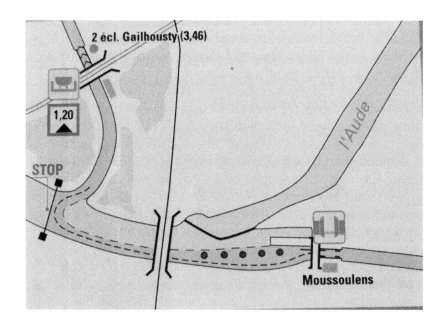

Diagram from the Du Breil guide showing the channel from the locks at Gailhoustie into the Canal de la Robine. Unfortunately I didn't have this until after the event

The difficulty is knowing who are the genuinely needy. These sort of people are social terrorists, preying on unsuspecting innocents. They are parasites and arseholes, worthless dregs that cannot be considered as human beings.

That little episode soured my opinion of Narbonne. I'm sure that despicable piece of dross was not typical of the majority of the good burghers of Narbonne but it left a very nasty taste in my mouth which lingered for a long time afterwards.

We were moored some way from the city centre and I cycled in to fetch a couple of pizzas on the first night.

I took the precaution of chaining up the Brompton outside the shop while I waited for the order. I returned to the boat via a different route and realised that there were far better moorings below the next lock, so we resolved to cut our losses and move there the next morning. I had decided not to risk getting to Port Nouvelle as I feared for the water level. It was midsummer after all when levels were invariably at their lowest. Narbonne Lock leads underneath the impressive Merchant's Bridge which is lined with houses and a bit reminiscent of the Glory Hole in Lincoln. After this there is a much more pleasant area of walkways and avenues adjacent to the Archbishop's Palace and the Town Hall. I asked the lock-keeper about a turning place and he told me that there was a suitable 'winding hole', although they don't call them that in France, rather an 'Aire de Virage,' about 5 kilometres further on. I decided to risk losing a mooring space to get the boat facing in the right direction. I wasn't al all sure how much water we might have underneath us and I wanted to get this manoeuvre over and done with sooner rather than later. In fact it turned out to be seven kilometres to the turn at which point we were only 13 kilometres from Port Nouvelle.

It was tempting to keep going but discretion ruled for a change, the canal had seemed to get progressively shallower and we unanimously decided to turn around and head back to Narbonne - we had come this far at least without getting stuck and we didn't want to chance our luck by going any further. Back in Narbonne there was still plenty of room alongside the wall and there was a lively market in full swing where we bought some fresh fish and vegetables deciding to eat aboard. We spent a couple of hours strolling around the immediate vicinity, visited the Cathedral of St Just and the Archbishop's Palace, and then found a shady bar that served up Kronenbourg in frosted glasses accompanied with two bowls of complimentary nuts. Maybe Narbonne had its good points after all.

The Glory Hole - Merchant's Bridge, Narbonne

We left at 09.30 the following morning and headed up through the lock underneath the Merchant's Bridge and on towards the river crossing at Gailhoustie. The water level was noticeably lower and we struggled at times to make headway through the mud. We passed the redundant dredger and came eventually to the point where the Canal de la Robine entered the Aude. I carefully navigated past the starboard buoys and stayed close to the left bank below the railway bridge until the rope that marked the end of the navigable section came into view. I then swung the wheel to starboard and followed the turn indicated in Merlot, keeping as close as I could to the opposite side on the approach to the lock, once again following the course mapped out in Merlot, but of course minus the buoys. And then we came to a silent and sticky end. Having now had the wisdom of the Du Breil chart, I can see that I was too close to the bank but unfortunately I had put too much trust in Merlot and paid the price. We were stuck good and proper. We tried the usual tricks - reversing, then shoving the gear into forward and opening the throttle. We tried pushing off with the shaft, first the bow and then the stern but that was futile. We commandeered a passing hire boat who took a line and then spun around on the end of it like a demented waterbug as it tried to pull us free. All our efforts came to nothing. The bow might move and the stern buried itself deeper in the silt, then when the stern moved slightly to one side the reverse happened and the bow refused to budge. We couldn't see anything through the thick bushes but heard a few choice words from the fishermen who had had their evening's sport buggered up by some idiot on a boat that was much too big to be here. I found the number of the éclusier and explained the position. He appeared through the jungle some minutes later shaking his head and shouted something I couldn't quite make out. Dave seemed to think it was something to do with fetching a large boat to help us out of our predicament but I wasn't convinced. After an hour or so of more fruitless revving and slewing, what should come triumphantly around the bend under the railway bridge but the redundant dredger, manned by a crew of Vikings thankful to be given something useful to do at last.

I had to groan at the irony - the very thing that should have been put to use to prevent such a catastrophe - it beggared belief. Ropes were attached, orders shouted excitedly, arms were raised - hadn't we been through all this before somewhere. The dredger driver, obviously delighted to be given the chance to show just what this beast was capable of, pulled levers this way and that and sent his charge backwards, forwards and   sideways all at the same time until the ropes strained under the weight and slowly Saul Trader was dragged back into water that was deep enough (just) to float again. The rest was simple and straightforward, and we were soon around the bend and into the lock. I dearly wished I had enough French to be able to convey all my emotions to the crew - frustration, anger, gratitude, relief, but in lieu of that I asked Dave to get a dozen beers from the fridge to give to the boys by way of thanks for their efforts, but by the time he got up to the wheelhouse with the bag they had disappeared, turned tail and headed back from whence they had come in a cloud of black smoke. In the end we left the bag of beer with the lock-keeper at Salelles d'Aude but I wondered whether they ever reached the gang.

Our rescuer -Dredger - TOO90115F

We completed the return trip from Salelles to Carcassonne in three days. There was a very useful facility on a website that was run by the magazine Fluvial which provided a lot of information regarding the planning of trips. It gave an estimated time for the journey - 66 kilometres and 23 locks, as 14 hours. This assumed an average speed of 5.5 kilometres per hour, which was a bit optimistic to say the least. It may be possible with a small plastic hire boat with a crew of six and with no hold-ups, but I always allowed a good bit of leeway on the Fluvial estimates. In the event it took us 23 hours. We stopped overnight in La Redorte where Monsieur Merlot was again found wanting. The guide said that Wifi, electricity and water were all available but all we could find was water at the somewhat over-the-top price of 2 Euros for a 30 minute trickle.

Rob drove up from Ventenac to crew with me on the last stretch to Toulouse where I had arranged for Serge to finish the outstanding work for the TRIWV certificate. We made steady progress through Bram and overnighted once again at Castelnaudary. We called into the port at Lauragais for lunch and were then held up for nearly two hours at the Embourrel lock when another idiot had pressed the wrong button on the automatic control panel. These were clearly marked as 'montant' - uphill, and 'avant' - downhill, and were accompanied by arrows indicating up or down but still people managed to get it wrong. There was nothing for it in these situations but to sit it out and the VNF van with the rescue team finally arrived at 3.00pm. Our mood did not improve as at the very next lock we were held for another hour as the bloody trip boat from Renneville fannied about in front of us, obviously delighting in causing aggravation and feeling extremely important.

There was a rubber dinghy tied on the pontoon at the top of Gardouch Lock, with a couple of lads obviously waiting their chance to lock through with a larger boat - us as it turned out. I think their problem was that their boat was too short to trigger the radar mechanism that set the lock. They indicated to us that they wanted to follow us in and initially I saw no problem with it. They buzzed in behind us and motored to the far end of the lock obviously intent on going out in front of us and speeding off in the hope of catching another boat and getting ahead. I wasn't happy about this and when we arrived at the next set of locks there they were again, ready to jump into bed with us. I agreed to this but told them that I would want to exit the lock first. I was worried that if they set off the radar when they left, the gates may close before we had time to follow. I thought they had understood but apparently had chosen not to as off they zoomed again as soon as the gates were open wide enough for them to pass. We couldn't leave until the gates were fully open, by which time our friends were half way down the next pound. Then as we slowly exited the gates began to close, and trapped us firmly in their grasp.

I was bloody furious and alerted the lads with a long blast on the horn. To their credit they did come back when they saw the damage they had caused and floated around sheepishly outside the lock. We were half in and half out of the lock, clamped firmly in the jaws of the unrelenting gates. l really didn't know what to do as I had never been in this situation before. We couldn't get off the boat to call for help and it was difficult getting any message across to the dinghy. There was no way they would be able to pull us out anyway, and any attempt at trying to force our way would more than likely damage the gate hydraulics. It did occur to me that another boat coming from the opposite direction may cause the gates to open but that could take hours. The canal was very quiet and we had only passed a couple of boats all day. More worrying was the thought that if a boat approached from the same direction would the lock start filling, with us wedged in the gate. We decided that the only thing to do was to call out the VNF but to do this we would have to somehow get off the boat and on to the lockside. Rob volunteered to go and clambered up the inside of the gate, swinging himself precariously onto the walkway. Realising what was about to happen, the dinghy raced off into the distance, abandoning us to out plight. They obviously didn't have a licence to be on the canal and didn't want to be caught by an irate lock-keeper.

Ten minutes later l'homme arrive and Rob explained how we had managed to get ourselves into this predicament. He by-passed the automated system with his hand-held controller and the gates obediently parted, relinquishing their grip on the boat and releasing Saul Trader back into the canal. I was definitely not going to let the dinghy anywhere near me again and we had a little chuckle as we approached the lock at Negra to see that they had indeed been caught by the éclusier and were forlornly dragging their little craft out of the water. There was a long pontoon above the lock which was used by a Locoboat hire base and I got the OK to stop there for a couple of hours. I wanted to touch up the black before we returned to Toulouse. I didn't want another chiding from the ever watchful Serge about my boat driving capabilities.

At Montgiscard we were lured on to the mooring by the prospect of beer and pizza and sat outside the café next door with a glass of the former while the latter was being prepared for us. We laughed about our friends in the rubber boat and I wondered what had become of them. I had no idea where they were from or where they were going and would have gladly helped them if they hadn't been so bloody-minded and not listened when we asked them to let us go first out of the locks. Had they done so all would have been well as they could have followed directly behinds us and passed through the gates unmolested.

We turned into the harbour at Ramonville where I had arranged to leave ST while Serge did his worst, and the Capitan, Michel, looked at me blankly when I reported to his office. Even though I had watched him write down the booking a few months ago he had absolutely no recollection of it and for a moment I thought he would not be able to find us a space. After a few minutes of indecipherable muttering, he pointed to a vacant space between two concrete walkways which was just about wide enough for us. There was a mass of herbes mauvaise and I managed to clog up both the prop and the bow-thrusters as I tried to reverse into the tight space. Rob, and Serge, who had magically appeared, took a line each and hauled the boat into place and I switched off the engine. I couldn't mess about clearing the weed now as I needed to get Rob back to his car in Carcassonne and I needed to start the long drive back to Calais and Angleterre. I left Serge with a duplicate list of the jobs that needed doing and told him I would return in a couple of months. I needed to get the boat to Castelsarrassin where I had pre-booked a 'hivernage', or winter mooring.

There was another small job that was required before the certificate could be issued and that was a gas installation certificate. Serge unusually knew nobody locally who could do this and Rob suggested an Englishman Michael Tubb , who was apparently qualified for this sort of thing.

"For God's sake don't call him Tubbsy," warned Rob, 'I did once and he refused to speak to me for a month.'

I flew back to Toulouse from Heathrow a few weeks later with British Airways, the expensive version of Ryanair, and was met at Blagnac by Serge who gave me a hug and kissed me on both cheeks. It was a sign. A sign of what exactly I wasn't sure but I was grateful for the lift as Ramonville is some way from the airport. I had acquired a pair of brass stars which I wanted Serge to fix to the bows of Saul Trader. These were traditionally fixed to the bows of Dutch barges to indicate that the vessel was free of debt: in other words, paid for and owned outright. Unfortunately they were too big to fit in the space in the bulwarks and I sold them to Serge for the price I had paid. Serge lived on a 30 metre former working barge, 'Stella', with his wife Vanessa, their daughter and two large dogs. The boat was unconverted and I think Serge had taken on a bit more than he could chew. It was after all a massive job, and although I knew that Serge had the necessary equipment and skill, it was a lot to ask after a hard day's work on other people's boats to muster the enthusiasm to spend all his spare time on his own work.

He had completed all the jobs on Saul Trader and I stuck the various labels I had acquired in England in their appropriate positions around the boat. There was no argument now as to what we could and could not do aboard - smoke, duck our heads, turn off the gas valve and/or the engine from outside, swear, fill the diesel and/or the water tanks, pump out the heads and isolate the batteries. What else could a man desire! Mick Tubb arrived as arranged the following day and did a cursory check of the gas system before signing an official-looking form and collecting his 100 Euro fee - in cash. I don't know how official it was but it seemed to satisfy Herr Van Dyke who in due course, having looked at the photographs of the various jobs, sent all the necessary documents proving that Saul Trader of Gloucester, British Waterways Registered No 51589, Small Ships Register No 94899, European Indentification No 03800317, SI (Technical Requirements for Inland Waterway Vessels) No 17101NL, was now fully certified and official - well for another seven years anyway.

I celebrated with Andy over a Guinness or two in De Danu before setting off single-handed in beautifully bright, clear Autumnal weather to Castelsarrassin, arriving three days later and slotting into my allotted space on the quay. The wheelhouse had developed a bit of a leak of late, probably caused by expansion and contraction of the wood around the foldable sections, and I took the precaution of protecting it with the canvas cover that came right down past the windows and secured to the side rails. I hadn't used it for some time as I was worried after the break-in at Landrecies many years ago that its presence aided the intrusion of burglars. There were plenty of other boats in Castelsarrassin with live-aboard owners and I concluded that it would be safe enough. I went through my check list of things to do when closing down for the winter - valves closed, water drained, fridge door open, gas off etc etc, paid the 685 Euros for a six month stay at the

Capitanerie, packed my carry-on bag and headed across the footbridge to the station and the 11.35 to Toulouse Matabiau.

Chapter 9   Navigable Tri-Lite and Dead Alternators

I drove back to Castelsarrassin at the beginning of June 2016. I needed to get the boat moved out of the port as my mooring was only for the winter and actually expired on the 1st May. I settled up with the Capitan for the excess period, and headed off west once again.

I stopped on the conveniently placed pontoon adjacent to the industrial area just outside the port of Castelsarrassin and went off to buy a couple of starter batteries. I had a useful little fold-up two-wheeled shopping trolley which I had bought a few years back in the Casino supermarket in Valence and this came in very handy to transport the two new batteries back to the boat. The engine started on 24 volts which was produced by two 12 volt batteries connected in line, or was it in series? Either way I drew a diagram showing where each lead joined each end before I disconnected the old ones. I had still not got used to the idea of using the iPad to take photographs of the set up which after all was a far simpler and more accurate way of doing things. Old habits die hard.

I called in at the port in Moissac to find that there was a new Capitan. Iain and Caz had left to go off to the Dominican Republic to set up in business growing herbs and spices, a brave adventure which as it happened didn't quite work out as planned. I was somewhat surprised when I heard this as they had been doing a great job in the port - Iain supplementing the income with a few maintenance and repair jobs and a periphery enterprise providing courses afloat in boat handling and navigation. The role had been taken on by our friends Jim and Sandra, long-standing residents of the port who lived on their small wooden boat. They had taken to the task like ducks to water and Jim had quickly stamped his authority on the port, something which did not necessarily please everybody. He told me that he was insisting on a deposit from anyone wanting to reserve a winter mooring as he had been let down by a number of people not turning up. Some selfish boaters had apparently been reserving space at several different ports, leaving it to the last minute to cancel, a habit that was unfair to everyone else. Mooring space was always at a premium in the port, especially over the winter months, as Moissac was a very popular town with all facilities. He had apparently upset more than a few with this policy and I really couldn't understand why, unless of course they were the very ones that had booked several different ports.

I got to know and like Jim over the next few years. He kept an eagle eye on the comings and goings in the port but was always very helpful and obliging, usually being able to find enough room for Saul Trader to squeeze into, and always coming along to guide us alongside and welcome us with a shake of the hand. I had a bit of time to spare in the port and made use of it by installing the new engine start batteries. I was heading to Sérignac where Dave and Becky were due to join me in a few weeks time. On the way I had a rather strange encounter with a small tug-like vessel called 'De Brave Anna' which was coming from the opposite direction. I altered course slightly to starboard and waved to the skipper as he passed by. In return I got a shake of a fist and a mouthful of something I didn't quite catch. The Brave Anna was flying a Swiss ensign and he was obviously aggrieved at something I had or had not done. Just what is was remained a mystery. As there was a space on the short and free pontoon mooring at Pommevic I decided to have an early night and avail myself of the electricity, kindly provided FOC. This was a very nice gesture on behalf of the Mairie of the village of Pommevic, designed to bring a little bit of trade to the few local businesses. The proviso was that it was for a maximum of 48 hours and this was clearly marked on a signpost alongside the mooring. Unfortunately this was blatantly abused - largely by Brits it has to be said, and the facility is now in danger of being withdrawn. What is more, I was told by Jock that the new Maire is also the president of the Village Mooring Society and has threatened to ban known offenders and advise all the member villages to do the same. I can only applaud this action and hopefully it may serve as a lesson to those selfish few who have done their best to ruin it for everyone else. You can be sure that these same people rarely ever patronised the local shops anyway, and and probably the same ones that book several winter moorings at the same time!

There was a shabby little craft that was lived on by a miserable scruffy Scotsman which I know for a fact stayed on that mooring for at least three weeks. He thought he was being very clever and actually tied just off the pontoon with one rope attached to a bollard and ran his electric cable to connect to the borne after dark, removing it in the morning. It's these sort of creeps who spoil things for all the other decent law-abiding boaters. According to my old mate Jock, the new Maire has apparently made up a black-list of the over-stayers. Good for him I say.

As was becoming the norm now, Pommevic presented me with another little surprise the following morning. I showered and made some breakfast, and while sitting in the wheelhouse I suddenly became aware that the water pump was still whirring its head off. This could only mean one thing - a leak somewhere in the line. I left my breakfast to investigate and as I opened the door to the engine room I was knocked back by a cloud of hot steam and the frightening sight of boiling water running down the bulkheads. I managed to quickly switch off the pump which at least stopped the flow and then stood with my head in my hands considering the possible cause while the engine room cooled down. My first thought was that the hot water cylinder had split, followed by all sorts of misgivings about the cost of a replacement, how and where to get a new one, not to mention the hassle of removing the old one and installing another. The first person that came to mind was Tubbsy - er, Mick Tubbs. I had his number somewhere and I knew he was still in France. It was still fairly early in the morning but this was urgent and I risked waking him up to make the call.

Mick's first thoughts were reassuring. A new one would be very expensive but he suggested that it was unlikely to be the cylinder, but more probably a split hose. He told me to wait a while to let things cool down and then turn on the pump again for a few seconds and look for a leak. I did this after about fifteen minutes and sure enough, a fine jet of water spurted from the plastic pipe that connected with the head of the cylinder. The pipe was only about eighteen inches long and had developed a tiny pin-prick hole. By chance I had a few spare bits of pipe saved from the time we had suffered the disaster in Bath, many ions ago. I retrieved a piece from the forward locker, cut it to length , connected it up and voila: the pump started and stopped as soon as the pressure was regained. I felt very pleased with myself and sent a text to Mick to thank him and report that the job had been successfully completed. I went merrily on my way, overnighting at Valence for scallops, Agen for Indian and finally L'Escale at Sérignac and the adorable Claudine for prawn omelette and chips. I took a taxi to the station at Agen where I caught the train to Castelsarrassin and the car.

When I got back to the boat I noticed a strange looking craft moored on the opposite bank. My first thought was that it was a sort of floating stage. It was basically a platform covered in synthetic grass with a canopy supported by tri-lite frames - the sort of stuff that you see on the side of the temporary stages at outdoor festivals. It had an array of lights attached to the upper frames and looked for all the world as though it was the set of some sort of musical show, with an incongruous looking bell tent in the middle of the deck. It turned out that this was the domain of one, Marcus, a Belgian self-proclaimed adventurer and inventor, and it was propelled by two outboard motors that were apparently solar powered. Well if you believe that you'll believe anything. Marcus had sailed this latter day Kontiki raft all the way from Belgium and was on some sort of promotional voyage to try to convince potential customers of its viability. I must say that it didn't particularly convince me and when I walked across to have a chat with him he was standing on the frame that supported the motors, raking around with a boathook and wrench trying to straighten out one of the shafts that had been bent when the craft had fouled on the cill in a lock, and cursing the bloody éclusier who had opened the paddles too quickly, ramming the boat against the lock gate. The weird looking contraption was called "CAPTAIN SUNSET", the name hung from one of the tri-lite beams in the sort of coloured letters that you see wishing someone "HAPPY

BIRTHDAY!" Another sign said 'Camp on Water', a message that I thought could well be misconstrued.

David and I gave him a hand while he contorted himself over the stern of the raft - my contribution not much more than a few grunts of support, and eventually it was knocked back into some sort of shape. Marcus invited us all for supper on Captain Sunset and we spent a pleasant evening chatting with him about his plans. He was meeting some tycoon or other somewhere who he hoped to persuade into funding the project by injecting a few million Euros.

"What's his name," I thought to myself, "Walter Mitty or Fred Carno?"

The food was cooked on a small camping gas ring but was nevertheless very enjoyable and we managed to demolish the complete case of 24 bottles of Kronenbourg that we had contributed to the party together with some sort of alcoholic prune juice fuelled fire-water that Marcus produced. And he also provided the music through his expensive looking state-of-the-art sound system which enhanced the feeling of sitting back stage at a rock concert.

He told us that he was planning to take a token demonstration load of beer from Agen to Belgium as a publicity stunt and casually described his vision of a large factory production line churning out up to a thousand Captain Sunset's per year. I can't say that I've ever seen another one but that is not to say that they don't exist!

As we staggered back to Saul Trader well past midnight we could hear him humming to himself as he clambered into bed in his little tent. I woke the next morning at 8 o'clock with a throbbing head and looked out to see an empty void where he had been moored. There was no trace of Marcus or indeed the raft. I had to pinch myself to make sure that I hadn't dreamt the whole thing. We never saw or heard of him again. I hope he survived the long slog up the Rhone, and who knows, maybe he's lording over his growing workforce in a factory on the outskirts of Liége, celebrating the launch of the one thousandth Captain Sunset. The world would be all the poorer without eccentric characters like him. Whatever floats your boat!

Captain Sunset and Robinson Crusoe

Dave and Becky paid me another visit - they must like life on Saul Trader - gluttons for punishment maybe. This time they had come by train to Bordeaux and I picked them up from the station. Back at Sérignac, another small boat arrived and I went over to take a line and help him tie up. It was none other than the Brave Anna. I introduced myself and took the opportunity to ask him about our little encounter.

"It is because you do not give me enough room," he protested, "you stay in the middle of the channel."

I tried explaining to him that we had at least a metre of gap between us when we passed and I had moved over far enough to the right.

"There was plenty of room for both of us and it is quite unnecessary to veer off close to the bank where the depth might cause one of us to go on to the ground."

I think he eventually got the message and we shook hands. I remembered reading an article in the Barge magazine some years ago written by the wife of Roy Scudamore of the 'Pedro', which said that as a loaded peniche they preferred oncoming vessels to stay in the middle of the channel as long as possible before moving over in order not to cause any undue conflicting wash. This would take a pretty nerveless steerer I thought at the time and although I probably did stay in the middle as long as I could , I had never yet collided with an oncoming boat.

We set sail next morning and on the way to Buzet I noticed the tell-tale sign of a fault with the alternator - again!

No rev counter and a flickering charging light. There must be something about me that Buzet doesn't like. I had changed the batteries so I was pretty sure that wasn't the problem. We managed to tie up outside the port office and went below to deliberate. After a lot of looking at it, pulling it this way and that, head scratching and generally procrastinating, we decided we knew exactly what the problem was - us. We hadn't really got a clue what was wrong with it. It was a case of resorting to the expertise of someone who did know - Alain, the Aquitaine mechanic. It took Alain all of ten minutes to declare the alternator dead as the proverbial Dodo, like the Monty Python parrot.

"It was no more", " it had ceased to be", "it was bereft of life, it rested in peace". It was an ex-alternator."

After careful deliberation I decided there was only one thing for it

"Hello. Is that Bob?"

"No it's his brother Jim. Is it Bob you're after?

"Er - yes please.

"OK - right you are. 'ang on a tick.

Once again the dependable Bob came up with the goods. I sent him some pictures of the defunct unit and Bob said he had a reconditioned alternator in stock.

"Well he's not exactly the same as he's a later model like, but I think he'll do the job."

As clever as Bob was with good old-fashioned solid things like alternators he still hadn't quite mastered the modern technology of getting things organised via t'internet, so it was left to me once again to organise the collection and delivery. For £65 DHL delivered the unit unmolested into the office at Buzet the very next morning. Safari so goodee.

Except that when Dave and I offered it up to the place where it was all supposed to join up - it didn't. There were all sorts of differently coloured wires that seemed to bear no relation whatsoever to the bits that they were supposed to connect to.

Dave doing his Jack Hargreaves impression

"So what do we do now then?" said Dave.

"Buggered if I know," said I, and with that Dave sauntered off to fetch his fishing rod.

"What are you hoping to catch?" I asked, as he baited up the line with a piece of stale cheese.

"Buggered if I know," he replied, which rather summed up our day really.

Then while I sat in the wheelhouse with a cup of coffee, idly contemplating my navel, two things happened almost simultaneously. Dave's rod bent at a ridiculously impossible angle and he strained with the winder to reel in his catch. Then the line snapped with a ping causing our intrepid fisherman to almost lose his balance and topple off his perch. He had caught the hook around the skeg of Saul Trader and had the line been of a better quality breaking strain could easily have lifted the stern out of the water.

At that very moment a large Australian appeared, stopping outside to pass the time of day - something I think he may have come to regret.

Brian was a (very) large Australian on a boat that he had bought two years ago and on which he had spent most of the intervening years completely refurbishing the interior and sorting out the electrics.

"I know a bit about about it," he said, " as I spent my whole career in Australia in the auto-electrical industry."

"That's amazing," I said, as nonchalantly as possible,"we have got a slight problem ourselves with our alternator."

If you read about it in a book you would put it down to fiction, but this was real. Here was our Roy of the Rovers - in person. I produced the gleaming new instrument and presented it for inspection.

"The thing is," I explained, "we've got this recon alternator and it's a bit different from the one that came off - and to be honest, we haven't got a fucking clue how it goes back on."

I thought it only polite to slip in a bit of Aussie vernacular. Brian needed no more encouragement. He retuned to his boat and I must say that I thought for a moment that he'd decided to do the sensible thing and forget that he'd ever seen us, but having warned his wife of the cause of his imminent disappearance, he returned with a bag of objects that only electricians know what to do with - pliers that looked more suited to pulling teeth, wire strippers and cutters and instruments with leads sticking out of them and weird numbers and flashing lights. Two minutes later he had stripped to his vest and squeezed himself into the space where the offending part needed to be re-united with the dangling wires.

It wasn't a simple job by any means and Brian had to do a lot of thinking. He drew several diagrams of the existing wiring and positioning and jotted down some hieroglyphics and complicated calculations until he was finally ready, after a second cup of coffee, to start the job. In a strange sort of way I felt a bit exonerated. There was no way on earth that Dave and I could have done it. His wife came by, wanting to know how he was getting on, and I thought it best to spare her the gory details and reassure her that everything was going according to plan, as if I knew anything about it. In the end it was two hours before I got the OK to fire up. Brian had lost at least 2 kilos in sweat and I had begun to feel a bit guilty at having involved him. He had only been out for a quiet stroll and a social chat after all. Thankfully, for all concerned, the engine burst into life, the red warning light disappeared and the rev counter needle flew up to its correct position. Um - hadn't we been through all this before somewhere? The white man's magician extricated himself from the engine-room and appeared in the wheelhouse glimmering with sweat and looking like a Sumo wrestler at the end of a twelve round bout. I really didn't know how to thank him enough. The offer of money was emphatically declined and he went off back to his boat for a shower and a lie down in a darkened room, after inviting us to call in during the afternoon for a tour of the boat and a look at the work he'd done on it. Brenda had showed some interest in the posters that were still in the window advertising the books so when we went to see them I took a couple of bottles of wine and copies of the books by way of a thank you. It wasn't much, and the phrase "booby prize" came to mind, but the gifts were graciously received.

"I hope I can do something for you one day," I said, the emphasis more on the hope than the expectation.

We had another fleeting visit from the Rev'd Peter, vicar of the parish church of St Michael's and All Angels, Winterbourne Daauntsey. This time he had driven all the way from Auxerre, which had taken him a bit longer than anticipated. He had got lost several times en route but eventually the Lord had shepherded him safely to Buzet, albeit not until 1.30 in the morning. Some vicars will go to great lengths to keep in touch with their flock. Dave had spoken to him several times on the phone to monitor his progress. It amused me to hear Dave, who had the broadest Wiltshire accent you have ever heard, speaking to Peter in a voice straight from a BBC Home Service war-time news broadcast. However our intrepid vicar arrived in his usual ebullient mood, seemingly unphased and undaunted by his arduous journey, bearing gifts of French biscuits and chocolate. It was too late even for Peter to suggest a nocturnal round of boules - what's the correct term for it, a fling maybe, or a toss? Nevertheless his appetite had not diminished and he gratefully devoured the supper we had kept for him before finally turning it at close to 3 a.m. I looked out of the window at 7.30 and there was Peter tossing off in the gravel beside the port office, humming the tune of 'Heavenly Father strong to save, Whose arm dost bind the restless wave."

We spent the next few days revisiting places between Buzet and Meilhan, before returning to Sérignac, where I had arranged another 5 week mooring with Mdme Cholet at 15 Euros per week. I did try to secure a hivernage but all the winter moorings had been bagged. I just hoped all those who had booked actually bothered to turn up.

In October I came back with my grandson, Percy, aka Dylan, who had grown somewhat since his last trip - he was nearly 20 now, and in the meantime had acquired amongst other things a diving instructor's licence, a girlfriend and an iphone - the latter to become a bit of a bone of contention and the girlfriend left behind in England.

The first problem arose at Heathrow Airport when his giant bright yellow diver's holdall was deemed too large for the overhead locker and cost me £35 to be put into the hold. We were only spending a week away and I had to wonder what the hell he'd packed - full wet-suit, flippers, goggles and air tanks? He actually proved a very capable and enthusiastic crew and luckily was never called upon to put his diving skills to use. The iPhone was a constant distraction, sometimes to the detriment of his concentration when working through locks, but all in all we got on very well together.

We were heading back to Toulouse and our booked hivernage at the port of Ramonville, where I had arranged for Serge to do another few jobs over the winter. Dylan was a big sports fan, but in spite of that had become a follower of Spurs. His father had a friend who was a long-established buddy of Harry Redknapp and Dylan had been taken as a treat to watch the Spurs team at their training ground. Dylan got the five star treatment and had his picture taken with all the players before sitting down with Harry for tea and buns. The result of all this blatant propaganda had turned the young Dylan in to a life-long and dedicated fan, quite oblivious to my attempts at converting him to support a proper team, like Southampton, the Saints, for instance.

At Montech I happened to see that there was a French Ligue 1 match taking place the following evening in Toulouse, where the local team were taking on Monaco. Dylan knew as much about European football as he did about the Premier League and could name half the team. I explained that if we made an early start we could probably get to the ground, which was close to the canal, in time to get to the match. It was the stadium that I had read about in the guide, where a footbridge over the canal closed during games.

This proved enough incentive for him to be up at 7.30, cycle into town for the baguette and cakes in the drizzling rain, and be back at the boat in time for us to cast off at 8.00 and head for the game. We made good time, eating our Boulangerie lunch on the move, and arrived within striking distance of the bridge at 5.50pm. The game was scheduled to kick off at 7.30pm which gave us enough time for a bit of dinner before setting off. We found a mooring at Garonne kilometre poste No.1, a few hundred metres from the footbridge, and just far enough away from the more down-at-heel areas of the Toulouse approaches. I peered through the binoculars now and again at the bridge which surprisingly stayed in the open position. This did seem a bit strange and got a bit more worrying as the time approached for us to leave for the ground. As we left the boat it started to drizzle which didn't serve to make the shanty shelters that straggled the towpath any more welcoming. The scattered rubbish and packs of stray dogs didn't help either. Dylan put his iPhone to use and logged in to some app (I think that's what they call them), that would show us the way to the stadium.

"Six point five kilometres," he said, peering at the tiny screen.

"What is?"

The stadium - it's six and a half kilometres away. At that point the drizzle developed into a persistent shower, and I suddenly realised why the footbridge hadn't been slid into place across the canal.

"Agh," I confessed, "you know what we've done, don't you?"

Well, at least what I'd done. It was unfair to implicate Dylan in this cock up. It was the wrong bloody stadium. This of course was the rugby ground and the football stadium was some way across the other side of town. There was a busy main road that ran parallel to the canal here and we climbed the bank to see whether there might be a chance of hailing a taxi, but the traffic was swishing past in the rain and it didn't look promising. After a few minutes getting slowly soaked, we decided unanimously to call it a day and admit defeat. Dylan took it all very calmly. I said I was sorry to have got him up early for nothing and he answered with a nonchalant shrug.

"We might be able to listen to it on the radio," I suggested hopefully, but we both knew there was little chance of that, and by then I think we had both lost interest. It had seemed a good idea at the time, as they say.

Next morning we moved the five kilometres into the centre of Toulouse, tying up at Ste Sauveur on the fuelling pontoon reserved for us by the newly installed Capitan, Allesandre. In the evening we met up with Andy in De Danu who told us he had been at the match, which Toulouse had won 3-1. Pity we hadn't contacted him earlier as he would have been able to pick us up. Easy to be wise after the event. As it happened he still had the programme in his pocket which he kindly gave to Dylan. Looking through it as I write I notice a couple of names in the Monaco line-up who have since made their presence felt in the Premier League - Fabinho at Liverpool and Bernado Silva at Manchester City. There was also a young lad on the subs bench for Monaco who might have a bit of a future - one Mbappé.

We stayed in the port on the Sunday and Dylan went off to explore the city. He came back in the afternoon with a replica Toulouse shirt and some photographs of the TFC stadium, which he had found just a couple of kilometres or so from the port. On the Monday we motored the seven kilometres to the Port de Plaisance Port Sud at Ramonville, where surprise surprise, the Capitan Michel, had no record of our reservation. Even though just a few months earlier I had watched him write down the details of the boat, the date of arrival, the length and breadth and the times I went to the toilet each day, he still insisted he knew nothing about it. He gave me a bewildered look as though he had never seen me before in his life, muttering continuously and sifting through a pile of papers on his desk. I wondered how he ever managed to stay in the job. It was simple enough. Most of the boats were moored permanently and there were only a few spaces for visitors. He worked from 10.00am till 12.00, took a three hour lunch break and retuned from 3.00 pm until 5.30. Hardly taxing work. What is more he lived on a boat not fifty yards from the office. To call him hopeless was too kind - he was an absolute bloody nightmare. I called Serge in the hope that he might be able to get some sense out of the idiot, and he turned up ten minutes later. After a lot of conflab and head scratching they finally agreed that I could moor in the narrow dock right outside the office which was just wide enough - and the exact place where I had been before. Why all the fuss and confusion I can only put down to the fact that c'est La France!

Serge explained to me that things weren't good at the port. Residents in the flats around the basin had been complaining about noisy work taking place on boats and the management had imposed some stringent restrictions. Serge did most of his work at the dry dock at Demoiselles or in the Port Technique, as it was known, a few hundred metres from Port Sud.

Chapter 10   Overheating and Hospitality in Beaucaire

In May of 2017 I flew back to Toulouse with postman Dave. Serge picked us up at the airport and after showering us with garlic flavoured kisses, told us all about his annus horribilis. He was full of apologies. He had been beset with a plague of problems over the winter and had been unable to do much of the work. His right hand man Ahmed had crushed his foot under a heavy steel plate and had to take two months off work to recover, and another member of the team had had a nasty accident with a high pressure hose that had taken half the skin off his leg. Serge was very down and I think he had also taken on too much work - a bit more than he could chew - a problem exacerbated by the absence of his key workforce. It wasn't the end of the world for Saul Trader as the jobs had been largely superficial. The main one being a repaint of the hull above the waterline. He promised me that he would make up for it next year and we left it at that. It did mean that I would have to spend another winter at Ramonville. Was it worth trying to book a mooring with Michel? I somehow doubted it.

I had made the decision to go back east this year. I had originally thought it might be time to bite the bullet and head back up the Rhone but the latest developments with Serge had ruled that out. In truth I needed very little encouragement to remain in the south. I had a few friends booked in for trips over the summer and I thought it was a good opportunity to explore some parts of the Midi that we'd bypassed on the way down, and have another look at the Petit Rhone, maybe going as far as Avignon. I had a French friend, Gerrard, who owned the apartment on the floor above me in Thailand, and who lived in Tarascon on the Rhone during the summer months, and we had tentatively arranged to meet up.

So with Dave aboard as number one, captain of the heads, token yokel (pc requirement checklist for the use of), bollard tosser and cribbage opponent, we set off to the East. We had only got about two kilometres from the port when I suddenly realised that the key to the security gate at Ste Sauveur was still in my pocket. The realisation came with the sort of start you get when you have nearly finished your Sudoko and notice that you have two of the same number in the same column. The Capitan at Ste Sauveur was very possessive of her security keys not unnaturally and there was nothing for it but to take it back. There was nowhere I could turn the boat round and Dave volunteered - well was pressed actually - to run back with it. I continued slowly onwards and I think Dave came to regret his foolhardy gesture as he didn't catch up with me until an hour and a half later.

"Phew - needed the exercise," he wheezed as he jumped back aboard.

We had a relatively trouble-free passage to Ventenac - quiet couple of beers and moules frites in the Place de Verdun at Castelnaudary followed by some harsh words at our peaceful overnight halt at Villepinte beside an attractive lavoir and opposite the eight arched overflow sluice. Peaceful that was until the approach of three German pocket battleships of the Kriegsmarine Locoboat hire fleet one behind the other sending three feet high waves across the towpath, came crashing towards us towards us flat out. Led by the Graf Spee, her Capitan standing aloft in a reversed black baseball cap, leading the charge like Boadicea at the siege of Colchester. This band of vandals had apparently been attempting to do the whole of the Canal du Midi , there and back, in seven days, and were obviously desperate to get back to their base at Castelnaudary before they lost their deposit! My shouts and gesticulations went largely unheeded until the last vessel of the convoy suddenly saw me and General van Klinkerhoffen slammed on his brakes, the sudden deceleration almost throwing him off balance. I managed to part with a few choice words which I'm quite sure had no effect whatsoever as the charge resumed unabated. We shook our heads, cursed the bloody Germans and the hire companies who failed to tell their customers about the rules and the etiquette, and walked into the pleasant little town for a take-away pizza fruits de mer, which we finished off over several games of crib and a few bottles of Kronenbourg. After stops at Carcassonne, two nights at 54 Euros,

Marseillette (closed) and Homps (extremely expensive dinner) we tied up at Ventenac once more, where we found another nice deepish mooring and a couple of conveniently sited wooden posts. We dined on the scallops at Le Grillade purely for research purposes to ensure that they were up to the usual standard and were entertained by the antics of David, the frivolous waiter.

One of the drawbacks with Ventenac was the lack of any convenient public transport. The nearest railway stations were at Lézignan and Narbonne, and there wasn't much to choose between them as far as distance was concerned, but obviously Narbonne had a better frequency of trains and routes. We had to get back to Toulouse and Dave went to the famous wine cave that sits alongside the canal at Ventenac on the following morning to avail himself of some of the produce and at the same time enquire about any local taxi firms that might be able to convey us to Narbonne Gare. Not an unreasonable request you would assume but Dave's question was answered with a rather unhelpful and unfriendly retort.

"Monsieur this is a wine cave where we sell wine. We are not a Tourist Information Centre,"

That was the gist of it and it aggrieved Dave somewhat (or pissed him off actually) to the extent that he immediately withdrew and abandoned any idea of buying any of the product on offer.

"Bugger him," said Dave philosophically, "if he can't be civil with me I'm bloody sure I'm not going to part with any money in his establishment." - or words to that effect anyway.

By chance he had bumped into David the waiter on the way back who gave him the calling card of a firm based not too far away in Bize.

I spoke to Bernard who was obviously the owner, and who sounded like Paul Robeson, who told me that he would pick us up at 12 noon. He arrived five minutes early and was standing beside his smart new Mercedes GLS in a chauffeur's cap and driving gloves, which he removed to shake our hands before loading our cases into the back and settling us into the air-conditioned leather luxury. Bernard told us that he was originally from Mauritius and had lived in France for 15 years. He spoke excellent English and drove us sedately to the station at Narbonne, 16 kilometres away, before relieving us of 40 Euros. It was a bit on the expensive side but the service was exemplary and Bernard the epitome of the gentleman chauffeur. I took his card and promised that we would contact him again should the need arise.

Sylvan passage near Argeliers

I drove back down a month later with six brand new Lumax 110 amp/hr batteries with a 12ft long shaft that I had requisitioned from the narrowboat strapped to the roof. Ours had been stolen many moons ago in Cambrai and I had never replaced it. After our ordeal on the Canal de Robine I thought it wise to find another one. We seldom needed one on Wat Tyler and I had rubbed it down in my garage at home and given it several coats of varnish. Sod's Law would probably dictate that we never ever had a use for one again but you never knew what challenges lie ahead. Alan and Dawn were moored in Roanne which made for a nicely convenient half way stop and Airbus Andy and tour guide Jeanette were coming with me from Valence and we were due to pick up another couple, Frank and his Thai wife Kung, at Béziers. I had never met either of them. I knew a German guy who lived in the same complex in Thailand who was a keen sailor and I had

146

shown him some pictures of Saul Trader. He told me that he had a friend from Dusseldorf who would love to come with us for a week and the trip had all been finalised via Email.

I was a bit apprehensive about it to say the least. Would the wife want four showers every day and would Frank laze around the boat and get in everybody's way and on everyone's nerves? There was little point in fretting about it now. I had made the commitment and would have to 'suck it and see.' If the worst came to the worst I could always use my authority as the Master of the vessel and chuck them off.

I replaced all the domestic batteries, changed the engine oil and filter and topped up the hydraulic steering fluid. Andy and Jeanette arrived and we were ready to go. At Capestang there was the small matter of the low bridge to tackle - this time we would not be able to duck the issue and turn around. There would be enough hands available to take the roof off if all else failed, as Rob was going to meet up with us for a meal that evening with Julian and a couple of friends. With Andy strategically in place on the fore deck monitoring the situation, we cleared the bridge, wheelhouse in situ, with just a couple of inches to spare. The port was fairly busy but we were directed to a space on the right hand side opposite the Capitanerie, and moored in front of a small plastic cruiser that would definitely qualify for a top ten place in the list of silly boat names, "Aresquiers!" This was not named after someone with a diverse sexual leaning but a small settlement on the Canal du Rhône á Séte.

Rob finally arrived an hour after the arranged time with Jules and a friend who was known as 'Dodgy' Phil with a girlfriend with legs that went up to her armpits and who looked like Joni Mitchell, and another Phil, who to avoid confusion was known as Phillip, and who as far as I know didn't have any dodgy connections. It was a rare pot-pourri of personalities. Phillip had recently retired from a career with an international firm of investment brokers and was pursuing a lifetime achievement award by trying to bed at least one woman from every country in the world. So far he was up to about 10 and currently trying hard to increase this number chasing a young lady from Japan. Dodgy Phil was a complicated sort of character who had earned his nickname from a time when he had owned a bar in a ski resort in the Alps which he had called 'Dodgy Phil's Bar' and the name had stuck. He was currently involved with several unconnected projects - a pig farm in the sticks on the outskirts of Bangkok, a wooden yacht which he was building in a shed on the island of Phuket with which he planned to sail around the world, and a project to refurbish a row of three run down houses he had recently acquired at Roubia, a village on the Canal du Midi a few miles west of Ventenac. The yacht had so far been en plan for 10 years and still had neither engine and running gear, or interior in place. If that wasn't enough to drive him crazy, he was taking lessons in the suicidal sport of Thai boxing. Reading between the lines, I think he had got himself somewhat bogged down with all this and was having difficulty keeping all his balls in the air. As you might imagine the conversation over dinner was a total bore! The Filet de Bouef and frites, followed by a very good Café Gourmand, helped to lessen the ennui. We were thankful to wave them all goodbye to get on with their mundane lives!!

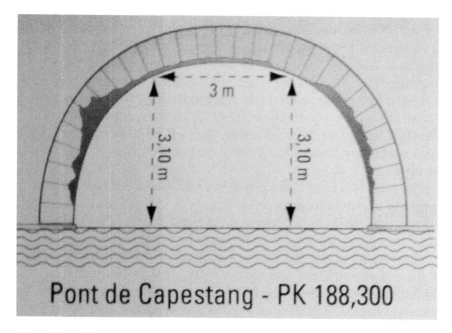

Pont de Capestang - PK 188,300

Not a lot of leeway here

From Capestang we continued on our way to meet up with our German friend at Béziers. This involved a further 17 kilometres of lock-free pound, passing through the short 160 metre Malpas tunnel which presented us with no problem being over 9 metres high and 6.5 metres wide. It was one-directional and boats are warned to sound the horn before entering. Béziers is approached through the 7 downhill staircase locks at Fonserranes which lower the canal 20 metres to the impressive Pont Canal, a 198 metre long aqueduct which carries the canal across the River Orb. These locks are worked on a 'boats up and boats down' sequence and we were lucky to arrive at the top just in time to join the downhill flotilla as tail-end Charlie. We had encountered the Fonserranes locks some years earlier when we made the trip in the opposite direction, and it still presented an awesome and in some ways quite frightening spectacle. The difference with these locks and all the other staircases that I'd ever come across was that here the middle gates were left open so that when the paddles were lifted a torrent of water was released that ran all the way into the two open chambers.

Going downhill as we were was not quite so daunting. It just meant waiting for the signal from the éclusier once the levels had evened up and the centre cill was clear before moving into the next one and so on. It did save time and meant that we literally flew through the flight in minutes and were finally released on to the aqueduct. After crossing this impressive structure which was completed in 1856, the canal descends through one more deep lock into the port of Béziers. A small and seemingly insignificant rider in the footnotes of the Du Breil reads :

"Note that trip boats who provide a regular service here have priority over all other craft."

This small insignificant piece of information was something that we were to discover to our cost. The canal widened before a right hand sweep led to the entrance of the last lock. The light was showing red and we tied with a single short line to a bollard, on the inside of the bend assuming that we would have to wait for an uphill boat. Time for a quick coffee, and Jeanette went below to prepare a bit of lunch. Then without warning the stern began to swing out in a current that was so strong that before we had time to to react had completely snapped our single rope. We were sent out of control into the middle of the cut. There was no time to start the engine and we were bowled sideways across the canal eventually coming to rest on the opposite side. Still not understanding exactly what was happening we tied another short line on to a concrete bollard and waited for the green. Nothing happened for several more minutes and then a trip boat appeared astern coming across the aqueduct, overtook us, and entered the lock. So that was it - another bloody trip boat causing havoc. I watched as they descended the lock into the Béziers port and waited. Another ten minutes and still no sign of anything happening, then another trip boat entered at the bottom and after what seemed like an eternity finally emerged at the top and passed us on its way to the staircase. At last I thought it's our turn. No such thing as the light remained obstinately at red. I was starting to get a tad annoyed by this time and I was on the point of walking down to the lock to complain when there was another sudden surge and the boat started to move forward at an alarming rate of knots. This time I was able to flick off the rope before it too was torn in half and started the engine, reversing at full revs to keep the boat away from the gates which were still closed. The reason for all this turbulence became apparent as yet another bloody trip boat appeared from behind coming across the aqueduct. The surge was caused by the flow from the staircase locks as they were emptied to let the jolly boats through and we were left sitting helplessly at their mercy. This time the swirling current sent us back to the side of the canal that we had been tied against originally. It was like being caught in a whirlpool. Trip boat number three passed and entered the lock without so much as a thank you and I was starting to get somewhat pissed off to say the least. Jeanette appeared with a plate of cheese baguettes and asked what the hell was going on

"Bloody trip boats." I said, "think they own the bloody place. We've been held up here for over a bloody hour."

At this we all started to laugh at at the very moment that I picked up a welcome piece of baguette and cheese and was about to eat, the gates creaked open and the light turned to green.

We were directed to a mooring in the port of Béziers by the lovely vivacious Capitan, Clare. I paid for two nights and was pleasantly surprised by the very generous rate. Just after noon on the following day a silver Merc slid into a space right alongside the boat and out jumped a smiling Thai lady followed shortly afterwards by a tall ganging Hitler youth lookalike, all of seven feet tall with a floppy Tilley hat jauntily askew on his head that gave him at least another six inches. This, it goes without saying, was Herr Frank.

"Wow," said Frank, after we had all been introduced, "She is a vonderful Wessel to be sure."

This didn't get me off to a particularly good start with Frank.

I had always regarded barges as 'he's'. 'J' Class yachts and cruise liners I suppose you could describe as she's - but barges, well they were masculine through and through. Nothing effeminate about a barge. I let it pass however, not wishing to start an international incident at this early stage, and we helped them unload their gear into the forr'ard cabin. Andy and Jeanette, who both spoke fluent German after their time in Hamburg, engaged them in some friendly chatter, and I suggested we make an early departure. Frank's wife, Kung (the word is Thai for 'prawn'), evoked the essence of Thailand, the land of smiles. They had brought bags loaded with goodies from Germany which was added to the overkill of supplies that Andy and Jeanette had contributed, and we had difficulty fitting it all into the galley.

We cast off and entered the first lock at the end of the port and waited for the gates to close. At that point a man ran out of the office and came towards us brandishing a piece of paper. This turned out to be the real Capitan who had been on his day off when the lovely Clare had charged us for the mooring. I'd had a strange feeling about that, thinking it may have been too good to be true - and it wasn't true. Clare had made a mistake somehow and undercharged us by 20 Euros. My futile attempts at arguing the point were just that - futile - and I reluctantly had to part with the balance. This did not do anything to help my mood.

"Mi prenrai," I said to Kung who was standing beside me, trying to make her feel welcome with my pathetic smattering of Thai, "ca ne fait rien - never mind - macht nichts aus!"

Oh you could almost touch the cosmopolitan camaraderie aboard the good ship Saul Trader.

Frank had already started to insert his five eggs where they were not required, suggesting that I hung the fenders from the side rails rather than from the deck cleats. He had a small dinghy he told me which he sailed on a lake near Frankfurt and I think he regarded this as sufficient expertise to give him the authority to tell me how to operate the barge that I had been running with reasonable success for the past thirty years. I wanted to tell him that there were two ways to do everything - the right way and the Harris way , and never the twain shall meet.

After the lock there was a four kilometre pound and it was half way along this that I first noticed that the temperature gauge had started slowly rising. Normally the running temperature hovered around the 70 degree mark but it had crept up to 75. Immediately I became aware that the exhaust note had changed to the more hollow echo that always indicated that there wasn't enough water going through the system. The most likely cause was that the filter tube had become clogged up so we tied to the waiting pontoon at the top of the next lock so that I could investigate and clean out the muck. This was a simple job which just entailed closing the cooling water intake valve, removing the cap from the top of the filter tube, taking out the tubular gauze filter and giving it a good wash through. A simple job that had the filter actually been blocked up could have been solved and put right in a matter of minutes. Unfortunately though, the filter was as clean as the proverbial whistle, which probably meant that the impeller itself had packed up. There was one more lock before the small town of Villeneuve-lès-Béziers and I decided to find somewhere there to tie up and investigate further. At least there were a few things there that would keep the 'guests' amused while I tried to fix the problem. It was all a bit embarrassing to say the least. Frank and Kung had driven all the way from Germany and Andy and Jeanette were on their summer break. Although they weren't paying guests as such, I still felt a certain responsibility for their enjoyment. We motored gingerly to the lock, all the while keeping a close eye on the engine temperature gauge.

Luckily there was an ideal mooring directly below the lock, alongside a small restaurant, and that is where we tied.

I suggested that the guests went for a look around the town but Frank and Andy insisted on staying behind to help. I checked to make sure that I had the correct replacement part. That was one thing I always made sure of - as soon as I had to change anything I ordered a new one. The first job was to remove the old impeller, which in itself was no easy task. It was located at the bottom of the engine and held into place with a brass plate with six retaining screws. The plate was situated such that it sat at right angles as you looked at it which meant that the screws had to be loosened with the screwdriver in the left hand - another clever tactic by the manufacturer to ensure that any work would have to be done by a qualified mechanic in possession of all the right tools at an exorbitant hourly rate.

This is how a nice new impeller should look

This is how a nice new impeller should look

The other thing to watch was that the screws didn't fall into the bilge as they came out. I wedged a small plastic tray underneath to hopefully catch any stray screws trying to make a getaway. Partly because of the awkwardness of accessing the screws, and probably also due to the fact that the job had been undertaken too often in the past by amateurs - me - some of the heads had burred making it difficult to get a decent firm purchase.

Eventually I had six screws safely in the tray and gently eased the plate with its attendant gasket away from the assembly. So far so good. The next stage was to extract the impeller. There was a special tool for this but needless to say I didn't have one. It was one of those things that I had put on my Father Christmas list of presents to myself but so far he hadn't delivered. Egged on my an enthusiastic Frank I twisted and pulled at the offending object until at last it wriggled free.

I have resorted to showing a picture of an impeller at the risk of boring people as I had given up trying to describe one in words. It was quite obvious that this was the cause of our problem.

All the blades were badly chewed and several had disintegrated completely. Just what had caused this I wasn't sure. We had experienced some problems with shallow water and silt and I can only assume that over the years of putting extra strain on the blades running hot with a restricted flow of water, had culminated in their present rather sorry state. The last time it had been changed was five years ago at Argeliers when Chris had done the job and I watched but regrettably didn't inwardly digest. After several frustrating and unsuccessful attempts at squeezing the new one into its hole, I stood up for a stretch and a breather. This was obviously the moment that Frank had been waiting for and he immediately took control. I was too deflated to argue and although I had some reservations, I let him get on with it.

"What I sink ve vill vant is a wot you say 'jubiwee cwip.

Easy for you to say Frank.

Actually I'm being unkind here. Frank's English was very good and I understood him quite clearly. What I didn't understand was what the hell he was going to do with a jubilee clip. Frank explained that if we could tighten the blades with the aid of the clip we could make it small enough to slide into the aperture. Brilliant!

As luck would have it I found one of just the right size and Frank, who had now taken over the job, fastened it around the outside half of the blade area. The added advantage of this was that we could be sure that all the blades were bent in the correct direction. Next he smeared a small amount of washing up liquid onto the area of the blades that would be inserted first. Once this was set up the impeller slid into the hole with ease, the outer half following as soon as the clip was removed - job done! At this point I made a mental note to order another impeller - and an extractor tool. So all we had to do now was re-open the fresh water intake valve and start her up. Doddle.

Except that as soon as the engine started I knew that the problem had not been solved. The exhaust still sounded hollow and instead of the whoosh of water passing out of the side there was a desultory trickle. What's more, after a few minutes ticking over the temperature gauge started to rise above the norm. There was more work to be done.

For a moment, even Frank seemed baffled. The girls had returned from the shops with fresh bread and cheese and we decided to have a break for lunch while we pondered our options. This was getting embarrassingly serious. Our resident aircraft technician, Andy, next volunteered a suggestion. For all I know they may have the same problem with the 380.

"There's obviously a blockage somewhere and I would think its being caused by all the broken bits of rubber from the old impeller," he said, and with the wisdom of hindsight, we all readily agreed with his theory. The next problem was where to start looking for these wayward little offending bits.

"We'll just have to disconnect it bit by bit starting from the pump," he said, "there's nothing else for it".

This was mid-summer in Southern France and the outside temperature was in the high eighties. In the engine-room it was probably nearer 100° - not a particularly inviting prospect when you consider that there were five separate sections of various pipework that fed the cooling water through the engine and out of the side. This was just another challenge for Frank who stripped to his underpants, (not a pretty sight), and stood ready for action.

He and Andy excelled themselves with a devotion that went far and above the call of duty. There were four separate sections that were meticulously dismantled, cleared of debris and replaced. The copper pipe from the pump up to the header tank, the heat exchanger on the top of the cylinder head, and then two more sections that fed the water to the outlet in the side of the hull.

Once each section had been cleared we tried the engine and the result was the same - lack of a through-put of water and a rise in engine temperature. The heat exchanger was like the boiler in a steam locomotive, a hundred small bore tubes. At

156

first we tried to clear them by shoving a length of metal welding rod through each one in turn, then Andy had the bright idea of using the dinghy air pump. This had the desired effect and blew hundreds of tiny pieces of rubber out of the ends of the tubes into a bucket. Then after reconnecting the rubber hoses to each end and trying again the result was the same. Finally the last resort. We disconnected the last piece of the jigsaw, held the bucket against the end of the pipe and briefly started the engine. After a couple of goes at this, and a bucket half full of boiling water and bits of rubber, we connected everything back up again and voila - success. The whole exercise had taken over two hours in searing heat and I think we all shed more pounds than Lewis Hamilton at the 2013 Hungarian Grand Prix.

When I apologised to Frank about spoiling his holiday he said "Please - it is not a problem I love mechanical things and I am so happy working on the engine more than I want to sit in the sunshine or walk around these places. I am very happy now we have the done the work".

Well! I had to admit I was starting to warm to Frank.

The girls had been amusing themselves as well and had found a little canalside bookshop which the proprietor, an Aussie, was having to close down because his lease was about to expire. He was more or less giving away all his stock - books, DVD's, CD's, pictures and various items of bric a brac. They insisted that we go and take a look and I had a nice chat with Gary and picked up a couple of interesting books, including one entitled "How to quickly solve engine overheating problems." No - I'm joking, but I did find the odd Ian Rankin novel and a brilliant Peter James novel that I hadn't read, 'Absolute Proof.'

I tried to return the favour in the afternoon and presented him with a couple of copies of my own work.

"I'm sorry mate - but I really don't want anymore. I'm trying to get rid of the stuff, not take in any more for Christ sake."

"But these are my own," I pleaded, "what I wrote. They're for you - a present."

Gary eventually relented and accepted my offering as graciously as might be expected in the circumstances. I didn't like to ask him whether he would like me to sign them! For all I know they might still be there. If you're passing and find one please take it with my compliments. If nothing else you could always tear out the pages and hang them from a piece of string in the heads.

Then I had my fifteen seconds of fame moment when just as we were about to cast off, a boat came out of the lock and as it passed the skipper, who I had never seen before in my life, shouted,

"Hi Keith - reading your book - good stuff."

I waved back at him and then hid my face in my hands with embarrassment. I suppose this must be how the likes of Paul McCartney and Mick Jagger feel every time they walk down the street.

Our next destination was Agde and on the way we passed through the weird flood barrage that was built to protect the canal from the River Libron. Apparently the surrounding countryside was too low to enable the construction of an aqueduct and this strange structure was designed by a Monsieur Magués and incorporates large gates at each end that can be closed in times of inundation.

Rob had volunteered to 'pilot' us across the Étang de Thau and he met us in Agde, where we found the only available mooring against a low wall at the foot of the Round Lock, the Bassin Ronde. This was at right angles to the canal and entailed a delicate piece of reversing. It was just about long enough for us, leaving Saul Trader's bow protruding a foot or so into the tail of the lock. I was pretty sure we were going to be asked to move but when the lock-keeper peered over the top his only reaction was a perfunctory nod - the sort I took as being as good as a wink.

Robert arrived by car shortly afterwards and we all went for a stroll to look at the wonders of the Round Lock and do our gongoozler bit. The lock has three exits, two for straight through passage of the canal and the third to allow access to the river. It was originally built round but modified to allow the passage of 38 metre barges in 1984. I believe it was Bernard Cribbins who told them that they had 'dug it round and it ought to be square!'

Elaborate flood barrier over the Libron

We then followed the path alongside the River Hérault into the centre of the town. The third exit from the lock allowed access to the river and I noted that there seemed to be plenty of available mooring - another thing to be added to the 'have to do' list for the future. The river is navigable with care for about eight kilometres to the north and the village of Bessan, and south to the Mediterranean at the port of Le Grau d'Agde. There are a number of very good boatyards and chandleries, as we were later to discover. We retired to a small bar and sat in the warm sunshine with a beer or two.

From Agde to Pointe des Onglous, where the canal du Midi enters the large lake known as the Étang de Thau, is about ten kilometres. We had of course crossed this on our way from the Rhone but I was following 'Pisgah' at the time and leaving the navigation to Jules. I vowed to take more interest in the passage this time as I would have to return without any guidance from the Whitaker clan.

As it happened there was little to gain from our experience as Rob promptly lost his way and at one point led us rather too close for comfort to the shallow area in the south. The channel is buoyed but the markers are few and far between and difficult to pick out. It was the sudden realisation that there was no buoy where there definitely should have been one that led me to instigate a severe change of course to port. It is about 15 kilometres from the Midi to the Canal du Rhône a Sète and the width of the lake varies between two and three kilometres. There are vast oyster and mussel beds in the north which cover almost half of the Étang and shallows in the south. We had steered much too far to the south and lost sight of the navigable channel, which runs close to the southern edge of the oyster beds. Once back on track we managed to pick out the buoy - it was actually buoy number six, and from thereon the channel route became clearer and we soon had the next buoy sighted through the binoculars. We eventually passed through the middle of the two cardinal buoys and tied up once again on the lake side of the bascule bridges at Sète and the two ships 'engineers' and their respective wives went off to explore the fascinating port while Rob and I discussed where we had gone wrong in the passage of the Étang. I made a mental note to disregard any advice that Rob had to offer and vowed to trust my own judgement on the return trip. The tourists arrived back at the boat with bags full of fishy things they had found in the port and Jeanette sauteed a large bowl of prawns in garlic.

We spent the night in Frontignan on a mooring which was 'reserved for commercial vessels.' Rob assured me that the commercials never came through this way now as there was a new deep draft by-pass cut that led directly to the Med, and somewhat surprisingly on this occasion he was actually proved right and we had an undisturbed night. Frontignan is a pleasant town and we found a lively restaurant nestled in the square below the   shadows of a fortified church. We were moored close to a very busy railway bridge and I wiled away an hour or so watching freight train after freight train clatter across and disappear into the night. Rob caught an early train back to Agde the next morning and we cast off in time to catch the opening of the very low road bridge which only operates twice a day, at 8.30am and 4.00pm, and headed off towards Aigues-Mortes.

The Canal du Rhône à Sète extends for over 60 kilometres from Frontignan to the Petit Rhône at St Gilles, running almost dead straight in a channel bordered on both sides by a series of Étangs.

These vast salt water lakes were very shallow and full of submerged fishing nets and powered craft were warned not to encroach. We gave ourselves as wide a berth as possible past 'Aresquiers' which was coming from the opposite direction, and sounded the horn for the quaint little manually operated swing bridge at Manguelone. I gave the wheel to Andy and after an hour or so to Frank, who was so excited by the prospect I thought he was going to kiss me. There is a varied birdlife here and we saw grebe, coots, cuckoo jays (according to Jeanette) and pink flamingo. There were Étangs from left to right stretching for miles on end - L'Arnel, Prévost, Méjean, Pérols and the vast expanse of Mauguio. We crossed the junction with the Lez where a narrow channel led to the small seaside resort of Palavas-les-Flots, which according to Du Breil boasted a railway museum that featured the history of the branch line that once connected the resort with Montpelier. For once in my life I had to pass up the opportunity but stored the information for use at a later date. There is another museum here dedicated to the work of cartoonist Albert Dubout. Aigues-Mortes is approached from the canal via two channels that form a 'Y' and we took the first one and were met by the port Capitan in a rubber dinghy who escorted us to a berth on the visitor mooring, where we stayed for two nights.

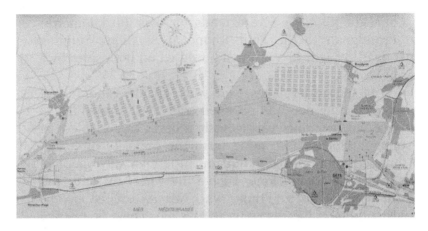

Du Breil chart of the Étang showing the buoyed channel parallel to the edge of the oyster beds

Saul Nomad was still there in the same place opposite the port but I saw no sign of John.

A branch line crosses the canal here on a swing bridge and we caught the two car diesel unit to the end of the line at the Mediterranean port of Grau-de-Roi. Frank and I took our swimming trunks in the hope of a nice cool dip but only lasted for a few minutes as the water was akin to an ice bath. Strange really as the air temperature was in the high thirties but I had found this before at Narbonne Plage. We just about managed to get everything submersed but soon abandoned the idea for fear of frostbite. We warmed up with a beer - well the rest of us did: Frank was tee-total and sucked a lemon smoothie through a straw. We sat at a table alongside the river and watched as a fleet of huge stern trawlers brought in their catch and unloaded it on to the quay. I thought of the Common Fisheries Policy and the fact that our fishermen were confined to port for long periods and forced to throw back perfectly good but underweight fish. Le Grau du Roi is the second largest fishing port in the Mediterranean and by the look of things the industry seemed to be doing very nicely thank you. And woe betide any jumped up British fishermen who might try to muscle in on their grounds. We might well be all part of the European Union and equal. It's just that some are more equal than others.

We walked back the five kilometres back to Aigues-Mortes. In the evening we booked a table at a restaurant in the corner of the square St Louis where most of the party slummed it with burgers and frites and Frank insisted on footing the entire bill.

In the morning another little problem raised its ugly head. There were three separate showers on Saul Trader. The one in the aft cabin pumped into its own dedicated holding tank, and the two forward showers drained by gravity into a tank that was hidden somewhere under the floor which was emptied by a submerged pump triggered by a float switch - something we may have a problem with in the future as France attempts to get more eco-friendly.

It was this pump that had started to play up and every time it was activated by the switch it tripped the fuse which in turn cut the lights in the saloon. I had never found the tank, let alone the pump, and I really had no idea where it was or how it was accessed. This was exacerbated by the fact that there were now four people using these showers, and with the extreme heat, sometimes twice a day. I illogically blamed Frank for this although of course it had nothing to do with him. It would have to wait anyway and just meant that every time somebody showered I had to go into the engine-room and re-set the switch. A minor inconvenience I suppose in the grand scheme of things.

We left Aigues-Mortes via the East channel, passing through the railway swing bridge and re-entering the canal at Pont Soulier. We covered fifty kilometres that day, with Andy and Frank sharing the steering. This was Camargue country and we passed several groups of the famous white horses, as well as spotting heron, egret which sat on the backs of the horses feeding off the ticks, and at one point a kingfisher who came and actually sat on the rail for a few moments. We turned left at St Gilles, negotiated one lock at Nourriguier, and arrived into the large port of Beaucaire in time for tea. I knew that mooring in the port was difficult and I had spoken to my friend Gerrard who told me he was a good friend of the Capitan and would arrange something for us.

"Materelle, she is my good friend. She will make something for you - no problem."

Gerrard often had trouble with gender when speaking English which was strange as he generally spoke very good English. The Capitan was a young man called, believe it or not, Frank, and he told me that he had never heard of Gerrard! Nevertheless he managed to squeeze us in to a space at the far end of the port where we had to moor stern-to, Mediterranean style against a wall. It made getting off a bit difficult as we had to climb over the rail and step over the gap but everybody made it safely. Even Gerrard himself, a downwardly immobile portly 70 something bridged the gap, no doubt egged on by the promise of Thai green curry with prawns that Kung had prepared for us as a parting gesture. They were leaving the following morning and Gerrard kindly arranged to pick them up from the boat and take them to the station at Tarascon where they were catching the train back to Béziers. As they sped off Frank opened the window and wildly waved his hat in the air until they were finally out of sight. I had mixed feelings. Frank had been a godsend with the impeller problem and he had certainly gone out of his way to contribute financially. On the other hand he did get on my nerves sometimes and was prone to sitting cross-legged on the foredeck wearing a sarong eating Thai food - pappaya pot pot, an obnoxious evil-smelling very hot dish that in my opinion was one of the main causes of a minor epidemic of IBS in Thailand.

We stayed in Beaucaire for three more days. The original plan to go on to the Rhône to Avignon had been blown out of the water due to the time factor caused by Frank and Kung needing to get back home. Gerrard showered us with hospitality which went way above the call of duty. He took us for lunch at his favourite restaurant beside the harbour and drove us to Avignon where we spent the day exploring this beautiful town in searing heat before returning to Tarascon by train. On our last day he invited us to his house in Tarascon for lunch where his 'woman who did' provided a wonderful meal of seafood accompanied with an exotic salad, complete with a couple of bottles of Gerrard's favourite locally produced Vin Rosé.

On the way back we stopped overnight at St Gilles where I got chatting to a French couple who had parked alongside in an ancient Citroen motorhome. Jean-Claude was a retired railway signalman. He spoke pretty good English and told me that he and his wife Nellie divided their summers touring in the van or sailing on the Med in a small dinghy which they kept at Aigues-Mortes. He told me that he had worked in traditional signalboxes until the last few years before he retired when he was transferred to a large signal control centre. The advance in railway technology and the advent of very high speed trains had forced signalling into the digital age and France had been at the forefront of some of this development. Drivers of trains travelling at 200 mph could not be expected to be able to pick out and react to traditional signals and sophisticated in-cab control systems had been progressed.

I asked Jean-Claude about something that had been puzzling me for sometime. which was the purpose of the boards I had seen on the side of high speed train routes, both in France and on the Channel Tunnel Rail Link. They were square with a blue background incorporating a yellow triangle pointed towards the track. They seemed to be positioned quite frequently and I thought they might have something to do with coasting sections. The practice of coasting had been in operation for many years on electrified lines, and allowed drivers to decrease power without losing speed, thereby saving energy and cost.

My yellow triangles, however, were nothing of the sort. They indicated block sections where drivers were given an automatic signal inside the cab to show that the next area of line was clear, or where they had to reduce speed. They were in fact virtual signals. Jean-Claude attempted to explain exactly how this worked but because of the language barrier and the complete absence of a technical side to my brain I wasn't that much wiser. I got the distinct impression that these trains hardly needed a driver at all and it wouldn't be long before the railway operators were pushing to make them redundant. I thought that the fear of this happening was another reason for the disruptive strikes by railwaymen that had crippled France over the past few years, ostensibly a protest over proposed changes to the long-established labour laws that ensured jobs for life and healthy pensions for railway workers.

Another thing that always fascinated me when travelling by TGV at 200 miles per hour, was the frequency with which trains passed in the opposite direction. With a closing speed of up to 400 mph these trains flashed past at a seemingly ridiculous proximity to each other, sometimes just five minutes apart on the busiest routes. A quick calculation and I realised to my surprise that they were probably more than 30 miles apart. It didn't take a lot to work out that even at 180 mph we would have covered a distance of 15 miles in five minutes and of course the train that had passed us in the opposite direction five minutes ago would also have covered the same distance. This meant that the gap between them would be an incredible 30 miles. (*thank you Einstein...Ed*)

I imagine you would need to be pretty much on the ball controlling trains running at these speeds and you wouldn't want to be coming into work with a giant hangover. I suppose the job was similar to that of an air traffic controller, but at least they had the benefit of an extra dimension, the vertical as well as the horizontal. On the railways there was no such leeway.

Paris bound Eurostar. The yellow board block indicator for trains in the opposite direction can just be seen above the first coach behind the leading power car.

We stopped overnight in Aigues-Mortes again and lo and behold who should come running across to greet us but Jean-Claude. He invited us to join him and Nellie for beer and we found a pleasant café in the square where we passed a couple of convivial hours. Conversation was not too difficult as Jean-Claude had a good knowledge of English but his wife had none at all. We parted as friends - Jean-Claude gave me his card, and we promised to keep in touch and meet up again somewhere. Another ship that passed in the night. The next thing I had to worry about was navigating the Étang. The guide suggested that boats should not attempt the crossing if the wind was above Force 3. I checked the forecast which was showing winds of Force 4-5 coming from the west in a few days. This would mean that we would be heading into the weather and although I didn't have any doubts about the capability of Saul Trader I would prefer it a bit more settled for my first solo crossing. We arrived at Frontignan too late to get through the bridge and tied up to the wall. There was a small wooden boat on the opposite side flying a red ensign and I decided to walk across for a chat. Ron was an amenable Irishman from Cork and he invited me aboard and introduced me to his attractive, buxom partner, Moira, who hailed from Liverpool and was clad in nothing but a small towel. Before I had a chance to say anything, Ron passed me a very large gin and tonic. I asked him about the weather and the Étang which he dismissed with a wave of his arm.

"it's a piece of wee wee," he said, "done it meself a hundred times. Do it with me oiyes closed. No problem at all at all."

I wasn't so convinced but my confidence seemed to grow with each G&T that was forced on to me and by the third I had made up my mind to go for it. We passed an hour or two slating everything that came into our heads - governments , cost of living, French incompetence, the VNF, hire boaters, mooring charges, rip-off boatyards - when they see you coming from a boat they double the bloody price. There wasn't much that we didn't have a good old moan about. Ron said that he was heading for the small port of Mèze but thought it might be a bit small for us.

Joust a minute!

"You'd be best to go straight across," he told me - be a doddle to be sure."

In the evening we were entertained by some jousting practice. Not horse mounted jousting but waterborne. Two strange gaily decorated wooden craft appeared with eight oarsmen in each and a peculiar raised platform at the stern at an angle of 45° which resembled the sort of ramp that Evil Knievel used to propel his motorbike over the top of a row of cars.

I was informed by a passer-by that they were practising for the annual Sète jousting festival. As the boats are propelled towards each other, accompanied by musicians with horns and drums, the jousters, one to each boat, climb to the top of the ramp brandishing a 10 ft pole with an iron tip. The object of the exercise, as far as I could make out, was to strike the opponent with enough force to throw him off balance into the drink. This is a serious sport in these parts and has been going on since the 17th century when the canal was first opened. I wondered whether they might look at recruiting some of the fat Dutch boaters I had encountered, some of them pretty lethal with a boathook.

After supper I drew up a simple course to follow to get us safely across the lake by using the parallel rule which we still had on board but hadn't seen the light of day since we had navigated the Ijsselmeer several years ago. It was a rudimentary calculation to say the least but I had a course to steer from the exit of the canal to the cardinal buoys at the start of the navigable channel (280°, then 250° for 4 kilometres to buoys 1 and 2, followed by a final 8 kilometres at 215° to take us past the mussel beds and into the Midi at Pointe des Onglous. It wasn't rocket science but at least we would have some idea of where to go if the weather did close in. In the event we sailed across in two and a half hours with a fresh but steady breeze sending up a refreshing spray over the foredeck bulwarks. As it turned out Ron's prediction was quite right. It was a doddle.

At Agde we did go on to the river and found a good mooring close to the centre. This was fortunate as there was some sort of festival taking place and the town was packed with revellers.

We came across a New Orleans style jazz band playing outside a bar in a narrow street and listened to the music for over an hour, transfixed by the wonderful atmosphere. The band were a motley bunch of musicians who had all seen better days, and had probably had better gigs. Some with white trousers and some more off-white, ice cream jackets and straw boaters. The fat curly headed conductor reminded me of Dudley Moore, tattered white shirt hanging down over the back of his trousers, polka dot neckerchief, grubby trousers and sandals that tapped out the beat. They played their hearts out and the small crowd gradually thickened.

"When the Saints Go marching In," "Five Foot Two, Eyes of Blue", "Sweet Georgia Brown," "Everybody Loves My Baby", "Bugle Call Rag" and the appropriately titled "Riverboat Shuffle." The tunes came thick and fast reverberated gently off the terraced buildings that lined the lane and the crowd swooned and swayed to the music. I watched one elderly lady with a shopping bag in one hand who waltzed and smooched around in front of the band for a good half hour, eyes closed and oblivious to everyone around her. It was magical and true France - and it was still only 3 o'clock in the afternoon. A policeman strolling around and obviously recognising some distant aunt in the crowd, went over and gave her a huge hug and kiss. Some beautifully eccentric freaks jumped and jived around, people clapped out of time with the music but nobody cared or told them to shut up. This was the sort of thing that France did with laid back aplomb. We might think they are 25 years behind us but they get their rubbish collected three times a week, not once a fortnight. They must be doing something right.

Oh when the Saints Go Marching In

On the way back to Villeneuve we had a strange experience approaching the lock at Portiragnes when a figured clad in black with a helmet that looked too big for his head, appeared running alongside the boat gesticulating madly. Who the hell was this crazy idiot. My first thought was that it was a boat-spotting anorak who just had to tick off Saul Trader to complete his sightings of the entire RW Davis barge fleet. Then another thought crossed my mind. Maybe it was someone who had bought one of my books and was about to demand his money back. I did my best to ignore him hoping he would go away as I concentrated on getting us into the lock. Then as we slowly ascended all was revealed. He had now removed the helmet and was standing on the lockside jumping up and down like a madman. Then it suddenly hit me. It was indeed a madman. Our old mate Phil Dipple, erstwhile bass player with Meet on the Ledge, raconteur, naturist and piss artist.

All bass players are a little bit crazy and Phil would probably have made the top ten. He was holidaying with his lovely wife Rose in a nudist campsite on the coast at Sérignan Plage and had (luckily for everyone) put on some clothes to go out for a tour around on the motor scooter. We stopped on the pontoon above the lock and Phil and Rose came aboard. We didn't have a lot to offer them but Jeanette conjured up some scran and we found a few bottles of Kronenbourg. It was a lovely surprise

171

and we spent a pleasant couple of hours catching up and gossiping about all our friends in the Leamington/ Warwick fraternity, before they sped away into the sunset and we cast off and headed for Villeneuve.

Another shock was in store as we passed another British flagged barge - not the one we'd seen before, who waved and shouted that he'd read one of my books. Bloody hell, my notoriety was spreading. Needless to say I have never come across anyone else, before or since, who was remotely aware, or it seemed interested, in my classic offerings.

Our next overnight stop was at the small hamlet with the somewhat ambiguous name of Poilhes. I imagined the scenario when a lad on a boating holiday telephones his mother in Dudley, West Midlands.

"Allo soon. Noice to 'ear from yow. Where'm yow be now then?

"Poilhes ma."

"Sorry to 'ear that soon. Can't yow get soom crame for that!

Another feature of the Canal du Midi is the thousands of crickets that sing endlessly in the trees and we had the full orchestra in Poilhes. It must be similar to tinitus. Rob was back at Ventenac when we arrived and Andy and Jeanette left to go back to home and work in Toulouse. I wanted to sort out the problem with the shower pump switch and explained the problem to Rob who volunteered to help me with it. The first thing we had to do was to find out exactly where the tank was situated. I had a small inspection hatch in the floor of the corridor between the cabins and from this I traced the outlet pipe into the top of the tank. It then entailed rolling back the carpet and removing half a dozen screws around a likely looking panel which when lifted out exposed a rusty steel tank with an electrical wire feed in the top. Well that was the first step. We then had to remove 24 rusted bolts that more than likely hadn't been touched for almost thirty years in order to take off the lid and see what was inside. This was a delicate operation. They were so encrusted that we were worried that they might sheer and it took several squirts of WD40 and some gentle coaxing with the socket wrench aided and abetted with a few grunts and choice obscenities before they grudgingly yielded their hold. Once we had removed the lid the problem became all too apparent. The pump itself was completed clogged up and the wiring to the switch had virtually disintegrated. The reinforced plastic pipe from the pump to the outlet had welded itself together and in attempting to get it off we managed to break off a piece of the connector. When we got it out, closer inspection revealed terminal damage and it was agreed that a new pump was required. Another example that bore out the truth of the adage that owning a boat was akin to standing under a shower tearing up twenty pound notes. I know it used to be fivers but with inflation and all that.

While we were pondering our next move there came the ominous sound of metal on metal that emanated from outside. I ran up to the wheelhouse to find and his 'mate' peering anxiously at the side of my Discovery. Cyril had a multi coloured Renault Master van which was his workshop, and since the time that his wife had buggered off with the milkman, had also served as his living quarters. The reason for the psychedelic colour scheme was not that Renault had produced an expensive limited edition of their iconic workhorse but rather that Cyril had been involved in so many prangs that he had replaced half of the original vehicle with bits found in various scrapyards. The base colour, in manufacturer's speak, was 'tangerine orange' but Cyril obviously didn't like this and rather that just repaint the whole thing and have done with it, was systematically adding bits of varying hue as and when they were needed. Hence the driver's door was a faded 'burnt chocolate',the nearside rear door a shade of 'moss green metallic', the bonnet a rather becoming 'nutmeg brown' and the offside front wing a fetching 'Prussian Blue.' Unfortunately he had yet to find a replacement offside mirror for the one that had unluckily shattered when he misjudged the entrance to his former garage - the garage that was attached to the house that was attached to his estranged wife. All in all you can probably deduce that one way or the other poor old Cyril was in a pretty sorry state. How he had managed to reverse into the side of my car however was a mystery, as the track was at least three times the width of his van.

When I leapt off the boat to survey the damage I found him desperately trying to re-fix the very expensive electronically controlled remote wing mirror with rain censor , automatic de-misting device and parking fold-up, (£1250.00 plus VAT at your friendly Land Rover dealer), that was dangling despondently over the side of my once beautiful moon mist metallic grey Land Rover Discovery which was now adorned with a three foot long gash in the side, embellished with an artistic brush of tangerine orange. So the question was - what to do next ?

Rob appeared and discovered that Cyril apparently had insurance, which was a bit of a surprise, but any claim would take an age to sort out and would probably mean that the repair had to be done in France. I was planning to return to England in a few days time which seemed to rule out that option. Cyril was in enough trouble with his personal life and I was reluctant to make things any worse for him. I reported the incident to my insurance company, Allianz, and they assured me that I would be covered even if the damage was done in my absence. I didn't really see any point in naming Cyril as I imagined he was probably high on the black list of all major international insurers. They duly recorded the accident and told me to contact them again when I got back to England.

A more pressing problem for the moment was to sort out the shower pump. An added complication was that the electrics on Saul Trader ran on 24 volts and it was sometimes difficult to get replacement parts. Rob called a chandler at Agde on the side of the Hérault that he had used before, and they told us that yes indeed they had a suitable pump in stock at the not so unreasonable price of 235 Euros. They were used to dealing with commercial fishing vessels which were also equipped with 24v systems.

We drove to Agde in the afternoon in the Discovery. Cyril had managed to force the mirror back into place and at least I could see behind me. Being on my nearside meant that it was on the offside while driving on the right and an essential piece of equipment. The electrics had been ripped off which meant that every time I switched off the engine, the mirror folded itself inwards, but had to be manually re-set every time I started up again. This was a bloody nuisance but I suppose in the grand scheme of things just another minor inconvenience. It didn't stop me cursing Cyril every time when I forgot about it and had to get out of the car and walk around to push it back into place.

The assistant at Chantier Allemande at Le Grau d'Agde was very helpful. He had already put the part aside for us and we added a suitable piece of hose to replace the damaged one. I also took advantage of the comprehensive range of Du Breil guides and added a No 12 in the series that covered the Aquitaine region to the shopping list. They were far superior to the Merlot guides that I had been using.

Back at the boat we gave the holding tank a thorough clean and burnished the wire connections from the float switch to the pump. The brackets that had held the original pump had corroded and we had to use a heavy lump of iron that I found in the bilge to hold the new pump in place on the bottom of the tank. With everything in place and connected we tried the acid test by running the shower and watching as the level rose. As soon as the water reached the point that floated the trigger for the pump it was swiftly expelled over the side. Voila - mission accomplished. Another job bites the dust. The old pump had served for almost thirty years so I suppose we couldn't complain. Another advantage of the exercise was that I now knew where the tank hides and how to get to it again should the need arise.

Rob and I both needed a diesel top up and we arranged a tanker delivery for the following morning. When the time came to settle the bill, Rob suddenly 'discovered' that he didn't have enough money and I had to lend him 100 Euros.

"No problem - I'll let you have it back this afternoon. Got to go to the Bank."

A favourite Yorkshireman's ruse and I had fallen for it - hook, line and sinker. I was half way back to England before I suddenly remembered that he hadn't paid up and after several attempts I told him to forget it. Call it a thank you for helping with the pump. He had earned it after all.

Cyril arrived with a hangdog look to discuss how we were going to resolve the little problem of replacing a thousand pounds worth of mirror. I seriously doubted whether he had ever seen that amount of money in his entire life. He was a sorry mess and this latest disaster can't have helped his state of mind. I had spoken to Rob Carter at R and E Land Rover in

Salisbury that I had used for many years. Rob was a former mechanic at the local dealer and had branched out on his own and established himself as an authorised Land Rover repairer. His rates were about half those at the 'official' dealer and as a result he was always busy. It was estimated that the cost of the whole job - apparently the mirrors came in primer and had to be sprayed by the garage, including repainting most of the near side would be £1250 plus the dreaded VAT. The chance of Cyril coming up with anywhere that amount were akin to Scunthorpe winning the Premier League. (originally I had intended to use Leicester City for this example, but the best laid plans !!)

The excess on my insurance was £250 and I suggested to Cyril that if he could come up with that we would call it a day. We shook hands on it and I thought I caught a glimpse of a little tear in the corner of his eye. I too felt a bit of emotion - silly as silly Cyril was, you couldn't help a bit of feeling for his situation. Contrary to popular belief, I did have a heart hidden away somewhere in the depths. Cyril redeemed himself very slightly by agreeing to take all the rubbish - pump and hose, a few odds and ends that I had accumulated over the past twelve months or so, a couple of used oil filters, and a five gallon drum of waste oil, to the décheterie.

Dylan and I took the boat back to Ramonville in September, where surprise surprise, our dependable Capitan Michel could find no record of our booking, and did his usual impression of a jabbering idiot, before eventually realising that there, right in front of his eyes outside his control tower, was the very space where we had moored on at least three occasions in the past. Doh!

On the way from Ventenac we had had more problems with the engine overheating and had systematically taken the whole assembly apart section by section blowing out more of the little obstinate pieces of rubber that were still hiding away in the pipework determined to block up the works. Dylan worked like a Trojan and I treated him to a couple of beers and a whole large pizza all to himself at our favourite mooring in Montgiscard. Serge took us to the airport promising that he would make sure all the outstanding work was finished over the winter. Famous last words.

Chapter 11   Home Sweet Home in Moissac

This time it was the weather that was the fly in the ointment. Most of the jobs I had left with Serge involved outside painting and France had suffered one of its worst winters for many years. When I met him at the airport he told me that it had rained every single day from early January until the end of March. This scuppered any ideas I had of taking the boat back to the Garonne but I needed to get away from Ramonville and managed to reserve a mooring for seven days at the old fall-back haven of Ste Sauveur. As soon as I had left the harbour of Ramonville and turned into the canal, I realised there was a problem with the steering. There are residential boats moored on the towpath for over a mile and I was suddenly heading towards the first one and the rudder was refusing to answer to the wheel. Luckily I wasn't going very fast - as we know there is a mandatory speed limit of 3 kilometres per hour passing moored boats, and I managed to avoid an embarrassing collision by using a combination of reverse and bow thruster. There was nowhere to turn and in any event I didn't want to go back to Ramonville. If I was going to be stuck anywhere I would much prefer to be in the centre of Toulouse.

I made slow faltering progress and managed to stay roughly in the channel by constant tweaking of the thruster until I had finally cleared the line of moored boats. The next mild panic occurred as I approached the narrow bridge at Demoiselles where the channel divides for two-way traffic. To my horror I saw at the last minute the unmistakable shape of the Toulouse bateau-mouche, the 'Occitaine', an ugly looking thing at the best of times that resembles a half-sunk space shuttle. It was coming towards me at what appeared to be a dangerously fast speed. The thought did cross my mind to give him the international signal "keep clear of me, I am manoeuvring with difficulty" but I didn't have the "Delta" flag immediately available. I always thought that four short blasts on the horn conveyed the same message but research has revealed that this has for some obscure reason, been made obsolete. All this flashed through my mind as I touched the reverse gently and moved the bow to starboard with the thruster. In a flurry of wash, 'Occitaine' passed me on its way to Mars, with a wave from the skipper, none the wiser about my incapacity. I was very relieved to tie up at last on the end pontoon at St Sauveur and check the problem.

There had always been a minor leak of fluid from the reservoir tank at the back of the wheel which I had tried unsuccessfully to cure, and for this reason I kept a small plastic container underneath. When I shone the torch in behind the console it revealed at least two inches of the luminous green fluid in the tray - it had virtually lost the lot, and presumably filled the vacuum with air. Apart from anything else it would need a thorough bleeding. I had already arranged to meet up with Andy at De Danu the following evening and I called him to tell him about the latest developments. He didn't hesitate to offer to come over in the afternoon so that we could have a look at it. I think I had been born lucky as every time I was in trouble it seemed that there was someone there to help me out. If I ever got around to writing my autobiography , I would like to have entitled it "Lucky all my Life," but this had already been used by Harry Westlake, the founder of the Rye based producer of racing cylinder heads. Andy had intended using the weekend to work on a car he had bought in Germany - a 2.0 litre petrol BMW, or BM Troubleyou as he liked to call it, and he had volunteered to pass up the opportunity to come and help me out. Good friend or what?

Andy was the epitome of the aircraft engineer, meticulous and thorough, and he treated the job with the same attention to detail as he would before sending a trainee Italian pilot into the air in a Tornado over Salisbury Plain. By the time he arrived at the boat he had researched the Internet and discovered how many times we needed to turn the wheel and in what direction, in order to correctly bleed the system. This was all written down and followed to the letter. He arrived with pukka bleed bottles and plastic hoses and carefully explained the procedure. When I had performed this operation in the past I have to admit that I had simply turned the wheel willy nilly and enlisted anyone who happened to be around to open and close the valves until the air bubbles stopped and clear fluid emerged. Andy first analysed the cause of the problem and thought it may have been the fact that I had been using a universal EP90 hydraulic fluid rather than the official Vetus product. This had come about after a conversation I had had with the oracle, Phil Trotter on the subject. He had advised me to use the Vetus stuff but when I had mentioned this to Craig, he said that what Phil had told me was rubbish

"He don't know what he's talking about," he said of the man he once referred to as 'The Master.' "you can use any hydraulic fluid - it's all the same anyway."

I was somewhere in the depths of France at the time and many miles from the nearest Vetus dealer, so I took the line of least resistance and bought some from a local garage which it seemed now, had been the wrong option. In the interim however I had obtained a couple of litres of the proper Vetus stuff and it had sat untouched in the stores - until now. The job took just over an hour under the guidance of Andy, after which we gave it a good test and then as all self-respecting aircraft technicians do when finishing their work, adjourned for a pint of well-earned Guinness. It seemed that on this occasion, the 'Master' was right all along.

I had a nice relaxing week in Toulouse and spent some of the time masking up around the green paintwork. It seemed unlikely that Serge was going to be able to do this and I would have a few months in the summer to hopefully get the job done. It wasn't that difficult, but a bit tricky around the handrail stanchions - just a bit of patience required - something that I had to admit that I was a little short of.

When I finally took the boat back to Ramonville I was an hour into the trip when I realised that I had inadvertently switched on the deck wash pump. This was next to the horn switch on the panel and I had stupidly pressed the wrong switch. The result of this was that as the intake valve was closed no water was passing through the pump and that had caused it to run hot - and, guess what, completely mash up the impeller. This was slightly worrying as the same pump also operated all the bilges and it was imperative to have this in working order. It was similar to the engine cooling impeller but in a much more awkward spot. This was another job for Serge. I told him that I would be returning in about six weeks so he needed to get the proverbial digit extracted and hopefully get a few jobs finished. On my return journey by car, my usual half-way stop with Alan and Dawn on 'Animo' wasn't possible as they had decided to explore the Moselle and were somewhere near Luxembourg, a little too far out of my way. Instead I booked a couple of nights in a small hotel in Bergerac, a beautiful market town on the banks of the Dordogne river. The World Cup was well under way and England had exceeded all expectations having scraped a win over Tunisia, thrashed Panama and narrowly lost to Belgium, to finish second in their group and reach the dizzy heights of the last 16. I watched the game against Colombia in a lively bar, the PQP (More than Perfect?), in the centre of the old town which was packed with fans, lots of them English. England went ahead early in the second half from a penalty scored by Kane and then Colombia equalised in the 93rd minute to take the game into extra time. This was exciting for everybody except the band that had set up their gear on the small stage at the back of the bar, expecting to start strutting their stuff. I had imbibed a few more pints of Guinness by this time than were probably good for me and bribed the drummer to let me have a bash on his drums. Nothing fancy - no Ginger Baker solo, but simply the old football fan beat of '

boom boom |
boom boom boom |
 boom boom boom boom |
 boom boom |

Hammered out on the floor tom, heralding the cry of 'England,' repeated three or four times. My performance gave me something of a hero status and I was besieged by offers of even more Guinness, which I obviously politely declined.

I don't think it was entirely due to this unprecedented support from the nether regions of France, but England actually won the penalty shoot-out, Eric Dier scoring the winning goal. The place erupted, backs were slapped and strangers were hugged. Football was coming home. We were in the quarter final!

Back at Ramonville Saul Trader was not at home. Michelle's side-kick informed me that Serge had taken it to the Port Technique. The nimbies had obviously won their battle to get all maintenance and repair work banned. Shades of city-dwellers buying chocolate box weekend cottages next to the village church and then complaining that the bells woke them up on Sunday mornings!

Serge had at least managed to get the hull blacked and had also fitted the new impeller to the bilge pump. At Ste Sauveur I watched the quarter final game in De Danu with Andy and England beat Sweden to reach the semi-final.We were really going places now!

Amazingly Frank and Kuhn had asked to come for another week and I was due to pick them up at Moissac. I stopped at Montech hoping to watch the first semi-final - Belgium against Le Blues. If there was a prize for the most boring town in France, Montech would have to be a strong contender. There is nothing of note in Montech - the only bar was closed for refurbishment in mid July, the height of the Haute Saison. There are several Banks, a pharmacy, a vetinerary surgeon next to a pharmacy for animals, a nondescript kirk, a pretentious and overpriced restaurant on the side of the canal basin, the usual plethora of boulangeries, hairdressers and florists, and that's about it. The only place I could find that was showing the match was the pretentious restaurant where I paid a fortune for a few blobs of fish surrounded with some red and green squiggles and some broccoli that was about the size of my thumb, for the priviledge of watching the French national team play a match in the semi-finals of the football World Cup, on a 12" TV hung in corner of the bar. I was the only person there. The outside tables were all busy and the only time anybody else showed the remotest interest was when they had to pass through to get to the toilet. Incredible. I can only assume it has something to do with the fact that there is no word in French for excitement, and rather too much sang-froid, or probably more down to the fact that rugby is the first love of the French.

Halfway down the Montech flight we were held up by a boat that had broken down. It was Sally and Greg on Boschplatz with a gearbox problem. Another English boater, Nigel arrived and took a quick look before deciding there was nothing he could do. We then agreed to man-haul the boat out of the lock so at least everyone else could pass.A short queue had formed either side of the lock. Nigel and I grabbed the end of a rope, heaving and straining to move the little Boschplatz and wondering why it was so heavy. Greg eventually realised that the bloody boat was still tied up to a bollard, and once he had released it Boschplatz slid easily out of the lock.

Apparently Nigel's wife had fallen overboard on the previous evening watering the flowers while they were tied up at Lacourte St Pierre.

"It was terrible," Nigel told us, "I was watching the football at the time and I couldn't get her out until half-time".

At Castelsarassin it came as no surprise at all to find that the only place that was open and showing the other semi-final, England and Croatia, was a little back-street pizza take-away café . Both town centre bars were closed at 8.00pm and down came the shutters, but the friendly proprietor let me sit in the corner of the café with my pizza and some very good vin rosé, to watch England, back to form, come in second, losing out to Croatia.

We arrived at the wharf at Valence d'Agen, where I was hoping to be able to leave Saul Trader for a couple of weeks. A new incumbent had taken up John and Judy's old mooring on the town side, but there was at least 30 metres of free space on the opposite side, where we had moored successfully on several occasions in the past. There was a small cruiser of about eight metres at the Toulouse end, a British flagged tjalk at the other end of the serviceable length of wharf, and a Locoboat type penichette which was another 8 metres long, flying a Swiss flag and obviously privately owned, bang in the middle. This left two free lengths of about 15 metres each, between the two extremities. Saul Trader is of course 21 metres long. No problem I thought as I stopped beside the penichette and politely asked the captain, who was sunbathing with his wife in deckchairs on the quay, whether he would mind moving a few metres forward to give me room to tie up. From his reaction I might as well have asked him if I could go to bed with his wife. He got up from his chair, rose to his full height, and said simply ,"NO." The more I tried to reason with him the more aggressive he became. It would only need him to shift a couple of metres but he was absolutely adamant that he was going nowhere. The main reason, I discovered, was that he had just set up his bloody TV aerial and to move would mean having to re-tune. It was 3.00 o'clock in the afternoon. A totally arrogant and obstinate bastard. There was nowhere else to go. I circled round a bit and attempted to get in on the opposite side but is was too shallow and there was nothing to secure to.

Exasperated I finally nosed the bow into the gap astern of him and tied the stern as best I could to the side of the small cruiser on the other end of the wharf. It was not ideal and not an easy manoeuvre and at one point I got very very close to his stern almost triggering an international incident, but I was determined not to be outdone. What made matters worse was that when I apologised to the English couple on the Tjalk at the far end of the wharf for disturbing their peace, I was given short shrift by a stuck-up wife who told me that he was in his rights, he had been there first, and why should he move. I gave up. I put it down to a simple case of 'Another Prick on the Wharf', with apologies to Roger Waters.

At least Skinny had a good crowd for the France/Croatia final. All tables were booked, inside and out, but she told us we could eat at the bar. Noix St Jacques? Désolée - Impossible - the chef had left and the only food available was burgers, which I declined in favour of a take-away pizza.

I had rather hoped that one or other of the immovable objects might leave the next morning but bloody-mindedness ruled that out and it became obvious that both boats were staying put. Even if they had originally planned to leave they certainly wouldn't be doing so now.

I needed to find somewhere to leave Saul Trader for a couple of weeks while I went off on another little jaunt to Portugal, and I obviously couldn't leave it as it was. The only alternative was Pommevic and so I made a U-turn and accelerated away in a cloud of smoke. Sod 'em!

I tied up to the tree roots just past the Haute Nautique pontoon. Please note that I did NOT connect up to the electricity. Whether this got me an entry into the Maire's blacklist I cannot say, but the boat was exactly where I had left it when I returned to go and find Frank and Kuhn.

I took them down to Buzet and back as they had not done this bit before. Frank was over the moon when I told him they could use the after cabin.

"Wow. We are so happy that you give us the master cabin," he said, and I thought again for an awful moment that he was going to kiss me. Nothing particularly untoward happened this time but we did have a rather amusing incident in Buzet when Frank, always trying to be useful, suggested that the rear tyre on one of the Bromptons was a bit low on pressure. I told him that it would be fine but he insisted on blowing it up. There was one of those exercise machines on the quay which you could use to inflate dinghies. Once connected to the inlet valve, pedalling the machine provided the air. Frank pedalled away until he was satisfied that the tyre was at the correct pressure, disconnected the lead and stood back to admire his work. Just as well as it happened, as seconds later there was an almighty bang and the tyre exploded into tiny fragments of shredded rubber. Frank was distraught, and I couldn't help laughing.

"I am so sorry. I must get a new one for you," he promised, despite my protestations.

"It was getting a bit old," I said, " probably needed changing anyway".

Frank was not to be deterred and went straight to the office to find out whether they might have such a thing. There were a few tyres for sale but none of the correct size for the Brompton. I implored him to forget about it but he was persistent. Later in the evening he came with a list of cycle shops he had found on the Internet. Most of them were in Agen and I told him that we would be passing through in a couple of days so if we had time we could have a look. This did not appease Frank however and next day at Sèrignac I saw him unfolding the other bike, the one with both tyres intact, getting it ready for action.

"Where are you going?", I asked. "You won't find any cycle dealers here - it's just a small village".

"I will go to Agen, there are three shops there and I have the map".

"But Frank," I shouted after him as he disappeared down the towpath in a cloud of dust, "it's at least 10 kilometres to Agen and then ...." - but it was too late. He was on his way and we could only hope that we would one day see him again.

It was nearly dark when he returned, riding like the winner of the Tour de France with a brand new tyre slung over his shoulder.

"It was at the third shop that I wisit," he said grinning, "65 Euros and they give me the tube for free."

"Result," I said, "you must have ridden at least 25 kilometres".

"Yes - my arse it is very hot," he conceded.

He then set about the task of reconnecting the tyre to the wheel.

Back at Valence I got a strange call from Jim at the Capitanerie in Moissac, asking me whether I was still in Castelsarrassin. I told him we were in Valence and hadn't been to Castel.

"OK," he said, "no problem. I'm looking for a boat."

Then he rang off. Ten minutes later he rang again.

"Hi Jim," I said, "I'm still in Valence".

"Yes I know. Can you see a boat anywhere called 'Matilda'?"

"I'm looking straight at it, " I told him, "it's on the opposite side."

Jim asked me if I could have a word with them urgently and get them to call him as soon as possible. Something to do with passports which he didn't elaborate on. I went straight over to 'Matilda' to give them the message. There were two women on board, Australians, who said their husbands were in the town and they would pass on the message as soon as they returned. They couldn't understand what it was about as they said that they all had their passports with them. I thought no more about it until the following morning when a man appeared outside the wheelhouse.

"I think I owe you a beer or two, " he said, and I must admit that was the sort of introductory comment I did quite like. He then proceeded to explain what had happened and to long a cut story short .... !

While they were in Toulouse they had met up with a fellow Aussie and had decided to visit the Airbus factory. They had had to leave their passports at the entrance desk and collected them at the end of the visit . Presumably at this stage they had each picked up a passport and put it in their pockets. It wasn't until the third member, who was still in Toulouse, checked in for his flight back to Sydney, when it was discovered that he had picked up the wrong passport - a small error that cost him over 2000 Euros, as he had to re-book a flight and travel by taxi to Valence to collect the correct one from the crew of the good ship 'Matilda'. An easy mistaker to maker.

It had been no trouble for me to run this little errand for Jim but it seemed to have cemented our relationship. Since then Jim has always gone out of his way to give us a good mooring in the port and welcomed us as old friends, which I suppose we were becoming after so many visits. I liked Jim. He was a diligent caretaker of the port and carefully monitored   all comings and goings,ensuring that nobody dared moor anywhere but where he told them to moor. He could be seen regularly patrolling his territory, looking like a guard in a concentration camp, on the lookout for any new arrivals who might try to sneek in under the radar and moor up just where they thought they could. Jim insisted that boats moor exactly where he told them they could moor. He seemed to have an inbuilt radar and usually anticipated any new arrivals, pacing up and down and shouting directions until they were settled to the nearest inch of their designated spot. Come to think of it I suppose it was the modern facility of the mobile 'phone rather that any hidden inner sense that alerted him to any imminent arrivals.

A lot of people didn't particularly get on with him. He called a spade a spade - are we allowed to say that now or should I rephrase it as 'he called a gardening implement a gardening implement ' - and some people couldn't take it. He was very fair-minded and had banned various people from using the port, including apparently a certain fellow boater who purported to be an electrician, who had relieved others of money for work and then abandoned them for months on end, in one case leaving them stranded without power after being contracted to do a complete re-wire on their boat. As in all situations where you get a band of people who form cliques, stories and rumours of skullduggery, clandestine conspiracies and illicit copulation abound and I usually steer well clear of all of them.

As it happened rather more of them than usual had turned up in Moissac, as there was an unofficial goat bothering taking place. Unofficial in the sense that it hadn't been organised by the Dutch Barge Association but by an interesting couple on a barge called Kanumbra, who apart from anything else, played upturned dustbin lids (sorry pans) in a steel band. They were expecting about 30 barges to attend and Jim was in his element charging around the port directing arrivals into their respective positions. My first thought was to get as far away as possible. Most of the boats that were attending seemed to be Piper boats, small box-shaped barges built in Stoke on Trent. The company had been building narrowboats since the seventies and was founded by David Piper. In fact this was where Phil Trotter cut his teeth. Since then David's son Simon had taken over the running of the business and they had rapidly expanded into the Dutch barge market. Although not particularly pretty to look at, they were comfortably fitted out with all mod-cons - Raymarine navigation systems, Oyster Remote Controlled Satellite receivers, wall-mounted televisions and modern fitted kitchens with full sized cookers and fridge-freezers. The entry model came in at about a quarter of a million pounds and there were no shortage of takers. Apparently they were now churning out one a month and had recently purchased a large site at St Jean de Losne. Fair play to Simon: he had seen a gap in the market and grabbed it with both hands, but I still preferred Saul Trader. It looked like a Dutch barge and it was a one-off, not one of your production-line look-a-likes, and it hadn't cost me anything like the price of a Piper. Good enough reason to make myself scarce. I know it was dangerous to generalise, but I tended to bracket these people with floating caravanners - seen it on the tele, sold the family silver to buy a boat on the never-ever, tried it for a year or so, got tired of it and returned to the time-share in Puerto Banus. Frank and Kuhn departed and Frank point-blank refused to accept my offer to pay for the tyre telling me that he would be most offended if I didn't let him pay. It was a nice gesture and I thought I would let him blow up the tyre on the other bike next year. One of those was starting to get a bit thin!

I rather turned my back on the festivities, preferring to spend a quiet weekend on a little mooring beside the river Tarn far enough away from Moissac and the madding crowd. There was a small landing stage that had been provided for disabled anglers but I had tied there before and never seen any fishermen, abled or otherwise, anywhere near the place. If one did appear and claim his rights I would have obviously moved but I was not disturbed at all over the three days of my solitude. I liked the spot: the river to one side and the railway that ran along an embankment opposite. Time for a bit of peace, maybe a bit of writing and some painting. The weather was a little cooler now and particularly during the morning provided ideal conditions in which to finish the green paintwork. I had a bit more time to kill and pleased with my paint job I decided to go and say hello to John and Judy who were now moored a few kilometres away at Malause. On the way there, without any warning, the engine faltered and died, and I was left drifting. This was the first time this had happened since we installed the day tank in St Jean de Losne twelve years ago. The symptoms were very similar and I feared the worst. Was this fuel contamination that had caused the problem. After a few minutes and several false starts the engine fired up again and I carried on. Over the next few days it happened a number of times and I was really starting to worry about things like fuel bugs. There was a separate filter in place now between the main tank and the electric pump that filled the day tank so I would have to check this first to see whether it was getting blocked. Jim had called to tell me that he had reserved a winter mooring for me at Moissac which was great news. It was the equivalent of securing a mooring on the Chelsea Embankment, and I gingerly made my way back to the port, constantly on guard and ready for any impending engine failure. There were several, but luckily each time the engine stopped I was well away from any other boats and it started again after the usual pregnant pause.

Iain, the former Capitan, who had returned from Dominca, came to have a look at it in Moissac and concluded that it was more than likely being caused by air getting in to the system rather than dirty fuel. This was certainly a relief but the mystery now was where it was coming from. After a closer inspection, Iain pin-pointed the problem to the lift-pump. Although the fuel was now delivered by gravity the lift pump still had to get the diesel through the primary filters to the injectors, and Iain recommended that I replace it.

"Ending is better than mending," according to Alduous Huxley.

I took off the pump and sent some photographs to another old-established firm in England that I had used in the past for such occurrences, Sleeman - Hawken, who were based in Newton Abbott. I spoke to Mike, another parts man of the old school and sent him as much information as I could. He searched his books and came up with one that sounded similar although had a different reference. Mike was concerned that the holes where the pump bolted on to the engine were situated differently and though we may have to bend the pipework to connect it.

"It looks though your holes are at 12 o'clock and 6 o'clock," he said, using the technical terminology, "and the ones of this pump are at 3 o'clock and 9!"

Looking at the pump it seemed to me that they were exactly the same and I went ahead and ordered it.

I now had for the first time in 20 years, a permanent home for Saul Trader at Moissac, where I knew it would be looked after under the watchful eye of Captain Jim. I was getting a bit long in the tooth for taking chances and leaving it in places where I really had no right. I had got away with it most of the time but it was reassuring to know that we were now officially official. I did the usual cursory winter checks, topped up the anti-freeze in the heating system and engine, closed down all the inlet valves and isolated the gas. I paid up for six months plus a bit for Iain to fit a meter to the power supply which would mean I would only get charged for the minimal amount used to keep the batteries topped up, covered the engine with some boiler cladding that I had left over from replacing the covering on the hot water cylinder, emptied the fresh water pipes and finally put the large canvas cover over the wheelhouse to keep out the rain.

So what of the future. I now had a 'permanent' mooring. Was it time to sell up? I had owned the boat for over 20 years and it had become inextricably connected to my way of life. What would I do in the summer without it? The next TRIWV certificate was due for renewal in three years time. Questions, questions. Maybe sell next year - or go back up the Rhone perhaps to St Jean de Losne. I was sill fit and just about able! Maybe the year after next. Or the ....??

We hadn't broken any speed records. It had taken us 20 years of a bit here and a bit there to cover 18000 kilometres and negotiate over 4000 locks. Many people had been more adventurous and covered more ground, even travelling as far as the Danube to the Black Sea. I don't know whether they had as much fun as we did, or met as many interesting characters, but I'm sure there are more books around that tell the stories.

Everything seems to be getting more difficult, or maybe it's just the age thing, but the old laissez-faire approach is slowly but surely being eroded. You now need a clean-air sticker for the car if you want to drive in Paris and some of the other large towns in France.

Failure could mean fine of up to 135 euros but the time it takes to sort it out had me thinking that it had cost me more in time than the bloody fine! And of course nobody has ever stopped to inspect it and I think I'm probably the only person in France who has actually got one. (*apart from my friend Alan Curnow who was the one who alerted me to the new rule in the first place*).

I took the old pump back with me and when I got home the new one was there waiting for me. I quickly unpacked it and sure enough all the fittings and all the holes were in exactly the same position. I checked the time - three o'clock. I would have to wait until nine to make sure that the other hole was in the right place!

All I had to do when I returned next year was to connect it up to the engine and voila - all would be well. Never say that with a boat as tomorrow something won't be!

Chapter 12 Almost The Last Final Chapter -

I returned to Moisaac a couple of times during 2019, flying down from Bristol.

I took the replacement lift pump with me and Iain attempted to fit it but it didn't take him very long to discover that the fitting on the end of the down pipe was incorrect so it couldn't be used after all. A bit of a waste of money. However he did put a new gasket in the old pump and found a possible source of a small air leak. He reconnected the old pump and, touch wood, it has behaved itself ever since. He also installed a small meter which monitored the electricity usage so that instead of the standard weekly charge I would only have to pay for the actual amperage used while the boat was connected to the shore power. I did a few short trial runs single-handed, to Valence d'Agen and back, and everything worked as normal - that's assuming things are ever normal with a boat.

An old acquaintance, Michael Mortimer, who I had not seen for several books, had fetched up at Moissac on his newly acquired Piper boat Icarus while I had been away and was moored opposite. I think the last time we had met was at Vincelles at the K&A Friends Rally back in Book 3. Michael had sold his beautiful Dutch motor cruiser and spent a few years living beside the Thames in one of those immovable mobile homes, before the lure of the Siren enticed him back to the water. While I was sitting with Michael in the wheelhouse of Icarus helping him dispose of a bottle of the finest Rosé, I became aware of an apparition that had suddenly appeared on the coach roof. With her long blonde hair and sylph-like figure she looked like a mermaid that had emerged from the depths of the ocean. The illusion was somewhat blurred however as I realised she was moving deftly around the boat brandishing, not a Triton, but a Kärcher pressure washer.

This I was told was Lisa, whose services Michael employed to wash the boat. Lisa was an English girl who lived locally and offered this service to boaters in the port. She did an excellent job and I immediately arranged for her to do the same for Saul Trader a couple of times during the winter. This proved to be very worthwhile. Lisa would call me when she felt that the boat was in need of a clean. Although the port was reasonably dust free, there was always the fall out from the trees and the occasional layering of sand dust blown in from the Sahara. Lisa would do a final clean a few days before a visit and what a boon it was to arrive and find a spotless looking ship, and not have to spend two valuable days cleaning up. Lisa's contact details can be found in the port office and I would highly recommend her to anyone leaving a boat for long periods in Moissac.

When I finally secured the boat for the winter and said my farewells to Jim and Moissac, little did I know that it would be almost two years before I would be able to return. The world was about to be turned on its head with the result that travel would be severely curtailed, and I would never see Jim again.

So in late November I followed the migrating birds bound for Bangkok and my usual winter hibernation in Thailand. Then by December the world as we knew it was about to change dramatically. I had always thought that the generation known as the Baby Boomers, those born as I was in the early years after the end of World War 2, were the blessed generation. We had grown up with the musical revolution of the sixties and seventies, we had enjoyed a carefree childhood free to roam the woods and play football on the greens with our jumpers used for goalposts, with nothing to worry about apart from getting home in time for tea. We had benefited from a growing economy and although we had little we wanted for nothing. We had never been summoned to sacrifice our lives in a major war and life in general was ordered and largely unhindered. We had discipline certainly, but only enough to ensure we grew up with respect for our society and our elders. Education was channelled so that the academics could study the arts and the sciences in Grammar Schools, artisans could learn a trade that would stand them in good stead for the future in Technical Schools and there were Comprehensive Schools for those who were less inclined in those directions, but would nevertheless receive the necessary support and adequate basic knowledge to find a path through the jungle of life. It was better to be top of the class in the D Stream in a Comprehensive than bottom of the A Form in a Grammar School. We also had a thriving military which afforded first class training for all abilities and a fulfilling career for life. Our Merchant Navy together with our engineering and manufacturing industries led the world.

A lot of that had of course already been decimated due to various factors - Beeching, worker's strikes and fundamental changes in teaching methods all playing their part in the start of the demise. Even so, nobody had been prepared for the bombshells that were about to hit us all. Events that would bring the entire world to a virtual standstill.

The first of these was Brexit.

On the 31st January in the year 2020, Britain finally left the European Union, after years of abortive negotiations and procrastination. In hindsight it should never have been left to an ill-informed and misguided public to decide the outcome of this momentous decision. But then hindsight is a wonderful thing. We had been fed lie after lie and politically charged propaganda for years, summed up by the blatantly untrue statement, plastered on the side of the campaign bus that claimed that leaving Europe would free up three hundred and fifty million pounds per week to spend on the NHS. Without getting too deeply into the pros and cons of Brexit it is clear that the result of the referendum came as a massive shock to the instigator of the vote.   True the Tories had promised to hold a referendum but it was the Prime Minister responsible who was the most surprised and shocked at the outcome. Cameron immediately resigned and ran into hiding, leaving Teresa May to dither , duck and dive her way through a bitter negotiating period.

After the dust had more or less settled, some real home truths began to raise their ugly heads, things which apparently hadn't been thought about clearly enough. Perhaps the one most relevant to us minority of part-time Francophiles, the European boating community, was that our freedom to roam around the Continent freely and unchallenged, was about to come to an end. Nobody, it seemed, had thought about that.

Would we need Visas? How much would it cost? These and many other problems suddenly appeared on the horizon. It certainly made everybody sit up and take notice and anyone thinking of buying a boat and living the life in Europe suddenly started to have second thoughts.

At the turn of the year all was well in Thailand and the skies were filled with the thunder and lightning of the New Year's Eve firework displays. In the middle of January 2020 I flew from Bangkok to Taipei for a two week tour of the Taiwanese railways. I enjoyed planning these trips almost as much as I enjoyed the actual travel. Taiwan has a compact railway network which utilises an interesting variety of motive power and rolling stock. The flagship trains run on the high speed line between Taipei, the capital, and the southern port of Kaoshiung. These 300 kph trains are built with Japanese Bullet Train technology and offer three classes of travel. The dearest, business class, costs around £40 for the 90 minute trip. At each end of the journey, the train is met by a small army of cleaners who stand three in line with military precision perfectly aligned at the point where the doors will stop. Each member of the carriage team has a distinct function. One goes through collecting up the rubbish, the second hoovers the carpets while the third, using a pedal at the base of the seats, revolves each pair through 180° so that they are facing the direction of travel for the return journey.

Another line that I had been looking forward to travelling was the 2'6"gauge Alishan Forest Railway, originally built to transport logs. The line climbs from the mainline station of Chiayi to a height of 7270ft. The line is 53 miles long and the uphill journey to the mountain resort of Alishan takes approximately three hours.

One thing that slightly amused me at the time was that nearly all the Taiwanese were sporting face masks. I had seen this practice before in Asia and put it down to a somewhat timid and wimpish way of avoiding transmitting or catching a common cold. Little did I know then that within a few weeks most of the world would be forced to adopt the same practice.

Pingxi Line train approaching Shifen station

TAIWAN RAIL TRIP SCHEDULE

Wed	15	BKK - TPE Eva L9XV7V.	Fullon Zhongli BKD
Thu	16	Zhongli	Fullon Zhongli BKD
Fri	17	09.00 Zhonglii - Taoyuan. 10 mins	
Fri	17	10.10 Taoyuan - Kaoshiung 11.45 (T621) Voucher 19KK	Chii Lih Hotel
Fri	17	Zuoying - Kaoshiung (15 mins) 14.06 - 17.25 Taitung (T7	Taitung BKD
Sat	18	15.02 Taitun - Hualien 16.56 Tze - Chiang (T427	Leaf Inn
Sat	18		Hualien. BKD
Sun	19	Taitung - Old Railway Culture Park	Issmy Hotel
Sun	19	15.29 Hualien - Yilan 16.34 - Tze Ch (T185) Coast Line	Yilan BKD
Mon	20	13.00 Yilan - TPE 14.12 - Taroko X (T219)	
Mon	20	15.00 TPE - Zhongli 15.39 Tze Ch (T135)	Fullon Zhongli BKD
Tue	21	08.41 Zhongli - TPE 09.16 (T278) 10.04 TPE - Ruifang 10.52 (T642)	
Tue	21	Ruifang - Shifen PINGXI Line Jingtong Shifen	
Tue	21	Ruifang - Shifen 30 mins Jingtong/Shifen Waterfall	Fullon Zhongli BKD
Tue	21	16.06 Jingtong - Ruifang 17.00. 17.38 Zhongli 18.35 (T1	Zhongli
Wed	22	08.45 Zhonli - Taoyuan. HSR Chiayi 11.45 Beimen Locor	Chiayi King Hotel BK
Thu	23	09.30 Chiayi - Fenqihu Carv4vSt 2/4. Bus Alishan. Zhaop	Shermuh BKD
Fri	24	14.30 Alishan - Chiayi 17.30 18.24 Chiayi - Zhongli (T14	Fullon Zhongli BKD
Sat	25	NEIWAN LINE -07.33 Zhongli - Taoyuan 07.42 (T102)	
Sat	25	08.09 Taoyuan - Hsinchu 08.56 (T5103)	
Sat	25	11.29 Hsinchu - Zhudong 11.43 - 13.10 Hexing 13.25 Ne	Shinn Yuan Park
Sat	25	15.47 Neiwan Zhuzhong - Hsinchu 17.20	Hsinchu BKD
Sun	26	Hsinchu - Miaoli 11.30 Mialoi Rly Museum 12.38 Miaoli - Changua 13.31	
Sun	26	Changua Roundhouse	Forte Hotel Hsinchu
Mon	27	JIJI LINE Changua - Ershui - Checheng (Jiji). 14.00	
Mon	27	15.30 Checheng - Ershui 17.41 Zhongli 20.56 (T522)	
Mon	27	Yuanquan, Zhuoshui, Longquan, Jiji, Shuili, Checheng -	Fullon Zhongli BKD
Tue	28	Zhongli	
Wed	29	Zhongli	Fullon Zhongli BKD
Thu	30	09.40 TPE - BKK 12.56 Eva L9XV7V	

196

In the December of 2019 news began to slowly filter through about a strange disease that was causing problems in some remote and unheard of city of Wuhan, somewhere in the depths of China. Nothing that was likely to affect us, or so we thought. It didn't take very long before this virus began its insidious penetration, creeping like lava from a slowly erupting volcano to gradually infect the entire world. We had never seen the like and we were totally unprepared for the devastation it would cause. The freedom afforded by mass travel quickly became the

harbinger of this deadly virus which would bring that freedom to its knees.

By the end of January 2020 the World Health Organisation officially declared a pandemic and two months later Boris Johnstone had announced the first lockdown in the UK and ordered people to stay at home.

In Thailand the authorities reacted remarkably quickly, closing all airports, bars and entertainment venues, imposing strict curfews and even banning travel between provinces. Those that had the wherewithal managed to escape back to their home countries but others, including myself, elected to stay put and ride out the storm. Free 30 day Visa extensions were granted when it got to the stage that no-one could leave the country anyway as there were no flights.

The results of this in the early stages at least, were twofold. Infections were kept very low and I remember seeing at one time, when most major countries were reporting deaths in the tens of thousands and hospitals overrun to the extent that temporary buildings had been turned into makeshift hospices, that Thailand reported something like 65 deaths. On the other hand, towns and cities were left ghostlike with businesses that relied on the tourist spend, shutting down and abandoning premises. There are no social services in Thailand and although the government introduced a scheme to help the destitute that had lost their means of income, this benefit only applied to those who were legally registered. The fact was that 75% were working illegally and this led to harrowing sights of thousands queueing in the harsh sunlight for meagre handouts of food and water provided by charities.

I finally managed to get a flight back to the UK in the June of 2020, having originally planned to return in April, after having several flights cancelled. By this time the UK had suffered from lock-downs, social distancing, working from home and bans on non-essential travel. The rest, of course is well documented history.

I suppose you could call that summer of 2020 a 'season of discontent.' Schools and non-essential shops were allowed to re-open in June and the Prime Minister announced that 'hibernation was coming to an end.'

Gradually other restrictions were lifted - pubs and restaurants re-opened, albeit on shortened hours, and you could Eat Out for £10 per head with the balance paid for by the Government. There were still a lot of somewhat complicated rules and regulations. The 'rule of six' for example that banned gatherings of more than six people and then in September entertainment venues were forced to close at 10pm. There were various tier systems introduced which meant that different areas were placed under different restrictions according to the severity of new cases in their respective areas. The rules were complicated and no less for people on boats. For one thing you were not allowed to travel unless it was absolutely necessary, so the question arose that if you had a call to say your boat was sinking would that be deemed a necessary reason to travel. I think you were allowed to move your boat to get water or fuel as long as you observed the 'social distancing' rule. It was all very frustrating and people began to wonder whether things would ever get back to normal.

Then came another blow as a second lockdown was announced at the beginning of November. This, we were told, was to prevent a 'medical and moral disaster in the NHS.' All around the country people came out in their droves to support the heroes who had been toiling ceaselessly in the most stressful conditions to tend to the sick. Flags and banners fluttered from buildings and people came out of their houses to clap the doctors and nurses at specific times to show their gratitude and support. There had been many murmurings and speculation from the media that a vaccine was being trialled in the UK, discovered by scientists from Oxford University, and in December this had become a reality and the first jabs were administered, initially to the aged and most vulnerable.

Roll out of the new vaccines took off in earnest and there were soon several variants on the market. Pop up centres were opened throughout the country offering Astra Zeneca and Pfizer jabs. Churches, leisure centres, theatres and village halls as well as GP surgeries were turned into vaccination centres. It was an amazing operation, manned by volunteers and retired nurses who supplemented the professional staff to provide, at least in my experience, a brilliantly efficient service. It was as though we were fighting a war, which of course we were in a metaphorical sense, and entire 'land armies' put their shoulders to the wheel for the cause - a wonderful show of British bulldog spirit. Even the mighty Salisbury Cathedral was turned into a virtual field hospital. By the end of January 2021 the 70's age group became eligible and I duly joined the queue for my first jab. I was utterly amazed at the organisation; registration, check in, seats wiped, orderly queues and marvellously friendly people going about the work in a professional and caring way. Just shows what we can do in Britain when our backs are against the wall.

There was a folk group from the north of England that had become very popular around this time. They were called Merry Hell and one of their best-liked songs was called 'Come on England.' It has a rousing chorus which seemed to sum up the spirit of those heroes of the NHS and the thousands of volunteers who gave up their time and risked their own health to man the trenches. It goes like this:

So stand up, come on England, live up to your history
Your heart can't be held in a flag or a crown
Raise your tea cups and glasses, you bold lads and lasses
And drink to the spirit that'll never lie down

Up until March 2023 almost 250,000 people in the UK had died from Covid-19 - a sobering thought.

I had been jabbed and I felt that I had been given a suit of armour to protect me from the evils of Covid-19. Emboldened by this, I decided to climb the mountain that was the path to a

Visa for Thailand. I really didn't relish the idea of any more of the British winter - and a mountain it certainly was. I had successfully navigated my way through the jungle of bureaucracy necessary to acquire a visa for Thailand for the past twelve years, but this one was different. Owing to the restrictions imposed during Covid the amount of paperwork and the whole process of application had changed. For a start you needed to obtain a Thai Pass before you could do anything else. After several attempts at a breakthrough I finally gave up and contacted an agency for help. Trunk Travel, a company headed by an Englishman and based in Bangkok, promised that they could handle everything and so for a reasonable fee, I put my fate in their hands. I still had to provide a dozen documents, which I had to scan and send to Bangkok, but they very efficiently took care of the rest. By mid February of 2021 I was in possession of a Thai Pass and a 60 day Tourist Visa plus a return ticket to Bangkok via Dubai with Emirates. I still had to get a test no more than 48 hours from departure which I took in the car park of Eastleigh Football Club and then had to undergo another test at Bangkok Airport before I was whisked by taxi to my quarantine ~~prison~~ / hotel, where I was to stay alone for 15 nights. It was somewhere around this time that I began to wonder whether it was all worth it.

The actual quarantine period wasn't as unbearable as I had envisaged. I had a reasonably sized room with a balcony (most essential), I had my iPod for my music and my iPad which allowed me to watch movies and, more importantly, sport, and keep up to date with Email and news. Alcohol was strictly taboo but I managed to get over this as a friend who kindly supplied me with little treats from 7-11 stores, would also bring a couple of litre Coke bottles filled with red wine. In fact the food that was supplied by the hotel, left outside the room in plastic throwaway containers three times a day, was more than I could eat. I had to tell them that I really didn't need the midday meal as I would only waste it but it took me three days to get this message across. I suggested that they donated it to the food banks for distribution to the hungry but I don't think this happened. I was not allowed to leave the room under any circumstances and all the hotel staff were dressed from head to toe in protective suits - the Urban Spacemen! I had to take a further test on the second day and a final one two days before I was allowed to leave. The results were conveyed to me by Line messages from the in-house nurse.

On day 15 at 06.00 I got the news that I was free to go. I was almost sorry to leave.

Being a somewhat anti-social sort of sod, I had quietly enjoyed the solitude of my own company.

I stayed in Thailand until the middle of June - in all my stay lasted for 130 days. Now if you have been paying attention you may well be wondering how I managed to prolong my stay for this length of time when I had only been granted a Visa for 60 days. Well I could have spent half a day queuing at the Immigration department with another pile of paperwork (the Thais really do love paperwork and I dread to think how many trees have to suffer for it), and obtained an extension of 60 days. This would have cost me 1900 Thai baht (roughly £45.00). Alternatively I could go to see my 'friend' Noi, who owned a small bar just around the corner, give her my passport and a few more Thai baht, and start the wheels of Thai enterprise turning.

Needless to say I chose this option, and three days later Noi rang me to tell me that the passport was ready to collect, freshly stamped with a further 90 days of stay.

When I asked where I needed to go to collect it she told me that it was not the Immigration office but to see the little man on the mango stall just opposite!

So that is how the system in this great country works. You can more or less get anything you want through the back door as long as you have the necessary lucre.

So what, I hear you cry, does any of this have to do with boating with a barge on the canals of Europe. Well nothing really. I have included this as part of the explanation as to why it was that I didn't get back to Saul Trader for two whole years. What is more is that I have imparted a few titbits of information that may be useful to anyone wishing to visit the 'Land of Smiles.' Tell me where you could find another book about barging with such gems of knowledge. Incidentally, the much vaunted myth about the Land of Smiles, is immediately extinguished as soon as you step into the airport and come face to face with the first

Thai individual that you meet - the Immigration Officer - welcome to the Land of Snarls!

My return flight with Emirates to London via Dubai on the 26th May was cancelled. The reason given was of course the dreaded Covid, something that had become synonymous as an excuse for poor service anywhere. I wasn't given the option of a voucher and instead received a paltry compensation which amounted to roughly 34% of the return fare. Thai Immigration granted me another 30 day extension free of charge and I had to re-book a flight with Singapore Air which added three hours to the journey. As transit passengers at Changi we were made to wait on the plane until all the 'locals' had disembarked, and then marched behind a security guard who looked like an alien from Outer Space, to be held in an isolation area for an hour and a half before a second route march that seemed to go on forever and then queuing again for another rigorous paperwork check and finally being allowed to board the connecting flight. Two weeks after my return to the UK I received my second jab at Salisbury City Hall and then, glutton for punishment that I must be, booked another flight, this time short haul with British Airways from London Heathrow to Toulouse. During that summer I did manage to get some time on my narrowboat, and took it down the River Severn to Saul for dry-docking and survey. Wat Tyler was now over 30 years old and my insurance company were insisting on an out-of-water survey before they would consent to a renewal of the policy. This was done by Mike Godding, who after a thorough inspection inside and out, pronounced the vessel 'as good as new' - a testimony to the fine standards of work of R W Davis. Mike is based in Evesham and I would not hesitate to recommend him should the need arise.

I had hoped to be able to visit the rejuvenated Saul Canal Festival, an event that I had been involved with myself 15 years earlier, but unfortunately this was not to be as Covid reared its ugly head once again to ensure a cancellation. There were a few other diversions that year. I visited the Bluebell Railway Collector's Fair in the July and actually had a small stand. This was the first time in many years and I was allowed my old spot beside the water crane on Platform 1 at Horsted Keynes where

I managed to offload a few bits of unwanted model railway items.

There was also the distraction of the Euros, where England excelled themselves to reach the final, only to be defeated on penalties after a one all draw with Italy. Then at the end of August I took Wat Tyler for a short trip around the Birmingham canals. From Stourport I was accompanied by the youngest grandson, Owen, as far as Brierley Hill. He worked his socks off, got a thorough drenching on the Stourbridge flight, and passed the test with flying colours. In fact he was so keen that after Blowers Green Lock, where the Dudley No 1 canal turns a sharp right, Owen marched dutifully on towards the first lock on the Dudley No 2 Canal before I shouted to him that we weren't going that way and he could have a short rest before we tackled the Delph. He had passed the audition and as a 'reward' I invited him to come with me to France for a week on Saul Trader.

I left Wat Tyler at Merry Hill for a couple of weeks in the care of my friends Pete and Marlene who are moored there with their boat, another R W Davis creation called Perfection, in the basin. There was always plenty going on there and Marlene dragged us for a curry in the Indian Tavern, where Owen, bless him, not only ordered the food via some new-fangled device on the table that allowed him to do the job with his mobile phone (something which was way beyond the capability of the rest of us), but also insisted on paying for the meal.

The tour of the BCN a few weeks later was a blast. I had two old (in both senses of the word) friends with me on Wat Tyler. Pete from Stourport, and the inimitable Kevin Day, he of the boat 'Nobody Knows' on which he lives at Withymoor Island which was where we picked him up. There were parts of the BCN that I particularly wanted to visit and we discussed our route over a couple of beers in the Withymoor club room. Kevin is the sort of bloke that once you have met him you will never forget him. He dresses in boatman's attire of dark corduroy trousers complete with leather belt and windlass holder, check shirt rolled to the elbows topped off with a flat cap. Kev is tall and gangly with a rasping Black Country accent and an opening gambit upon meeting anyone anywhere at any time of the day of 'It's a fine summer's morning' - the first line of a song written by John Richards and recorded by, among others, our good friends from the band Meet on the Ledge. When Kev walks into a room, or more often a pub, people take notice. The combination of the appearance and the voice invariably turn heads and Kev soon makes friends with everyone. He is possessed with the sort of amiable character and sense of humour that warms people to him. As you can imagine, we visited several of the BCN hostelries during our trip and became know by some as the three stoogies. Make of that what you will.

Our trip took in some of the lesser known parts of the BCN - Titford Pools, Brownhills, and the Daw End Branch, Ryders Green and the Tame Valley Canal where we crossed the M5 motorway on an aquaduct - something I hadn't done for 35 years.

Kevin knows the BCN very well, having done the 'Challenge' several times, and passed on a lot of his knowledge and experience as we went along. We did catch him out at one point though, when after a problem with the starter motor at Brownhills, we didn't manage to get away until 7.00pm. I asked Kevin how long it would take to get to the Masons Arms at Daw End and he said 'ah about an hour I reckon.' We finally tied up outside the pub at 10.30pm and it was only due to the welcoming hospitality of mine host that we were able to fully satisfy our thirsts.We left the premises at 11.45pm. Kev only intended staying with us for a week, but in the end left us at Wolverley Lock Inn. There will be more details of this little adventure in a book about my 32 years on Wat Tyler that I am in the course of writing. If I ever get it finished, that is!

Chapter 13 Back to France at Last

So having got through the Covid years with a few pages of waffle, it was eventually time to think about the possibility of returning to France. I had had my second jab and by the Autumn of 2021 the rules for entering France had relaxed slightly. After some periods of serious lock-downs, during which time the French even had to have written consent to leave their houses without a valid reason, travel from the UK became a little easier. There were still a number of hurdles to be cleared - proof of vaccination and medical cover for example, and a Declaration d'Honneur to testify that, and I quote.

I have not presented (sic) during the last 48 hours, any of the following symptoms:

- *fever or chills,*
- *a cough or an increase in my usual cough,*
- *unusual tiredness,*
- *unusual shortness of breath when talking or straining*
- *unusual muscle aches and/or body aches*
- *unexplained headaches,*
- *loss of taste or smell*
- *unusual diarrhoea.*

that I am not aware of having been in contact with a confirmed case of covid-19 in the fourteen days preceding departure;

And undertake on my honor (sic) to submit to an antigenic test or a possible biological examination on arrival.

I also had to take another anti-gen test within 48 hours of departure which on this occasion entailed a visit to another pop-up testing station in Andover. The fact that I wanted to take my grandson with me, who was still under 18 and therefore had only had one vaccination, posed another challenge as he had to have his test within 24 hours of departure. This meant that we had to book an appointment at the airport (Heathrow) on the day. The negative result was returned within the hour and at last we were cleared to go.

The flight was due at Toulouse Blagnac at 18.55 and the last train of the day to Moissac left at 20.17. All things being equal, this would give us a little over an hour to get to the station at Matabiau. The bus journey took about half an hour and under normal circumstances this would allow enough time but of course these were anything but normal times. I was worried that the immigration procedure might well take longer than usual so as a safety precaution I booked an overnight stay at the Ibis Hotel which is directly opposite Matabiau station. Now, under the rules of the law of Sod, had I not made this provision, we would have been held up for hours at immigration, missed the bus, and arrived at Matabiau to see our train disappearing in the distance. As it happened we landed ten minutes early thanks to a tail wind, and were on the bus twenty minutes later, arriving at Matabiau station with fifteen minutes to spare. Better to be safe than sorry as they say. There was no real point in staying overnight in Toulouse so we decided to catch the 20.17, which was waiting for us in the bay platform. We had just enough time to get a quick snack and a drink to take with us from the buffet and gratefully boarded the train. The journey time to Moissac is just under an hour which meant that we should arrive with a bit of daylight left. Lisa Butcher had been to the boat a few days earlier to give it a good clean and had left the keys in a safe place for us.

Ten minutes into the journey we were hit by the mother of storms. Zigzagging streaks of lightning crackled outside the windows followed immediately by thunder that exploded like gunfire. The rain lashed against the train in a cascading deluge and the wind battered the windows and rocked the carriages. It was absolutely relentless. The sky turned an ominous dark bluis grey pierced by the the sparkling flashes of lightning. It was exhilarating and scary at the same time. The first stop was at Montauban where a few passengers alighted to make their way home and a few more, looking miserable and bedraggled, silently trudged through the train looking for a seat. And there we stayed. Ten, fifteen, twenty minutes passed and a lengthy announcement was made which I didn't understand. I looked around to see the reaction from the other passengers. They weren't moving so I concluded that the stop was only temporary and we weren't being told to get off. We were held there for almost an hour. A couple more announcements, gloomy faces from all those that had understood the message, and finally the train made a stuttering start and we were on our way again. I never found out the reason for the stop. Whether there was a fault with the train, or a relief driver hadn't turned up, I will never know. Maybe it was just due to the horrendous weather. It was quite possible that they were worried about damage to overhead wires or flooding on the track between Montauban and Moissac, and needed assurances before we were allowed to proceed.

The result of this was that we finally arrived at Moissac at 22.30, one and a half hours late. The storm had not relented at all - in fact if anything it was worse.

We sheltered under the station canopy while I rooted out some wet weather gear from my case. The noise of the rain drumming on the roof was so loud we could hardly hear each other speak. While I was doing this Owen went to the end of the platform looking for a toilet. Then there was an almighty clap of thunder which was followed immediately by a blinding bolt of lightning and a sudden fiery spark as it hit one of the overhead catenary masts just yards from where Owen was standing. This sent a shower of sparks fizzing for several yards along the wires. My first thought was that the whole length of cable was about to come tumbling on to the track. My second thought was that we needed to get the hell out of the station before anything more drastic happened.

We trudged as quickly as we could through the deserted streets dragging our sodden suitcases through the puddles behind us to the port and the refuge of the boat. Lisa had left the keys where we had agreed and had also made up the beds for us. This was a welcome boon which meant that after a quick coffee we could turn in for some well earned and much needed sleep.

The next morning arrived with a gentle breeze and bright sunshine, the torrential storm of the previous evening a distant memory. I had allowed us plenty of time for the trip to Toulouse and planned a lazy four or five days for the passage of 68 kilometres and 29 locks. The best laid plans! We stayed in Moissac for the day to stock up with provisions, top up with fresh water and generally check the boat in readiness for the trip. I settled up with Lisa for the cleaning and introduced myself at the port office. Since Jim's sad and untimely death, Bruno, who we knew from Briare and latterly Castet en Dorthe, had taken over as the Capitan. This was good news. Bruno was an excellent Capitan whose heart was in the job and who had a respect for the canal and the boaters, which was mutually received. He had moved his boat from Castets and looked set to settle into the role. I don't know exactly what happened - whether there was a problem with the Mairie or whether Bruno decided for one reason or another that the job wasn't for him, but by the time we arrived Bruno had left and a new regime put in place. The encumbent at the time of our visit also ran a local campsite and I got the impression that he really didn't want the job. I have since heard that this appointment was on a temporary basis and as far as I know a permanent replacement has still to be installed. It's a real shame as Moissac is a beautiful little town with a plethora of shopping facilities, restaurants and bars, as well as the historic abbey with its cloistered gardens. Jim's loss has been felt deeply in the community. He had nurtured a wonderful camaraderie amongst the moorings which so far has not been maintained. It is difficult to see where another Jim might come from. RIP Jim. The phrase 'he will be greatly missed' has never been so relevant.

I have to say I was not sorry to be leaving.

Jim with his lovely wife Sandra outside the Port Office

I can't really explain why but I have always been a little bit wary of the three locks that carry the canal from Moissac up to the aqueduct that crosses the River Tarn. We had been bumped about once or twice and it was essential to make sure the ropes were secured tightly before starting the operation. For this reason I walked with Owen to explain the procedure before setting off. The bottom lock is situated just after the junction with the short branch that leads to the Tarn via a double lock staircase. The lock is normally kept empty with the gates open and the green light showing. I don't recall ever seeing a lock-keeper in attendance. The locks are operated from an adjacent borne alongside the lock with simple instructional arrows that point up or down together with a red emergency button. Although Owen had some experience of lock operation in England, the French system was completely new to him. The main difference with these automated locks was that once the button was pressed to start the cycle you were left at the mercy of the speed that the paddles were opened, and the resulting flow of water.

On the English canals the paddles had to be raised by hand which meant that the volume of water entering the lock from above could be controlled. I usually insisted on the ground paddles being half raised until the level covered the cill which would result in a steady ascent. In France this was not possible as the paddles were raised remotely. I explained to Owen that he should wait at the lockside. I would then bring the boat into the lock, starboard side to, walk to the bow and throw him a line, the eye of which he would drop over a bollard in such a position that would leave a 30 - 35° lead from the bow. I would then secure the rope to the bits, return to the wheelhouse and put the morse control into slow ahead with the rudder turned to port. This would bring the boat gently alongside the wall. Finally I would throw the eye of a shorter line for Owen to drop over a bollard as close as possible to the wheelhouse which would keep the stern against the wall in the event of any cross flow as the lock filled. When all this was in place I would give the signal for Owen to press the 'Up' arrow and we were on our way to the next level.

Simple! The locks here operated in a chain, which meant that the next one would readied for you. Owen would walk between each one and once the boat was secured start the process again. In this manner we arrived at the top of the three locks in a gentle and orderly fashion, ready to proceed across the imposing aqueduct and head for the next town en route, Castelsarrassin. The planned passage to Toulouse would mean overnight stops at Castel, Montech and Grisolle.

The locks all had landing stages conveniently sited above and below where Owen would leap off and take up his position on the lockside. He was really getting into the swing of things and we were soon working as a team without the need to shout instructions. He did worry me at times when instead of waiting for me to get the bow alongside he would leap a gap of six or seven feet on to the landing. I had to remind myself that he was a fit and agile seventeen year old. I would probably have done the same a few years ago - well 60 years ago to be exact!

I would always go down to the engine room an hour or two into a voyage to check that all was well and took the opportunity to do this whilst awaiting the gates of the next lock. When I opened the door of the engine room I was knocked back by a dense cloud of acrid poisonous fumes. I quickly jumped back and shut the door, trying to work out what was happening. I switched off the engine and soaked a towel which I put over my mouth as I cautiously opened the door again and shone a torch through the thick choking fumes. There didn't seem to be any sign of escaping oil or water This was no place to linger. I reckoned that any more than half a minute in there and I would be dead. Once I had satisfied myself that the engine wasn't about to seize up I closed the door again and went out onto the deck for some much needed air. I tried to think logically as to the cause and decided that it must be a leaking exhaust pipe. There was a short length of steel pipe and I thought that maybe this had split. It was far too hot (and dangerous) to do anything right then so I decided to carry on. The engine wasn't overheating and apart from the pipe deteriorating further I didn't think that any more damage would be caused.

At Castelsarassin we stopped for a breather and after waiting an hour for the engine to cool down a bit, I ventured back into the engine room for a closer inspection. Sure enough, I found a hole the size of a golf ball in the pipe. I cursed the fact that I hadn't got any of the old stand-by, a GunGum bandage, amongst my spares, warned Owen not to go anywhere near the engine room, and vowed to carry on as far as we could. There was nothing much I could do about the problem so I thought that the best bet was to get to Toulouse as quickly as possible. I switched on the extractor fan which helped expel the fumes to a certain extent but still rendered the engine room a no-go area.

So the best laid plans once more went ignominiously out of the window. Instead of the leisurely four day cruise, we would have to be on the move for as long as the lock opening times would allow. So we pressed on to Montech where we tied for the night. Owen took it all in his stride with a nonchalant indifference, as if to say well this is a boat isn't it, and it's Grandad's boat. What else would you expect? He spent most of the time when we weren't working locks sitting staring into his iPhone, thumbs darting rapidly across the key pad, oblivious to anything else. He was a bright lad who had been one of only two candidates out of 1000 applicants, to be awarded a tool-making apprenticeship with BMW. I told him that my brother had served his time in a similar apprenticeship and it had proved an invaluable education which had left him with a plethora of skills which had even enabled him to build his own house. Whilst chatting in the evening at Montech he told me that they had been studying electricity. That's white man's magic I told him.

"I think I could probably wire up a house," he said matter-of-fact. When he went below to do the washing up he called up to me.

"Grandad. How do you turn on the lights?"

"See that little white square thing on the wall," I suggested sarcastically, "it's called a switch. Just press it and see what happens, and when you've finished the washing up could you make some coffee please."

"Grandad," came the cry from the galley a few minutes later, "how do you make coffee?"

I find it sad that this generation seem to think the world revolves around their iPhones. When I pointed out things along the way like a kingfisher or the wonder of the Montech water slope I got a cursory glance and a nod before the attention was redirected to the small screen. Owen did have other interests it's true. He was a keen skateboarder and he loved coarse fishing so I suppose there were times when the iPhone took a back seat.

We left Montech early in the morning to judge arrival at the first lock for the opening time of 9.00am and soldiered on all day to Toulouse and the port of Ste Sauveur where we were tied up by 6.00pm. On the way we suffered another slight mishap whilst waiting for a lock to empty when the boat was swept by the by wash inexorably into the trees on the offside. I tried everything to get the boat back into the middle of the channel but it wasn't having it and the result was that as I went forward towards the lock the jackstay caught in a overhanging branch and snapped off at the base, sending it complete with the ensign into the cut. There were a couple of Eastern Europeans walking on the towpath and they found the incident highly amusing. The bedraggled ensign drifting into oblivion. I think they saw it as a symbol of the fall of the British Empire!

It now meant that we had an extra couple of days in Toulouse before our return flight. Serge came down to the port the following day with Lauren and with the engine now cooled down, managed to remove the offending piece of exhaust pipe.

Serge fabricated a completely new section and two days later the new part was fitted and that particular problem was solved. There were a few other jobs I had lined up for the winter which we discussed, and I left Serge with a new list.

- Fit new shower in forward bathroom starboard
- Replace generator impeller
- Treat wheel house roof and supply new winter cover
- Fit and connect solar panel - aft deck
- Replace galley sink mixer tap

I wouldn't be returning to France for seven months which should give them plenty of time to sort out these few jobs. I knew from bitter experience with boatyards however, that however long they had they would invariably leave completing the work till the very last minute. It was always best to tell them that you would need the boat at least a month before you actually did. We spent the rest of the time in Ste Sauveur cleaning up and readying the boat for its winter hivernage. Owen went off to explore the city and I took the opportunity to spray the decks and topsides with a 'magic' fluid that I had been told would keep the steel free from fungi and leaf mould over the winter. It was called 'Wet and Forget' and it had to be applied to a dry surface.

There was one other important thing that had to be done before we left and that was to get an anti-gen test.

The port Capitan told me of a pharmacy just a few hundred yards away where this could be done and I booked an appointment for the two of us for 10.00am on the day before our departure. We turned up at the pharmacy and were shown into a tiny cubicle at the back of the shop. The pharmacist dressed in full riot gear, full length operating gown, hair net, visor, gloves and rubber shoes. She looked as though she could quite easily have been doing a heart transplant. She rammed the swab so far up my nostril that my eyes started to stream uncontrollably and at one point I thought the end was going to come out through my eye socket. The good news however was that we were both passed 'fit to fly' and presented with certificates to prove it. What fun travel was in those dark days of Covid. I was amused when the pharmacist spotted a large mosquito on the wall and squashed it flat with one foul swoop of her hand, splatting a pool of dried blood on to the plaster. So much for hygiene!

Our flight was a mid afternoon departure which gave us plenty of time for the last minute checks and shut-downs before a 20 minute walk to the station where we caught the bus to Blagnac airport. I remembered the old Norfolkman who once told me when I was leaving the boat for a few weeks in Carassonne. "When you leave the boat you'll be worrying about it for ten minutes then you'll forget about it altogether," Turned out he was just about right.

Chapter 14 Ready for Inspection

I had been thinking about putting Saul Trader on the market for sale for five or six years. It was always going to be 'next year', but unfortunately next year is rather like tomorrow - it never comes. There were always reasons for fuelling the procrastination - just another couple of jobs to sort out, then of course the downturn in the market caused by the pandemic, and the irrefutable fact that after a couple of months of cruising I realised that I was still reasonably fit and agile and that I still loved the boat. So 'just one more year' evolved into seven years since the last TRIWV inspection, or to give it its full-blown title the 'Technical Regulations for Inland Waterway Vessels', and I obviously couldn't sell it before I'd renewed the certificate, could I? I could hardly believe that it was seven years since Rob van Dyke had flown from Holland for the inspection in the covered dock at Toulouse. Who knows where the time goes ?

I had spoken to my friend Rob Whitaker, of the barge 'Pisgah' whose TRIWV expired at the same time as mine. Pisgah moored at Ventenac en Minervois and Rob told me he had booked the unique dock at Gailhousty on the Junction Canal that branches off from the Midi a few kilometres east of Le Somail. Rob's son Jules lived permanently in the area and was well known to the local VNF staff. He told me that the week prior to Rob's booking the dock was free so I took the decision to secure it. Rob had used a surveyor who also lived locally for his last inspection. Johan did work on behalf of Rob van Dyke so it made sense to book him for the job which would hopefully save some of the costs of Rob having to fly from Holland. Jules also knew a guy who would be able to do the preparation of the hull for the thickness test and the subsequent blacking. This was all sorted and booked in the November of 2021.

So at the end of May 2022 I caught the early morning Brittany car ferry from Poole to Cherbourg. I took this option as I wanted to spend a couple of nights with my friends Andy and Janette who had recently moved from Toulouse and bought a camp site in the Vendee. Andy had taken early retirement after 30 odd years with Airbus to run the site which boasted camping pitches and spaces for motorhomes. It also had a gîte attached to the main house where I spent a very pleasant couple of days.

On arrival at the boat I soon realised that some of the work I had asked Serge to do had not been finished. The new shower had been fitted but there was a small leak and Serge had replaced the washer at the base of the hydraulic steering reservoir but unfortunately that still leaked. These were fairly minor problems compared with the genny cooling system that was still blocked and the new wheelhouse cover, which had been on order for several months, had still not been delivered. Serge gave the firm responsible a bit of a kicking and they eventually turned up with it the day before we were due to leave only to find it did not fit. After some rather heated debate they disappeared with tails between legs to return later in the day with the size corrected. C'est La France! Serge also delivered two 20 litre drums of two-pack tar for Will, who I had booked to do the work in the dock.

The trip from Toulouse to Sallèle d'Aude and the Gailhousty dry dock was fairly uneventful and took eight days to reach Ventenac where I arrived on the 3rd June with a couple of days to spare before the docking.

I completely forgot that the manned locks on the Midi close for lunch usually between 12.30 and 1.30 although this can vary. The Pizzeria at Montisgard was closed so dinner on board was called for. I had pre-booked a mooring at Castelnaudary and was allocated a space before the bridge which was about 6 inches longer than the boat. I had a couple of breezy days and have to confess that once or twice on the twisty sections between Béteille and Lalande I lost the stern on the shallow inside of the bends and had to fight with reverse gear at full throttle and bow thruster to get free. I stopped for a few hours at Carcassonne for supplies and the éclusier told me that the moorings in Trèbes were complet. I decided to stop for the night on the lock landing at Villedubert, about three kilometers before Trèbes. It was almost closing time anyway and I checked with the lock-keeper that I could stay. I knew I would be away first thing in the morning so no harm was done and nobody was inconvenienced. As it turned out the complet Trébes moorings had seemingly all been vacated just before my arrival which resulted in a queue of about six boats all waiting at the top of the staircase. I managed after some difficulty to get alongside at the back of the queue and soon realised that I would be going nowhere until after the lunch break.

Another five or six boats arrived in the meantime and formed an orderly queue. Then at the last minute another hire boat, one of those ugly box shaped unwieldy steel things where the steerer stands on the roof, steamed on past me coming to an abrupt halt in front of the top gates, skewing sideways across the cut. This is a three lock staircase and as the last boats before lunch had gone down, the first movements after lunch were the ones waiting at the bottom. Three hire boats were brought up in a prolonged exercise which meant that Johnny-come-lately was left hovering around and looking a little bit stupid for at least half an hour. Then when the last of the ascending boats had left the top lock, insult was added to injury as the éclusier ordered Johnny to give way and clearly indicated for me to proceed first into the lock. I had to concentrate on not looking too smug as I slowly passed a flustered looking Johnny. Once inside, the lock-keeper then decided that there was enough room for Johnny as well and in he came gently nudging alongside.

As is often the case, it is a mistake to pre-judge people and as the lock started to empty I got into a very pleasant conversation with Johnny skipper. He was American and told me he had spent five years sailing his 70 ft yacht around the world. The crew were all very sociable and as I listened to his fascinating tales I unforgivably took my eye of the proverbial ball. Saul Trader had started to take on a list and in a rush of panic I realised that we were trapped between Johnny and the lock wall - and the lock was slowly emptying. I blasted the horn and yelled for the éclusier to stop the descent. I couldn't see the lock-keeper and in my state of fright I thought he must have gone down to the next level. I blasted again long and hard before realising that there were two keepers behind me and they had got the message and re-acted immediately to stop the lock and start to refill it. I breathed a long sigh of relief and started to shake. Once we were afloat and level they got Johnny to move forward which then gave us both plenty of space. It was a timely reminder of the importance of paying attention in locks. I had suffered a similar sort of experience with my narrow boat ascending the locks out of Stratford on Avon. I was single-handed and following my usual practice of leaving the boat ticking over in forward gear with the bow nudging the striking plate. I was standing on the lockside chatting to a passing gon-goozler when I suddenly noticed that the bow was trapped and the boat had started to nose-dive. I managed to drop both paddles but not before a lot of water had cascaded into the well deck, breeched the doors and flooded the carpet. I put it down to the fact that the bow fender had caught under the bottom of the steel plate and the chain had failed to break. Normally there would have been a weak link in the securing chain for use in this exact situation. With a sort of perverse logic, rather than insert such a link, I removed the bow fender completely. I ran around like that for nearly 20 years before finally suc-cumbing to a new bow fender, supplied and fitted by Graham New, in 2022.

As is always the case, there were plenty of gongoozlers at the lock in Trèbes too. There was a restaurant right alongside the lock: it was lunchtime and all the outside canalside tables were full. There were a crowd of English lads on the nearest table and we exchanged a bit of banter.

"It's OK, " I told them, "I have an arrangement with the restau-rant to lay on a bit of entertainment for the diners. Get a free meal out of it."

I did notice that when descending the next few locks the éclusier seemed to pay extra heed to the stern quarter of Saul Trader, obviously having had the message passed down by the towpath telegraph. I wanted to tell them that it was nothing whatsoever to do with the boat. I had successfully negotiated over 4000 locks in France and never once had the problem. The rubbing strake would always slide gently from the lock side as the boat went down. The problem at Trébes was that we were jammed between the lockside and the boat that was alongside.

At Homps I met another of these ungainly craft in the shape of 'Bosun Higgs'. That was the name of the boat, not the owner. Once again there was very little room on the moorings. The good Bosun had at least 6 or 8 feet of space in front of him and as I hovered hopefully alongside the crew returned from a trip to the supermarket. Before I had even asked, they offered to bow haul the Bosun up a few feet which just about gave me enough room to get alongside the quay. I got talking with them and discovered that they were English and lived in Gloucestershire, not far from the birthplace of Saul Trader. One of them told me that he remembered seeing ST on the canal at Saul and knew Phil and Craig from the boatyard. I gave him a bottle of wine and a copy of my first book (bit of back-handed compliment I suppose) by way of thanks for their help. I was fascinated by the name of the Bosun. I first thought it may have been a character from the Captain Pugwash books and I asked them whether they had a cabin boy called Roger aboard. They had actually hired the boat and had no idea where the name came from so I had a quick Google and discovered that the only reference to any Bosun Higgs was in fact an English Country Dance Band, but why the name should have been chosen for a hire boat on the French canals is a mystery. The crew assured me that none of them was remotely musical. The other possibility is that it is a play on the term Higgs Boson, which according to Wikipedia is an "elementary particle in the Standard Model of particle physics produced by the quantum excitation of the Higgs field."   So there you have it. Notwithstanding all that my theory about these horrible boats was confirmed by the skipper who told me it was an absolute pig to steer.

I arrived at Ventenac on the Friday which gave me a couple of days to spare before the docking. I moored next to another friend Annie, who was the ex wife of Rob and the mother of Jules. Annie had bought a lovely little tjalk in Decize and sailed it down the Rhone with Jules. Annie was a great help and drove me to the shops and to Narbonne so I could catch the train to Toulouse and retrieve my car. The train fare was on some sort of special deal and cost me the princely sum of one Euro. Unsurprisingly it was packed to the gunwhales but I did manage to find a seat.

That evening we all ate in La Grillade alongside the canal - Annie, Rob and a couple of Annie's friends Ted and Gertrude, and I pigged out on the excellent Noix St Jacques. There was some confusion around the docking. The official start date was the Monday, 6th June, but this transpired to be a holiday in France. This was Whit Monday. France seem to have a holiday at the drop of a hat. If there's a Monday, chances are there will be a holiday. Father's Day, Mother's Day, Ascension Day, Bastille Day, Labour Day, Victory Day, Assumption Day, All

Saints Day, Armistice Day, as well as the usual ones around Christmas, New Year and Easter.

I called in to Sallèles d"Aude on the way back from Toulouse to check. There was a lady in the office who assured me that the docking would be at 09.00 on the Monday. So I moved the boat from Ventenac on the Sunday morning and tied up above the lock at Sallèle. Annie kindly came down to take me back to Ventenac to collect my car and we had a very pleasant lunch in the canalside restaurant Le P'tit D'Oc. On Monday morning it was quite obvious that we would be going nowhere. The office was firmly shut and there was nobody around apart from the lock-keeper who confirmed my suspicion that we wouldn't be able to get into the dock until the following day. I called Will to let him know and then moved through the Sallèle lock in the late afternoon the one kilometre to tie for the night on the landing stage above the Gailhousty lock.

In my experience the lock here is quite unique. It is essentially a double lock staircase which lowers boats from the Canal de Jonction to the short section of the River Aude which then leads into the Canal de Robine and thence to Narbonne and the sea at Port-la-Nouvelle. The difference here is that the lower chamber has a ledge about 6 metres wide set at 3 metres above the low water mark. This ledge is in fact a dry dock equipped with wooden keel blocks which allow boats to sit a few feet above the floor, and an electricity and fresh water supply. In order to get boats on to the dock, the middle gates are left open and the entire area filled to the upper level. The boat then enters the lock and is manoeuvred carefully to the side so that as the water recedes it sits on the blocks high and dry above the lower level. Once this has been done the lock reverts to its normal function allowing passing boats to traverse the staircase in the normal way.

I was summoned by telephone to present myself in the office at Sallèles at 08.30 on the Tuesday morning to complete the necessary paperwork and the crew then arrived to begin the operation. I then discovered that I would have to go through the locks and into the Aude in order to turn the boat around and enter the dock with the bow facing upstream. This apparently is to ensure the boat can exit quickly in the event that the river floods in times of heavy rain.

I had had some experience (not entirely pleasant) in the short river section several years earlier when I ran aground close to the entrance of the channel that led to the lock. In view of this I was a bit wary of the depth and anxious not to repeat the mistake. I knew there was a bank of silt in the middle of the river which wasn't buoyed and in the event I was a little over-cautious and turned the boat around too close to the entrance pier, actually touching the brickwork, albeit gently, with the stern. Had I known what I know now, I could have done this on the previous evening which would have saved an hour or so on the day. I watched Jules take Pisgah through this manoeuvre a week later and he in fact went right into the middle of the river before turning. Pisgah draws a foot or so less than Saul Trader so I still don't know how far into the channel I could have gone before getting stuck.

Once in the lock the VNF staff started the filling process and with the aid of a rope fore and aft and some use of the bow thruster, Saul Trader was gently pulled into position over the blocks. Will was already on the lockside and made sure that the rudder was clear of the aftermost block as we eventually came to rest as the water drained around the hull. Will had arrived at 08.00 and had already set up his gear and was hard at work with the pressure washer minutes after we had settled. By the middle of the afternoon he had all but finished when I got a call from Johan, the Dutch surveyor who was due to do the survey on the following day. He told me he would be passing by on his way back from another job and would call in for a chat. Johan rumbled up in his van an hour later. He was the archetypal old sea dog in his Yankee denim overalls and large floppy sea boots with a mop of curly hair. He greeted Will like a long lost friend although I later found out that they couldn't stand the sight of each other, and strode across the plank from the dockside into the wheelhouse as though he owned the place.

We passed the time of day with a coffee and he told me that this job and the one for Rob the following week were his last before he retired. Jonah, sorry Johan - I had an unfortunate habit of getting names mixed up, told me that he lived on his boat a few kilometres away in the Port de la Robine. He then said that he would return in the morning .

On the dock at Gailhoustie

"I will give you the certificate and a list of anything else you need to do. If you do these things it is up to you."

This did surprise me somewhat as at that point he hadn't even looked at the boat. It was true that we had been given a certificate after the previous inspection seven years ago but I thought he would have at least done a cursory inspection before producing the new certificate.

"Cost is 1800 Euros", he said, before adding emphatically "Cash!"

The following day Johan turned up as arranged, banged on the side of the steelwork in a few strategic places with his lump hammer, took a look inside the boat and made some notes, and after about 45 minutes produced the certificate and a foolscap page of scribbled recommendations, and held out his hand for his money.

"Oh, forgot to say," he said nonchalantly, "plus travel expenses of course, 200 Euros."

Of course - 200 Euros to drive 20 kilometres there and back - obvious really! As if this wasn't enough, he then charged me 30 Euros for six stickers that I told me that I needed to fix to things like fire extinguishers, pointing out that they were in fact fire extinguishers. When I looked at the packets I noticed that unbelievably he hadn't bothered to remove the price labels - 2 Euros each!

Rob always said that when you shake hands with a Dutchman, be sure to count your fingers afterwards.

The 'up to me' list contained a number of fairly insignificant things which were easily implemented but one thing that Johann did say which worried me was that the copper bush where the prop shaft enters the water had worn and needed replacing. I asked Will about it who told me that it wasn't desperate but we had been getting a small drip of water through the stern gland so I made a note to dry dock the boat again as soon as possible.

Johann disappeared into the sunset dreaming of his impending retirement and I counted my fingers. I saw him as a likeable rogue. He was tired of the work and fed up with the futility of it all. He saw it for what it was. A largely unnecessary set of bureaucratic rules and regulations that really achieved little more than relieving the oppressed boat owner of his hard earned sheckels. The test only applied to boats of 21 metres and over. Had I known this when I registered Saul Trader many years ago with the Small Ship's Register before the dreaded TRIWV had been thought about I would have shown the length as 20.9 metres which would have saved all this expensive palaver.

One undoubted benefit of the enforced docking was that the hull got two fresh coats of two pack tar and Will worked tirelessly to finish the job by the Thursday. The dock was booked until the following Monday but I contacted the VNF and arranged to leave the next day, and move back to Sallèles d'Aude. It wasn't that I particular disliked being on the dock. In fact the surroundings were quite imposing, overlooked as it was by the large and architecturally ornate building that formerly housed offices and the home of the lock-keeper. At each side of the lock four gracefully symmetrical sets of steps connected the upper and lower locks via an elegant stone bridge. A footpath led to the river where another surprise structure was a huge steel girder bridge that once carried a single line railway which connected the town of Bize with Narbonne and the Port la Nouvelle. The line was originally built to transport wine and pottery but after the demise of goods traffic the line was used as a tourist attraction that ran with a diesel railcar. This was discontinued in 2004 but the track seems to be mostly intact and probably wouldn't take much to re-open. I hope that it will be restored as I'm sure it would attract a lot of custom and I for one would be on the first train.

I was a little uncomfortable during the stay on the dry dock. It was high summer and a number of local youths and girlfriends were using the lock and the surroundings as an adventure playground, starting by jumping from the top lock into the bottom and then as there bravado got the better of them, and egged on by the girls, they had graduated to jumping from the ledge on the side of the building into the bottom lock, a drop of about 10 metres. I began to worry that sooner or later someone would get seriously injured, although I had to admit quietly that at their age I would probably have been doing exactly the same thing.

On a couple of occasions I was disturbed in the small hours by a strange activity close to the canal. I was woken at first by lights illuminating the building and when I got up to find out what was going on I saw a small crowd of what I assumed were youths dancing around a bonfire in what appeared to me as some weird and satanic sort of ritual. I watched for half an hour or so until suddenly all the lights went out and all went silent. It was three or four o'clock in the morning and I found it so disturbing that the next morning I walked across to where the activity had taken place half expecting to find a sacrificed body, but there was no sign at all of the goings-on of the previous night. I began to doubt my sanity and wondered whether I had dreamt the whole thing.

Nevertheless I was quite glad when the VNF arrived and filled both locks to re float Saul Trader and we motored slowly back to Sallèlles d'Aude, and civilisation. It's a pleasant little town with good moorings above the lock and all facilities within easy reach. A good bar where I watched the Grand Prix, several good restaurants, a large Casino supermarché as well as a Tabac and an excellent bakery. Diesel is available by delivery from the local garage. Annie, ever helpful, brought me back to the boat after I transferred my car back to Ventenac, with a visit to the Intermarché supermarket in Ste Marcel-sur-Aude to top up with supplies.

Back in Ventenac I had the devil of a job to get anywhere near the bank. The spot where I had tied previously was occupied and I spent half an hour shuffling about before managing to at least get the bow reasonably close with the stern sticking out a metre and a half from the bank. The VNF have spent years replacing thousands of plane trees that famously lined the Canal du Midi that have had to be destroyed after contracting a deadly and highly contagious fungus. The trees were planted in the early 1800's as a means of shade and it is thought that the disease first appeared as a result of contaminated ammunition boxes left by the Americans during the second World War. The consensus is that over 40,000 trees may have to be destroyed and the VNF has raised nearly half a million Euros from a public appeal and vowed to replace every tree with a more resilient variety. A lot of work had been carried out in the area between Capestang and Ventenac during the previous winter and this had left the canalside banks with loose unstable earthworks. Another reason for the trees in the first place was to help stabilise the banks. After the re-planting along this length at Ventenac, the VNF had installed about half a mile of wooden mooring posts. The problem was that they had merely been knocked into the soil with no foundation and were already beginning to work loose. The place where I had found to moor was equipped with several of these posts and I managed to get four ropes secured. I wasn't at all happy with this and my fears were soon realised as a hire boat went past with engine roaring and a three foot wash astern which pulled two of the posts straight out of the ground. This stretch of the canal is fairly straight and wide and although most boats pass at a reasonable speed there are many that think they are still on the autoroute and only seem to have one throttle setting - flat out. I tried to hammer the posts back into the ground but it was apparent that they wouldn't hold so the only alternative, and one that I thought long and hard about, was to tie the fore and aft ropes around the base of the trees. I knew that I was risking admonishment from the VNF for this, as another cause of the problem with the spread of the disease had been levelled at boats tying up to the trees, but there was nothing else I could do. What I hadn't foreseen was that one of the residents of the houses along the canal who obviously resented the fact that boats passed his house, actually came along and openly photographed my ropes, making quite sure that the boat's name also featured in the shots. Not very helpful - or friendly. I wasn't comfortable with the situation and I could see his point, but why not come and talk about it.

I was only there for a couple of days anyway and left before the inevitable visit from the VNF. I had arranged with Frank, my German pal and his Thai wife Khung to come with me for a week. They were going to be driving down from Dusseldorf and I had suggested meeting up with them in Agde. So I said my farewells to Annie and Rob and headed east.

This was the long bief, or pound - 54 kilometres of relaxing lock-free cruising. Just right for the lazy, and the single-hander. I stopped for the first night at Pont Sériège, about 10 kilometres from Capestang. There is a restaurant here and a convenient hotel boat mooring, which as it was after 6.30pm I gambled on the fact that it would be unlikely that any hotel boats would still be on the move. The restaurant was closed anyway. There are notices on the banks beside these moorings that state 'Bateaux a Passages'. Dear old John of 'Tressnich' always swore blind that this meant pleasure boats. Well we are boats that have passengers he would say. Of course this wasn't true. The signs were to indicate that the moorings were reserved for hotel boats - boats that carried up to eight or ten paying guests that cruised the canals on set voyages. I think there was an unwritten law that pleasure boats could use them as long as they were prepared to move if a hotel boat arrived. As it happened on this occasion no such vessel caused any disturbance to the peace and quiet of a very conducive mooring.

I stopped briefly at Capestang for some shopping after slowly and carefully negotiating the lowest bridge on the entire canal and found a made-to-measure space just in front of my old friend, the quaintly names Locaboat 'Les Aresquiere,' appropriately moored next to another Locaboat 'Condom.' The centre of this little town is just a stone's throw from the cut and I was re-stocked and underway again in less than an hour.

From here to the end of the pound at the Fonserannes flight of locks is about 17 kilometres and I arrived at around 5.00pm. After half an hour of wallowing about in mud and reeds I eventually found a suitable spot and tied alongside the bank. Fifteen minutes later I had to move up a few feet to allow enough space for a new arrival in the shape of a lovely small Dutchman called Stormvögel.

Alongside the canal a short decked pathway leads through a small wood lined with educative illustrated panels that explain the huge undertaking by the VNF to replace some 40,000 plane trees that have been destroyed by the highly contagious canker stain disease. At the end of the walk there is a large area that has been set aside for the raising of rows and rows of young saplings, trees of a hardier strain that are resistant to the disease which will eventually be re-planted alongside the canal. There are a large number of these nurseries throughout the south of France working to complete this immense project, which was started back in 2011. A truly monumental task undertaken by the VNF with the help of a considerable amount of help through donations to maintain the iconic status of the Canal du Midi and a great deal of credit must go to the dedication and perseverance of all concerned.

I cast off at 08.30 the next morning to motor slowly to the top of the flight. As soon as the top gates opened I made my move and luckily (and sensibly in my opinion) the éclusier indicated to the two hire boats that had arrived behind me to wait and closed the gates behind me - result!

The somewhat unique way of working these locks I have described elsewhere. The practice of leaving the middle gates of each pair open, although at first a little daunting, certainly speeds up the operation, and I was soon leaving the bottom lock and turning sharp to starboard to head for the very deep (6.19 metres) Orb Lock which takes boats down to the basin at Beziers. The lady éclusiere at the Beziers lock insisted that I use '2 cords', something that is not easy for the single-hander. After several minutes of protracted argument and explaining that I had come through the Fonserrannes flight with a single line, it became quite clear that this lady was not for turning. I reluctantly conceded, paid out enough of my centre line to cope with the drop, and threw an eye over a bollard next to the wheelhouse. I suppose I was being a bit petty but I knew damn well that my short line would not be long enough and after we had dropped half of the 4.24 metres I had to let go of my end and leave it dangling over the side. The look of scorn on the face of madame was met with a clever-dick told-you-so grin, as I went forward to tend to my original line. The boat, as always when going down hill in locks, sat obediently on the wall. No harm done, no emergencies, no drama. The only possible danger that could have ensued was from the look that could kill that I got from the nice lady as I waved my thanks as I motored slowly out of her lovely lock.

The VNF did have the last laugh though as at the next lock the éclusier, a male this time, who had obviously been briefed over the towpath telegraph about this stroppy boater who refused to abide by the rules, insisted on two ropes. I had no choice as it became quite obvious that until I had made sure that I had two ropes of adequate length, this one had a drop of just over 2 metres, we weren't going anywhere.

"Lamentable, monsieur," I told him as I left, my apparent knowledge of such a perfect expression leaving him completely speechless! He wasn't to know that I had secretly looked up the word for pathetic during the transit.

At Agde I explained to the lock-keeper that I wanted to turn right in the Bassin Rond, (round lock) and venture into the centre of the town on the River Hérault. I had never done this before and it had been on the bucket list for some time. In order to achieve this the lock had to be lowered a metre or so and this time I wished I could have tied somewhere as there was a quite considerable tow as the lock emptied. I reversed back to the wall as far as possible from the gates and there was absolutely nowhere to attach a rope. I had to use the engine in an attempt to keep the boat steady but with little effect. Once on the river I was confronted with a long line of moored boats on both sides and motored about three kilometres towards the sea at le Grau d'Agde without managing to find a single space. I had told Frank that I would be moored near the centre of the town but this was completely impossible. There was no alternative but to retrace my steps back on to the canal. Frank was due to arrive from Germany the next day so I would need to make sure he knew where I was. Upstream of Agde the lock is approached via a narrow shallow channel and as I got within sight of the lock I saw that the gates were closed. A glance at my watch told me that it was just about closing time so it looked as though I was going to be stuck in the channel for the night - not a very alluring prospect. This worry was accentuated when I tried to get alongside a rickety pontoon just below the lock. The boat ground on something hard and submerged and the flow from the lock leakage rocked the boat gently up against the obstruction. This was definitely no place to spend a night. Desperate measures were called for, the first of which entailed a risky jump from the boat on to the bank. I ran up to the lock and tried frantically to explain my predicament. Fortunately the lock-keeper was still in his cabin and thankfully understood my problem. He nodded sympathetically and started to empty the lock as I hurtled back to the boat and scrambled aboard.

The next problem arose as the gates were opened and I started to motor towards the lock when I realised to my horror that there wasn't enough headroom under the bridge at the entrance. My first thought was that there had been a rise in the river level - it was tidal after all - and I would still have to sit out the night where I was. Then I noticed more water flowing out of the lock and eventually the level lowered just enough to allow me to get under and into the lock.

To say that I was very relieved would be an understatement. The lock-keeper was brilliant and worked for at least half an hour past his closing time to get me raised up to the canal again and moored on to the lock pontoon, facing in the direction that I needed to take for my next little adventure. Needless to say I rewarded the lock-keeper with a suitably generous alcoholic offering.

Will at Gailhousty told me that he had successfully navigated upstream on the Hérault to the small town of Bessan, some seven kilometres from the junction with the canal, which is where I decided to head - and hopefully pick up Frank and Khung.

The trip upstream was uneventful. The river was calm and quiet and the banks were lined with a verdant forest of trees which added to the tranquility of the scene. I didn't pass another vessel on the move. At Bessan there was a perfect space on the pontoon which I gratefully accepted. As it happened half of the mooring was taken up by a kayak hire business which left just enough room for Saul Trader, albeit with about six feet of stern overhanging. I spoke to the operator of the kayaks who told me that I would be fine staying for a couple of nights. The next problem was to contact Frank who would be driving from Germany and heading for Agde town to rendezvous as arranged. The problem was two-pronged. I was no longer in Agde and the credit on my UK mobile phone had expired. With the sort of cock-eyed logic that was this 21st Century with all its built in miracles of science and communication, Vodafone had sent me a message to inform me that I had reached the credit limit that I had set on the phone. All I had to do they said was to log in to my Vodafone account and up the limit. Ah - but I couldn't log in could I because I had already reached my limit! I could almost hear one of the super-brains in the PR department at Vodafone headquarters muttering gleefully "Gotcha"!

I was beginning to get a bit worried now. How close was Frank, and what the hell could I do if I couldn't contact him? There was a restaurant right beside the mooring - La Guinguette de Bessan and I asked one of the girls whether they had an internet connection that I could use, but unfortunately there was no coverage here. I was pointed in the direction of the town but before I left I decided to book a table for the evening.

"Combien de personnes?" she asked.

"Trois personnes s'il vous plait," I said, ever the optimist, and trudged off towards the town with hope in my heart.

I tried a small bar and I tried in the Post Office, all to no avail. Then I noticed another bar on the far side of the small square.

My question was answered with a oui so I ordered a beer and sat outside in the shade. After a few minutes it became obvious that there was no Internet. I queried this with the barman who replied with the Gallic shrug. Things were getting more desperate by the minute. I was running out of options and I had no idea how near Frank was.There was another restaurant on the corner where a waitress was setting out tables in readiness for the lunch-time rush. My question brought another negative response but then seeing the look of dejection on my face she must have taken pity and offered me the use of her own personal network, via her mobile phone. This did the trick and within minutes I was connected to Vodafone, logged in and had added another 20 Euros to my account. Bingo!

I wanted to kiss the waitress but thought better of it and instead bought another beer and gave her 10 Euros for her help. I think at that moment I would have paid 50 Euros had I been asked. Kung answered the phone as Frank was driving and told me they still had about four hours drive to reach Agen. I explained the situation and Frank stopped the car to consult the map, put the new destination into his GPS and told me they should arrive by 5.30pm. Wow - what a relief. I took a sip of the beer and finally relaxed.

God's in his heaven and all's well with the world.

Chapter 15   Return to Ventenac

Frank and Khung arrived at 6.30, just an hour later than predicted by the GPS. Once they had settled in we had a very nice meal in La Guinguette followed by an early night. A guinguette incidentally is a traditional term for a café or restaurant that provides music and dancing. I think there are several in Paris that still maintain the custom. I suppose they are similar to the tea dances that were once popular in England in the 20's and 30's, and interestingly were also known as thé dansant. This particular guinguette held similar events throughout the summer months on Wednesdays and Fridays so maybe we were lucky that we were there on a Monday. It could possibly have caused some mild amusement to see Frank (7ft tall in his socks), cavorting around the floor with Khun (4'6" in her heels!). The mind boggles.

The trip back to Ventenac passed without any undue calamities. I think Frank was secretly disappointed that he didn't have to strip off and work for hours in the engine room in 100° heat but you can't have everything.

We overnighted at Beziers (30 Euros mooring and no convenient restaurants), Capestang (30 Euros mooring) where we ate in La Bateliere restaurant alongside the canal, and Sallèlle d'Aude where we stopped for two nights and sampled the excellent tapas in the P'tit D'Oc.

On the way down the flight on the Canal de Jonction we had a slight hiccup at the third lock when emptying the lock. When the bottom gates opened I was confronted with a situation similar to that at the Bassin Rond. There wasn't enough headroom below the bridge to get through and I had to call out the homme to sort it out. This entailed re-filling the lock and emptying it again, when by some miracle the water returned to its normal level and we exited the lock in the usual manner. I had become almost a regular in the Sallèles bar, the Café de la Paix, and was greeted by the proprieteur as a long lost friend. It was a weekend, there was another Grand Prix, this one the British round from Silverstone, and the TV was switched to the correct channel before I had even asked. Hospitality at its finest.

Back at Ventenac we all enjoyed a farewell dinner for Frank and Khung in La Grillade with Annie and Rob and being an incurable creature of habit I indulged again in the Noix de Ste Jacques. Aroy mach, as they say in Thailand. Very delicious.

I needed to leave the boat for three months as I had things to do back in England. In the past this had never been a problem in France but recently the VNF had began to tighten up on these things. I think they had been taking advice from the CRT in England who were doing their level best to make everything as difficult as possible for the boater. Rob kindly offered to come with me to the office in Sallèlle to negotiate with the Chef - and a brilliant job he made of it. The two of them chatted and joked for half an hour before I was given the 'nod' with a warm shake of the hand. A mooring for three months at Ventenac, gratis, free and for nothing. I must say this was largely achieved by the sang-froid negotiating skills, or to put it another way, the bullshit that Rob had spouted with the Chief and I was impressed and grateful in equal measure. All I had to do now was to find somewhere that I could tie up securely and return to England safe in the knowledge that the boat might be in the same place when I returned.

After three or four attempts I finally found a spot that fulfilled both criteria - adequate depth alongside the bank, and four secure posts to which I could attach my four lines - head and stern rope and two springs. I was pretty confident that it would withstand any onslaught from the Locoboat racers and the drag from the hotel boats. It was about 100 metres or so from Annie's boat and she kindly told me that she would check it every day. I could relax a little and pack up my stuff ready for the long drive north to Calais. I still had one stupid mistake up my sleeve. I had shut down all the valves and then decided to give the batteries a final top up. I started the engine and had run it for about half an hour when I suddenly remembered that I had shut off the cooling water intake. What a total prat! This of course meant that the impeller had been running hot and more than likely suffered damage to the rubber blades. It was too late to do anything about it but I did mention it to Nick who was going to do a couple of jobs for me while the boat was in Ventenac. Nick was a former engineer with REME who lived on his boat in Narbonne. He had done some work in the past and I found him very competent and reliable. I explained what had happened and asked him to check it for me. There was nothing else I could do at that stage, other than rue my utter stupidity.

We retuned in the middle of October, we being Dave the retired Winterbourne Gunner Postmaster General and Andy, who had taken early retirement from Airbus.

We met up at Toulouse airport as Andy had flown from Hamburg and Dave and I had come down with Easy Jet from Bristol. As it was too late for the last train to Narbonne we spent the night in the Ibis Hotel across the road from the station, and enjoyed a couple of pints and a Mexican burger in our old favourite bar De Danu. Unfortunately, like all things these days, the place had changed hands and was now owned by the Charles Wells brewery who in their wisdom had stopped providing Guinness and replaced it with a very poor substitute called Inkwell, that looked and tasted like Quink Ink! Nothing's sacred. The burgers were OK though.

To my immense relief Saul Trader was exactly where I had left it and was none the worse for being abandoned for over three months. Annie came up trumps again and took us to the supermarché in Saint-Marcel for supplies, and then to Ginestas for an excellent meal in La Table du Casino.

We cast off from Ventenac at 08.00 on the 21st October. The plan was to do the trip to Toulouse Saint Sauveur in seven days which would mean an arrival on Thursday 27th. This would give us the Friday to see Serge about the unfinished jobs, and discuss any new work that needed to be done over the winter. The first coloured person in the woodpile reared its ugly head just 200 yards into the voyage. At PK159, just a kilometre and a half from where we set out, there is a U-shaped bend where the canal crosses the River Répudre on a small aqaduct. And that was exactly where I suddenly discovered that the rudder was not responding to the helm, or in layman's terms we had lost the bloody steering. Shit and merde!

I reversed out of the bend into the offside bushes, with a multitude of scenarios buzzing round me head, none of them particularly appealing. We had experienced problems with the hydraulic fluid in the past and Serge had fitted a new plug and gasket to the bottom of the reservoir. I checked this and found that the level had dropped slightly and there was a small amount of oil in the tray that I always left underneath it. I topped up the level and immediately felt more tension on the wheel. We got underway again and the steering returned to normal. I made a mental note to check the level every day and report the failure to Serge. In the event it did need a small amount each day and Andy found another small leakage underneath the bed in the stern where the hydraulic arm joined on to the top of the rudder stock. So having established that there was no serious problem we soldiered on. The plan for day one was to stop at Homps but as it was still mid afternoon, largely due to some well-timed passages through locks, we continued for another five kilometres to La Redorte. I was not hopeful of finding anything open as I had experienced the town before but Andy and Dave went out to explore and reported back that they had indeed found a restaurant - and it was open.

This was Chez Bibiche, a tasteful little place with a decidedly American gay feel. Stars and Stripes hanging from a balcony, large red Mick Jagger lips adorning the walls and even a small stage which I imagined had hosted some wildly erotic gay cabarets in the past. Not on this occasion however as there was only one other couple in the place and they looked perfectly heterosexual. The owner cum chef looked pretty dejected and I couldn't work out whether it was because of the lack of business or dwelling on the good times of the past when he would be cavorting on the stage in a tutu with plumes of feathers in his hair. The food was sufficient and we were grateful for that.

Next stop was Trèbes where we found another bar with a difference. This one had a bit more atmosphere and a good crowd and featured a live band who weren't at all bad (for France) with an open mic so that various wannabe Pop Idols could get up and sing a song. Most were only allowed the one, which tells you something about the quality of the performance but there was one young lady who took the place by storm. She was still there when we left at 11.00 o'clock and with my cynic's hat on I thought she must have secretly been one of the band who had been lurking in the distance, ready to strut her stuff.

The following day we made it to Carcassonne. We were doing really well and were now a good half day ahead of schedule. The boys were doing a great job scouting for restaurants and this time found an Italian establishment close to the canal. The place was packed and as it turned out, not especially for the food, but the après-déjeuner entertainment in the form of the ubiquitous Karaoke. After the usual somewhat feeble and embarrassing attempts at Elvis Presley and Jim Reeves impersonations, up stepped what was to be a revelation in the form of David Baker of Winterbourne Gunner, Salisbury. We had no idea of the talent that Dave had kept hidden under the microphone. After a quiet word with the master of ceremonies, Dave started hesitantly with an old favourite, the Elton John number 'Your Song',

If I was a sculptor, but then again no.
Or a man who makes potions in a travelling show
I know it's not much, but it's the best I can do
My gift is my song and this one's for you

And then the crowd went beserk, voices uplifted to the rafters in a wild celebration of song.

And you can tell everybody this is your song
It may be quite simple but now that it's gone
I hope you don't mind I hope you don't mind
That I put down in words
How wonderful life is while you're in the world

Now I realise that France is not exactly known for musical excellence. I mean take away Edith Piaf and Charles Aznavour and what have you got? They've won the Eurovision song contest five times - that's how bad they are. Dave's performance was not exactly up there with the Joe Cockers or Neil Diamonds but the audience were enraptured and I thought for a minute they were going to besiege him for autographs. It was like the end of a Billy Graham Evangelist meeting after the masses had been saved and seen the light. Nobody was more taken aback by this new found adoration than Dave himself. The only other time he had been moved to sing in public was at the Women's Institute annual party in the Winterbourne Village Hall, and that was after someone had spiked his sherry. Buoyed by this wave of mass hysteria Dave felt quite understandably that he couldn't let down his new legion of fans and after another nod and wink to the MC launched into a raucous rendering of 'Walk of Life' by Dire

Straits before finishing his act on a more sober note with a classy version of the Bee Gees 'Words'.

I thought we may have to be escorted from the premises by armed police to save us from the screaming fans but luckily they had all returned to their seats, propped up their walking sticks, parked their zimmer frames and settled down. I did record some of this on Dave's mobile phone but he was somewhat coy about it when I asked him and told me he had erased it! Personally I think it's going to be used as a video on his next Top of the Pops release.

Back down to earth, or water in this case, we sat on the boat with our black coffees and discussed the plans for the following day. I suggested an early start. We had done very well so far but you never knew what may lie around the corner in this boating business.

"We've got about four kiloms to the next lock so if we can get away at eight we should arrive in time for opening," I suggested.

This brought a grudging response from Elton Knopfler.

"Shouldn't have drunk all that rum," he moaned, "those chicks just kept buying me drinks."

"Er well, for 'chicks' read "grandmas', I said a little unfairly.

We did get away at eight and I was grateful for having such a willing crew. We made excellent progress and kept going through my original planned overnight stop at Bram to tie up on the lock pontoon at Guillermin. We were now 11 kilometres and eight locks further than planned. Good work indeed, but as it happened, just as well.

We ate on board for a change - ham eggs chips and beans. I was reminded of a saying that Ron was fond of repeating. If we had any ham we could have ham and eggs if we had any eggs. It was quiet and peaceful, without a single karaoke within earshot.

We passed through Guillermine lock at 09.00, and then on the way to the three lock staircase at Vivier, we were caught up by a hire boat that had been moored in the pound. It was one of those huge Le Boat vessels that sleep about 10 people with a beam wider than Saul Trader. We got off to a bad start when the 'lady' lock-keeper kept us waiting for no apparent reason for 15 minutes before she deemed to open her gates for us. Andy jumped off at the pontoon and ran up to the lock as I motored slowly in and moored as I usually did whenever possible port side to the wall. Dave threw up the head rope eye which Andy dropped over the centre bollard and I gently eased forward to take up the strain with the rope leading astern at an angle of about 30°. Then Dave went aft and threw another shorter rope for Andy to drop over the bollard at the stern. Perfect! Except it wasn't perfect for Madame Éclusier.

There wasn't enough room for Le Boat's four and a half metre beam to get past me into the lock so the Madame insisted that we move Saul Trader forward. I went into insult mode. This entailed miming obscenities at the good lady - not actually saying anything but going through the motions as it were to get my feelings across. This had absolutely no affect whatsoever and so we had to adjust everything to accommodate her demands. After several attempts, with Saul Trader's bow virtually in contact with the upper gate, and Le Boat wedged against my stern quarter, resulting in more harsh and entirely unnecessary confrontations, madame finally realised that this wasn't going to work - something I tried to tell her 20 minutes earlier but she ignored with a dogged persistence. The final irony occurred as Le Boat reversed back out of the lock just as another hire boat appeared around the corner. I'm sure it wasn't totally because she was a large aggressive woman who had let a little bit of power go to her head. Maybe she had had a bad night and got out of the wrong side of the bed that morning.

Later in the trip over a beer, Andy, who was always calm and collected, told me that I should be more 'tolerant.' Patience of a saint more to the point and that I had to admit, I did not possess. So after successfully passing through the double staircase at Gay and the four that make up the St Roche staircase, we arrived at Castelnaudary in the middle of the afternoon. And there we stayed after a very friendly skipper moved his boat a metre or so to give us enough room to tie up on the quay opposite the ever busy headquarters of the local Pompiers. For the first time on this trip we now had a few hours to relax and while the boys went off to the town to explore the bars, I made myself known to the Port Capitan, paid my dues and received in return the magic swipe card for the electricity and the all-important code for the Wifi.

In the evening, after a couple of demi-pressions in the Grand Bar we made our way to Le Cassoulet Gormand restaurant on the quay where rather than the ubiquitous cassoulet I enjoyed an excellent pork filet mignon with gratin potatoes and petit pois followed by an equally irresistible Café Gourmand. If you've never experienced this sweet delight you really should give it a try. It is found on the menu of most restaurants in France, and although it varies from place to place, you can usually be treated to small tasters of such desserts as ice-cream, chocolate mousse, apple pie with cream, créme brulee, raspberry cheesecake and an expresso coffee. A perfect way to finish a meal without piling on excessive calories. Well that's what they told me anyway!

We were doing well and after a long day of 25 kilomteres and 13 locks, we tied for the night at Gardouche. For the first time ever there was a space for us right alongside the quay. Things were definitely looking up and with a fair wind we would be in Saint Sauveur on the following day, the Thursday, just as I had planned. This of course was a fateful mistaker to maker and I should have remembered the old sailor's superstition. Never predict your destination in advance. Never!

We set off early with the best of intentions and successfully negotiated the double staircase locks at Laval. There was a fresh northeasterly wind blowing across the canal which called for concentration to keep the boat in a straight line. Then after one kilometre I heard the dreaded hollow sound of the exhaust, which could only mean one thing. There was a blockage in the raw water intake that was preventing adequate cold water circulating the engine. A quick glance at the temperature gauge confirmed my fears. It was reading 100°. This could mean one of several things, the simplest of which was that the filter was blocked with silt drawn in from the canal. It was an easy enough job to check this. I slowed the boat down and stopped the engine while Andy took the wheel in a vain attempt to keep the boat as near as possible to the middle of the cut while I dived down to the engine room, shut off the intake valve and removed the filter. It was completely clear. This was the worst possible scenario. Had it been blocked I could have cleared it and all would have been well. As it was there was something else, something that would take much longer to fix, that was causing the problem. The next obvious course of action was to check the impeller for damage but in order to do this we first had to get the boat secured to the bank. The wind had already blown us into the bushes on the offside and there was a steep bank of trees on the towpath side. I started the engine and tried to gently manoeuvre to the opposite side against the wind. Andy managed a leap from the bow on to the bank and get a rope around a tree which Dave secured to the bits, but the strength of the wind prevented me getting the stern away from the opposite bushes. After about fifteen minutes of trying, albeit without risking putting on too many revs, we gave up. We would have to stay as we were sprawled across the cut. If any boats appeared we would have to get them to push their way past. There was nothing more we could do.

Back down below Andy set to work checking the impeller. Once he had removed the end plate he declared that it looked to be fine so we tried again with the same result. We were in a very isolated spot and luckily no other boats had appeared but I knew we couldn't stay where we were for much longer. We were about a kilometre and a half from the next lock at Négra, where I knew there was a long pontoon that was formerly used by a hire company. We gave it half an hour for the engine to cool down sufficiently before very cautiously heading off. Luckily no other boats had appeared during our enforced stay. Tying up securely on the pontoon at Négra almost felt like heaven. At least we could now have a closer look at things without the fear of being run into, or at the very least causing considerable inconvenience to other vessels.

The first thing as always in these situations - coffee, and in my case cigarette. Time to take stock and plan the next course of action. Andy was all too familiar with the cooling system as he had been with us when with Frank several years ago, he had spent half a day sorting out a similar problem. We were still miles from anywhere with no chance of finding any assistance. We were on our own. While Dave and Andy set about the job I fretted about what we were going to do if all else failed and we were stuck here in the wilds. We all had flights booked from Toulouse for the Sunday, and that was now looking ominously close. We were still some thirty kilometres and six locks from home.

The consensus was that there must be a blockage somewhere in the system so the first thing was to disconnect the copper pipe that led from the impeller to the heat exchanger. Having removed this we found piece of rubber about an inch long that had obviously come from a damaged impeller. When Andy had inspected it earlier he had only looked at one side and assumed it must have been OK, but this latest piece of evidence contradicted that assumption. Sure enough when the impeller was removed the inner end was found to have several chewed blades. After our last escapade I had always ensured that I kept at least two spares. The new one was fitted and the copper pipe reconnected and we started the engine with a renewed optimism. It ran for half an hour on tickover and the temperature remained at normal. It was too late in the day to move anyway and we resigned ourselves to another night of Dave's cooking. I have to say that I was not entirely convinced that we had solved the problem as the exhaust note did still not seem quite right, but I kept my thoughts to myself.

We had only covered less than two kilometres the next morning before the temperature started to rise again. The problem, as I feared, had not gone away.The only good thing was that we had a decent stretch of towpath side and the wind had subsided considerably. We managed to get a rope fore and aft around some tree roots, probably not fully sanctioned, and re-think our strategy. When I say 'we' I of course meant Dave and Andy. My main role was that of chief fretter and coffee supplier. The entire system had to be disconnected and washed through to clear any obstruction. The copper pipe - clear; the heat exchanger, all 70 odd tubes blown through - clear, and finally the length of pipe that connected the heat exchanger to the overboard outlet - all clear. Once it was all re-connected we started the engine again and - exactly the same result, no water getting through. Andy was beginning to doubt himself which was a serious problem with a highly skilled and experienced aircraft technician. Heads were scratched and shaken in disbelief and I looked over at the A61 motorway a few hundred yards from us and wondered what the chances would be of hitching a lift into Toulouse.

As a last resort we spoke to Serge to see whether he could offer any advice but he too was at a loss. He very kindly offered to come and find us but not before 5.00pm.

Things were getting desperate. Ten minutes later, while we were all dejectedly contemplating our navels, Serge rang back. "You must have an air lock," he said, "can't be anything else." Before he had rung off Andy leapt from his chair with a jubilant cry.

"Of course, of course," he exclaimed, already half way down the stairs to the engine room.

Ten minutes later, after a blow back of water that nearly drowned Dave, we had a lift off, or to be exact we had water gushing through the system into the canal ensuring that the engine kept nice and cool. We couldn't get the ropes untied fast enough. It was 1.00pm and I estimated that we could reach Ste Sauveur in about 6 hours. We might just make it before it got dark.

Once through the very last and very deep lock at Castanet, I switched on the nav lights and we crept slowly past the long line of liveaboard boats that inhabit the towpath for miles through Ramonville in the deepening gloom. There was no way I was going to stop now. The Capitanerie at Ste Sauveur had arranged for someone to show us our mooring and he appeared on the pontoon as we approached to take our lines and welcome us home. We had made it. Against all the odds we had made it.

By the time we had fully secured it was 8.00pm, Friday the 28th October. We explained our late arrival and were told that a lot of boats had suffered similar problems caused by the silt stirred up as a result of unusually low water levels.

I accepted this news as exoneration of the feelings of guilt I had been quietly harbouring over the past few days. So it wasn't the fact that I had run the engine dry in Ventenac back in July that had been the cause of the trouble after all. I thanked the boys for their unstinting devotion to duty in our hour of need and treated them to burgers and beer in De Danu that very evening.

Favourite mooring next to the Tarn - and the railway

Moissac. Our new Home Port

A study in front ends

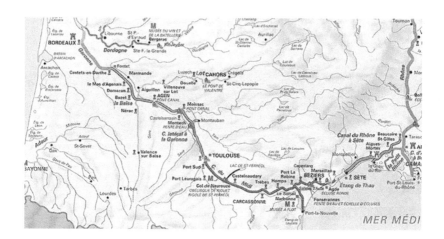

Footnote

In the Spring of 2020 I got the terrible news that Jim, the port Capitan at Moissac, had passed away. Everyone who knew him would be shocked and saddened at the news.

When I last saw Jim in the previous October, he was his usual boisterous, bustling self, always ready to stop for a chat or share a joke as he patrolled his territory along the quay.

Jim, and his lovely wife Sandra, had taken over the running of the port just a few years ago, and they were doing a fantastic job.

Rest in Peace Jim. We will all miss you.

I will never forget your friendly welcome and your performance at the Friday Karaoke nights in the Bluebell, singing your brilliant version of the classic Jimmy Buffett song, 'Margaritaville.

SAUL TRADER LOG - JUN 2012 - AUG 2018

BOOK 4 A LOT OF WATER			2972				14509.5		3294
13.07.12	1100	1630	4.5	2977	Ventenac	Capestang	29	14538.5		3294
14.07.12	1100	1500	4	2981	Capestang	Argeliers	25	14563.5		3294
16.07.12	0800	1100	3	2984	Argeliers	Salelles d'Aude	8	14571.5	5	3299
				2984	DIESEL 600 ltrs @ 1			14571.5		3299
05.09.12	1400	1800	4	2988	Salelles d 'Aude	Ventenac	13	14584.5	5	3304
07.09.12	1030	1530	4.5	2992	Ventenac	Capestang	29	14613.5		3304
08.09.12	1000	1800	5.5	2998	Capestang	Roubia	33	14646.5		3304
09.09.12	0930	1900	9.5	3007	Roubia	Marseillette	28	14674.5	11	3315
10.09.12	0900	1700	8	3015	Marseillettes	Carcassonne	22	14696.5	7	3322
11.09.12	1330	1700	3.5	3019	Carcassonne	Trebes	13	14709.5	6	3328
12.09.12	0830	1900	8.5	3027	Trebes	La Redorte	21	14730.5	6	3334
13.09.12	0830	1530	6	3033	La Redorte	Ventenac	23	14753.5	6	3340
				3033	OIL AND FILTER CHANGE			14753.5		3340
				3033				14753.5		3340
07.07.13	1000	1100	1	3034	Ventenac	La Somail	4	14757.5		3340
08.07.13	1030	1430	4	3038	La Somail	Capestang	25	14782.5		3340

245

SAUL TRADER LOG - JUN 2012 - AUG 2018

Date	Start	End	Hrs	No.	From	To	Km	Total		No.
09.07.13	0930	1430	5	3043	Capestang	Sallelles d'Aude	33	14815.5	5	3345
10.07.13	1030	1830	8	3051	Salelles d 'Aude	Homps	27	14842.5	10	3355
11.07.13	1000	1300	3	3054	Homps	Puicheric	9	14851.5	3	3358
12.07.13 1030	1500	3	3057	Puicheric	Marseillette	9	14860.5	3	3361
13.07.13	1230	1500	2.5	3060	Marseillettes	Trebes	9	14869.5	1	3362
14.07.13	1000	1600	5	3065	Trebes	Carcassonne	13	14882.5	6	3368
				3065	Left S/T outside po - 3 weeks !			14882.5		3368
04.08.13	1000	1100	1	3066	Carcassonne	Penhautier	3	14885.5	1	3369
06.08.13	1000	1700	6	3072	Penhautier	Bram	21	14906.5	4	3373
07.08.13 1000	1700	6	3078	Bram	Castelnaudary	16	14922.5	12	3385
				3078	Retrieve car from Ventenac - train an bike (10 kiloms)			14922.5		3385
12.08.13	1030	1500	4	3082	Castelnaudary	Le Segala	10.5	14933	5	3390
13.08.13	1130	1700	4	3086	Le Segala	Gardouche	15	14948	4	3394
14.08.13	1000	1630	4.5	3090	Gardouche	St Jouzy/ Castane	28	14976	7	3401
15.08.13	1000	1200	2	3092	Castanets	Toulouse	5.5	14981.5	1	3402
17.08.13	0900	1700	7.5	3100	Toulouse	Grisolle	32.5	15014	13	3415
18.08.13	1100	1400	3	3103	Grisolle	Montech	16	15030	1	3416
19.08.13 1130	1530	3	3106	Montech	Montauban	10	15040	9	3425

SAUL TRADER LOG - JUN 2012 - AUG 2018

20.08.13	1000	1730	6.5	3112	Montauban	Castelsarassin	23	15063	17	3442
21.08.13	1400	1600	2	3114	Castelsarassin	Moissac	8	15071	7	3449
22.08.13	1200	1600	3.5	3118	Moissac	Valence d'Agen	17	15088	5	3454
24.08.13	1200	1700	4.5	3122	Valence	Agen	26	15114	3	3457
25.08.13	1100	1400	3	3125	Agen	Serignac	12	15126	4	3461
26.08.13	0930	1730	7	3132	Serignac	Valence d'Agen	38	15164	7	3468
27.08.13	1230	1630	4	3136	Valence	Moissac	17	15181	5	3473
28.10.13	1400	1600	2	3138	Moissac	Castelsarassin	8	15189	7	3480
29.08.13	1000	1530	5	3143	Castelsarassin	Valence d'Agen	25	15214	12	3492
				3143				15214		3492
29.10.13				3143	DIESEL - 400 LTRS II 20 LTR DRUMS			15214		3492
				3143				15214		3492
04.07.14	1130	1300	1.5	3145	Valence	Pommevic	2.5	15216.5	1	3493
05.07.14	1030	1430	3	3148	Pommevic	Moissac	14.5	15231	4	3497
07.07.14	1300	1700	4	3152	Moissac	Valence d'Agen	17	15248	5	3502
09.07.14	1130	1800	6	3158	Valence	Serignac	38	15286	7	3509
11.07.14	1100	1600	4	3162	Serignac	Buzet	16.5	15302.5	3	3512
14.07.14	1200	1815	5	3167	Buzet	Mas d'Agenais - Villeton	27	15329.5	6	3518

247

SAUL TRADER LOG - JUN 2012 - AUG 2018

15.07.14	1000	1600	5	3172	Villeton	Meilhan	26	15355.5	5	3523
17.07.14	1100	1800	4.5	3176	Meilhan	Castets en Dorthe	18	15373.5	6	3529
				3176	Stern tube work by Adam Townsend and Fred good job but bloody expensive			15373.5		3529
25.07.14	1200	1500	3	3179	Castets en Dorthe	Fontet	11.5	15385	5	3534
28.07.14	1200	1500	3	3182	Fontet	Meilhan	7	15392	1	3535
31.07.14	1200	1800	5.5	3188	Meilhan	Villeton	26	15418	5	3540
01.08.14	1130	1500	3.5	3191	Villeton	Caumont	13	15431		3540
02.08.14	1130	1430	2.5	3194	Caumont	Tersac	8	15439	3	3543
03.08.14	1400	1500	1	3195	Tersac	Meilhan	3	15442	2	3545
05.08.14	1100	1400	3	3198	Meilhan	Villeton	26	15468	5	3550
06.08.14	1000	1330	2.5	3200	Villeton	Buzet	13	15481	2	3552
07.08.14	1200	1630	3.5	3204	Buzet	Serignac	16.5	15497.5	3	3555
08.08.14	0930	1230	3	3207	Serignac	Agen	12	15509.5	4	3559
09.08.14	1000	1430	4.5	3211	Agen	Valence	26	15535.5	3	3562
10.08.14	1430	1830	4	3215	Valence	Moissac	17	15552.5	5	3567
15.08.14	0930	1300	3.5	3219	Moissac	Valence	17	15569.5	5	3572
18.08.14	1000	1630	6.5	3225	Valence	Serignac	38	15607.5	7	3579

248

SAUL TRADER LOG - JUN 2012 - AUG 2018

19.08.14	0930	1230	3	3228	Serignac	Buzet	16.5	15624	3	3582
20.08.14	1500	1730	2.5	3231	Buzet	Vianne	17	15641	3	3585
21.08.14				3231	Vianne			15641		3585
22.08.14	1030	1500	2	3233	Vianne	Buzet	17	15658	3	3588
				3233				15658		3588
26.08.14	1200	1600	4	3237	Buzet	Serignac	16.5	15674.5	3	3591
27.08.14	1045	1815	7.5	3244	Serignac	Valence	38	15712.5	7	3598
				3244				15712.5		3598
				3244	400 litres DIESEL in drums - OIL CHANG			15712.5		3598
				3244	Genny battery replaced			15712.5		3598
15.06.15	1500	1600	1	3245	Valence	Pommervic	4	15716.5	2	3600
17.06.15	1000	1400	3.5	3249	Pommevic	Moissac	14.5	15731	4	3604
19.06.15	1000	1900	8.5	3257	Moissac	Grisolles	24	15755	8	3612
20.06.15	0830	1700	8.5	3266	Grisolles	Toulouse	33	15788	12	3624
23.06.15	0700	1000	3	3269	Ste Sauveur	Calle seche	2	15790	0	3624
23.06 - 09.07. 15				3269				15790		3624
09.07.15	0900	1000	1	3270	Calle seche	Ste Sauveur	2	15792	0	3624

SAUL TRADER LOG - JUN 2012 - AUG 2018

10.07.15	1030	1900	8.5	3278	Ste Sauveur	Gardouche	33	15825	9	3633
11.07.15	0900	1630	6	3284	Gardouch - Lauraga	La Segala	16	15841	6	3639
12.07.15	0830	1230	4	3288	La Segala	Castelnaudary	10	15851	8	3647
13.07.15	0800	1800	9	3297	Castelnaudary	Ecluse Lalande (37	33	15884	21	3668
14.07.15	1000	1300	3	3300	Lalande	Carcassonne	8	15892	5	3673
17.07.15	0930	1530	7.5	3308	Carcassonne - Treb - Marseilette		22	15914	9	3682
18.07.15	1000	1600	5.5	3313	Marseilette - Puich ic - Homps		18	15932	11	3693
19.07.15	1030	1730	4.5	3318	Homps	Ventenac	16	15948	6	3699
20.07.15 1300		1630	3.5	3321	Ventenac	Sallelle d'Aude	10	15958	5	3704
21.07.15	1400	1700	3	3324	Sallelle	Narbonne	12	15970	4	3708
23.07.15	0930	1900	7	3331	Narbonne	Sallelle d'Aude	12	15982	6	3714
24.07.15	0930	1800	8.5	3340	Sallelle	Homps	30	16012	12	3726
25.07.15	1030	1200	1.5	3341	Homps	La Redorte	6	16018	1	3727
26.07.15	1030	1900	8	3349	La Redorte	Trebes	20	16038	8	3735
27.07.15 0930		1830	8	3357	Trebes - Carcassonr	Lalande	20	16058	14	3749
28.07.15	0830	1800	8.5	3366	Lalande	Castelnaudary	33	16091	21	3770
30.07.15	0830	1800	9	3375	Castelnaudary	Gardouch	26	16117	13	3783
31.07.15 0900		1400	4.5	3379	Gardouch	Montisgard	14	16131	8	3791

01.08.15		1200	3	3382	Montisgard	Ramonville Port	13	16144	2	3793
	0900									
				3382				16144		3793
				3382	All TRIWV work completed by Serge	Gas Certificate done by Mick Tubb		16144		3793
24.10.15	1200	1400	2	3384	Ramonville	Ste Sauveur	2	16146	10	3803
25.10.15	1000	1715	7	3391	Ste Sauveur	Grissolles	33	16179	12	3815
26.10.15	1030	1330	3	3394	Grissolles	Montech	15	16194	1	3816
27.10.15	1100	1400	3	3397	Montech	Castelsarrassin	8	16202	8	3824
				3397				16202		3824
02.07.16	1100	1700	5	3402	Castelsarassin	Valence d'Agen	25	16227	12	3836
				3402	START BATTERIES REPLACED			16227		3836
04.07.16	1100	1830	7	3409	Valence d'Agen	Sérignac	38	16265	7	3843
				3409				16265		3843
				3409	STARTER MOTOR EN PANNE			16265		3843
27.07.16	1200	1600	4	3413	Sérignac	Buzet	16.5	16281.5	3	3846
28.07.16	1230	1600	3.5	3417	Buzet	Mas d'Agenais	21	16302.5	3	3849
29.07.16	1100	1500	4	3421	Mas d'Agenais	Meilhan	20	16322.5	4	3853
30.07.16	1100	1600	5	3426	Meilhan	Castets en Dorthe	17	16339.5	4	3857

SAUL TRADER LOG - JUN 2012 - AUG 2018

Date				No.	From	To					
31.07.16	1700	1830	1.5	3427	Castets en Dorthe	Pont de Bassande	4	16343.5	2	3859
01.08.16	1000	1400	3	3430	Bassande	Meilhan	11	16354.5	2	3861
02.08.16	1030	1730	6	3436	Meilhan	Villeton	25	16379.5	4	3865
03.08.16	1200	1530	5	3441	Villeton	Buzet	13	16392.5	2	3867
04.08.16	1000	1400	4	3445	Buzet	Sérignac	16.5	16409	3	3870
05.08.16	1000	1130	2.5	3448	Sérignac	Agen	11	16420	4	3874
06.08.16	1030	1530	5	3453	Agen	Valence d'Agen	25	16445	3	3877
08.08.16	1000	1130	1.5	3454	Valence d'Agen	Pommevic	4	16449	2	3879
				3454	Hot Water Cylinder pipe with pin hole			16449		3879
.10.08.16	1030	1530	3	3457	Pommevic	Moissac	13	16462	3	3882
11.08.16	1230	1730	4	3461	Moissac	PK 86 Lac Bleu Bergon	22	16484	5	3887
12.08.16	1030	1530	4	3465	PK 86	Agen Comm Port	22	16506	3	3890
13.08.16	1000	1230	2.5	3468	Agen	Sérignac	11	16517	4	3894
15.08.16	1200	1500	3	3471	Sérignac	Buzet	16.5	16533.5	3	3897
				3471	Dave/Becks Alterna or problem			16533.5		3897
18.08.16	1100	1430	3.5	3474	Buzet	Mas d'Agenais	20	16553.5	4	3901
19.08.16	930	1600	6.5	3481	Mas d'Agenais	Castets en Dorthe	36	16589.5	8	3909
21.08.16	1630	1800	1.5	3482	Castets en Dorthe	Bassande	4	16593.5	2	3911

SAUL TRADER LOG - JUN 2012 - AUG 2018

22.08.16	915	1645	7.5	3490	Bassande	Villeton	39	16632.5	7	3918
23.08.16	930	1330	3	3493	Villeton	Buzet	13	16645.5	2	3920
24.08.16	1000	1400	3.5	3496	Buzet	Sérignac	16.5	16662	3	3923
				3496	5 weeks mooring 75 Euros -			16662		3923
10.10.16	1200	1430	2.5	3499	Sérignac	Agen	11	16673	4	3927
11.10.16	930	1500	5.5	3504	Agen	Valence d'Agen	25	16698	3	3930
12.10.16	1100	1500	4	3508	Valence d'Agen	Moissac	17	16715	5	3935
13.10.16	1100	1700	6	3514	Moissac	Montech	21	16736	14	3949
14.10.16	900	1700	8	3522	Montech	PK1 Garonne	40	16776	10	3959
15.10.16	1130	1400	2.5	3525	PK1	Ste Sauveur	5	16781	3	3962
17.10 16	930	1100	1.5	3526	Ste Sauveur	Ramonville Port	86	16867	0	3962
				3526	DIESEL 600 ltrs @ 1			16867		3962
08.05.17	1430	1630	2	3528	Ramonville	Ste Sauveur	8	16875	0	3962
10.05.17	800	1800	10	3538	Ste Sauveur	Gardouche	33	16908	9	3971
11.05.17	930	1800	8	3546	Gardouche	Castelnaudary	26	16934	14	3985
12.05.17	1400	1800	4	3550	Castelnaudary	Villepinte	11	16945	15	4000
13.05.17	830	1600	7.5	3558	Villepinte	Carcassonne	29	16974	10	4010
15.05.17	830	1600	7.5	3565	Carcassonne	Marseillette	22	16996	9	4019

SAUL TRADER LOG - JUN 2012 - AUG 2018

Date				No.	From	To				
16.05.17	1000	1600	6	3571	Marseillettes	Homps	18	17014	10	4029
17.05.17	1100	1800	6	3577	Homps	Ventenac	16	17030	6	4035
				3577	6 DOMESTIC BATTEI IES REPLACE NUMA) 110 AMP/HR			17030		4035
				3577	OIL FILTER CHANGE STEERING FLUID TO UP			17030		4035
15.06.17	1130	1600	4.5	3582	Ventenac	Capestang	27	17057	0	4035
16.06.17	1130	1630	5	3587	Capestang	Béziers	20	17077	7	4042
18.06.17	1030	1230	2	3589	Béziers	Villeneuve	5	17082	3	4045
19.06.17	1130	1500	3.5	3592	Villeneuve	Agde	17	17099	1	4046
20.06.17	1030	1700	5	3597	Agde	Frontignan	28	17127	0	4046
21.06.17	1100	1600	7	3604	Frontignan	Aigues Mortes	40	17167		4046
22.06.17	700	1600	9	3613	Aigues-Mortes	Beaucaire	55	17222	1	4047
				3613				17222		4047
26.06.17	1400	1700	3	3616	Beaucaire	Ste Gilles	24	17246	1	4048
27.06.17	1030	1500	4.5	3621	Ste Gilles	Aigues Mortes	25	17271		4048
29.06.17	1400	1830	4.5	3625	Aigues-Mortes	Frontignan	40	17311		4048
30.06.17	830	1500	6.5	3632	Frontignan	Agde	28	17339	1	4049
01.07.17	1000	1400	4	3636	Agde	Villeneuve	17	17356		4049

02.07.17	1400	1830	4.5	3640	Villeneuve	Colombieres	13	17369	11	4060
03.07.17	1000	1200	2	3642	Colombieres	Poilhes	7	17376	0	4060
04.07.17	1000	1200		3642	Poilhes	Capestang	6	17382		4060
05.07.17	1200	1700	5	3647	Capestang	Ventenac	27	17409		4060
				3647	DERV 500 LITRES			17409		4060
21.09.17	1830	2000	1.5	3649	Ventenac	Bottom lock Argen	11	17420	0	4060
22.09.17	900	1730	8.5	3657	Argens	Puicheric	15	17435	9	4069
23.09.17	830	1800	9.5	3667	Puicheric	Carcassonne	19	17454	16	4085
25.09.17	1030	1900	5	3672	Carcassonne	Villesque	11	17465	6	4091
26.09.17	900	1800	7	3679	Villesquelande	Castelnaudary	26	17491	20	4111
27.09.17	900	1800	9	3688	Castelnaudary	La Segala	11	17502	7	4118
28.09.17	900	1700	8	3696	La Segala	Montgiscard	29	17531	11	4129
29.09.17	900	1400	7	3703	Montgiscard	Ste Sauveur	20	17551	3	4132
01.10.17	1500	1600	1	3704	Ste Sauveur	Ramonville Port	8	17559	0	4132
11.05.18	1100	1500	3	3707	Ramonville	Ste Sauveur	8	17567		4132
17.05.18	1100	1300	2	3709	Ste Sauveur	Ramonville	8	17575		4132
05.07.18	1400	1600	2	3711	Port Technique	Ste Sauveur	7	17582	0	4132
10.07.18	830	1600	7.5	3718	Ste Sauveur	Lamothe	36	17618	12	4144

SAUL TRADER LOG - JUN 2012 - AUG 2018

10.07.18	1600	1800	2	3720	Lamothe	Montech	14	17632		1	4145
11.07.18	1100	1600	3	3723	Montech	Castelsarrassin	13	17645		8	4153
12.07.18	1400	1630	2.5	3726	Castelsarassin	Moissac	8	17653		7	4160
15.07.18	1100	1600	3	3729	Moissac	Valence d'Agen	18	17671		5	4165
16.07.18	1430	1530	1	3730	Valence d'Agen	Pommervic	3	17674		2	4167
				3730				17674			4167
02.08.18	1100	1500	4	3734	Pommevic	Moissac	14	17688		3	4170
04.08.18	1300	1700	4	3738	Moissac	Valence d'Agen	17	17705		5	4175
06.08.18	1130	1530	4	3742	Valence d'Agen	Agen	27	17732		3	4178
07.08.18	1000	1630	5	3747	Agen	Buzet	29	17761		7	4185
08.08 18	1100	1400	3	3750	Buzet	Sérignae	16	17777		3	4188
09.08.18	800	1500	7	3757	Sérignac	Valence d'Agen	38	17815		7	4195
10.08.18	1030	1430	3	3760	Valence d'Agen	Moissac	17	17832		5	4200
13.08.18	1200	1500	3	3763	Moissac	Valence d'Agen	17	17849		5	4205
17.08.18	1200	1300	1	3764	Valence d'Agen	Pommevic	3	17852		2	4207
18.08.18	1100	1800	7	3771	Pommevic	Castelsarassin	20	17872		9	4216

256

With grateful thanks to all those who accompanied me on these trips for putting up with me and adding to the quality of the experience with their humour and knowledge and the bonus of their company.

Particular thanks to Allen Maslen for his input and encouragement - a legend and an inspiration.
Allen has written several interesting books which can also be found on Kindle.

Author Page

I was born and brought up in Hastings, beside the sea, and many miles from the nearest navigable canal.

It was not until 1976 that we hired our first narrowboat from North Kilworth and spent a week circumnavigating the Midlands. I was immediately hooked.

I had always had a keen interest in railways and the canals held the same fascination for me.

I bought my first narrowboat in 1984 and got the chance to add the replica Dutch Luxemotor barge to the "fleet", in 1998.

I still have both boats and I still get the same "kick" when I go aboard after an absence.

The lore of the Cut has stayed with me and will do so as long as I live.

Keith Harris

The Complete Saul Trader Series of Books

Available from my website: www.keithharrisauthor.com

And from Mortons Publishing: www.mortonsbooks.co.uk

Book 1 . We Don't Go Far but We Do See Life
Apr 1998 - Oct 2002

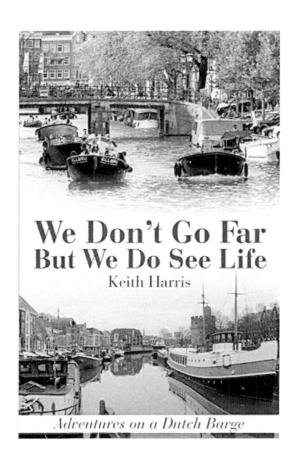

This is the first of a series of four books that follow the voyages of the Dutch barge 'Saul Trader' from the River Severn in Gloucestershire to Bordeaux in the South West corner of France. Stories of the people and the places, the ups and the downs of travel on a barge around Europe, told with a liberal helping of tongue-in-cheek and enlivened with a fair smattering of anecdote and humour. We navigate the sometime treacherous waters of the Severn Estuary and drag the bottom of the Kennet & Avon Canal to the River Thames and London, before braving the busy shipping lanes of the English Channel to reach France. We suffer the first of several flooded bilges, climb through the four Belgian boat lifts and get serenaded at a music festival, dodge the massive ships in the water motorways of Holland and enjoy the spectacle of the Dordrecht in Steam weekend, before savouring the delights and dangers of Amsterdam to Friesland along smaller more typical Dutch waterways , lockless and lined with windmills. Finally we return to France after a hairy passage of the turbulent Albert Canal and the excitement of the Ronquierres Plane and brand new Strepy-Thieu boat life, to winter in Cambrai.

Also available in the Saul Trader Series by Keith Harris

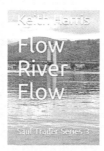
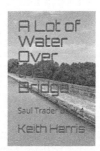

In the second book we venture back into Belgium and the Chantier Naval boatyard at Namur. Then to Paris via the River Meuse, the Oise and Seine. From Paris we follow the Marne to Epernay and Chalons en Champagne before returning to Landrecies for the Winter.

The following Spring we go south to Nancy and Toul before heading East on the Marne-Rhine canal to Strasbourg and thence to the mighty Rhine for a somewhat hairy two day passage to Mulhouse.

After that we travel the equally hairy River Doubs for our next wintering at St Symphorien. - after some expensive renewal work, we explore the central canals of France including the Nivernais before our next winter resting-place at Jo Parfitt's base in Laroche Migennes.

Our escapades include running aground, flooded bilges and a burglary, getting banned from driving, and held up for miles on end by obstinate éclusiers.

I can tell your mouths are watering in anticipation. Come aboard - you're more than welcome - but take off your shoes first please.

The third book in the series about the voyages of Saul Trader on the waterways of Europe. Flow River Flow covers our travels on the Nivernais in France before a return to Holland for a repaint and a circular trip around the Netherlands before returning south via Belgium and the River Meuse to the Canal de L'Est and River Saone. Finally we bite the bullet and take the one-way street that is the mighty Rhone to the Camargue and Canal du Midi. Once again the book describes the characters that we encounter and attempts to describe the scenes with anecdote and humour. It is a social account of our travels rather than a detailed record of the history or the geography of the places we pass through. The primary object was to record the adventure with a touch of humour and a sprinkling of satire which I hope will put a smile on your face and even at times cause some outbursts of laughter.

This is the fourth and (probably) last in the Saul Trader series. We have now reached the sultry summer climes of the south of France and seem reluctant to return to the frozen north. We travel to the western end of the Midi encountering more characters in the shape of an enterprising Belgian hippie and his crazy Dutch girlfriend, a naval officer that goes by the name of Tommy Trinder and a boules-obsessed English country vicar. In the cosmopolitan city of Toulouse, a city of contrasts, we find amongst the hubbub a real Irish bar and suffer once again at the hands of the kleptomaniac. There is solace on the Canal Garonne and an expensive and nearly disastrous repair job at Castets en Dorthe.

Pretty towns come and go as we pass through the peaceful settlements of the Garonne - Moissac, Meilhan and Mas d'Agenais with its secret treasure. There are more characters, some good and some not so - a gift from the skipper of a hotel barge for being 'nice', and a wonderfully helpful and proficient repairer of all things boat. We retrace steps back to the Rhone, crossing the large inland sea, the Etang de Thau, and are held up by more breakdowns resulting in parts having to be sent from England, and our guests bravely enduring 100° heat for hours on end to sort out problems with, of all things, overheating! We finally return to the lovely welcoming port of Moissac where we find a permanent year- round mooring.

You can buy direct from my website: www.keithharrisauthor.com
Or contact me on keith.arris@outlook.com

Book 2 . We'll Cross That Bridge When We Go Under It

Apr 2003 - Nov 2008

In the second book we venture from Cambrai back into Belgium and the Chantier Naval boatyard at Namur.

Then to Paris via the River Meuse, the Oise and Seine.

From Paris we follow the Marne to Epernay and Chalons en Champagne before returning to Landrecies for the Winter.

The following Spring we go south to Nancy and Toul before heading East on the Marne-Rhine canal to Strasbourg and thence to the mighty Rhine for a somewhat hairy two day passage to Mulhouse.

After that we travel the equally hairy River Doubs for our next wintering at St Symphorien.

The following year, after some expensive renewal work, we explore the central canals of France including the Nivernais before our next winter resting-place at Jo Parfitt's base in Laroche Migennes.

Our escapades include running aground, flooded bilges and a burglary, getting banned from driving, and held up for miles on end by obstinate bateliers.

I can tell your mouths are watering in anticipation

Come aboard - you're more than welcome - but take off your shoes first please.

Jun 2009 - May 2012

The third book in the series about the voyages of Saul Trader on the waterways of Europe. Flow River Flow covers our travels on the Nivernais in France before a return to Holland for a repaint and a circular trip around the Netherlands before returning south via Belgium and the River Meuse to the Canal de L'Est and River Saone. Finally we bite the bullet and take the one-way street that is the mighty Rhone to the Camargue and Canal du Midi. Once again the book describes the characters that we encounter and attempts to describe the scenes with anecdote and humour. It is a social account of our travels rather than a detailed record of the history or the geography of the places we pass through. The primary object was to record the adventure with a touch of humour and a sprinkling of satire which I hope will put a smile on your face and even at times cause some laughter.

Book 4. A Lot of Water Over the Bridge

July 2012 - Aug 2018

This is the fourth and (probably) last in the Saul Trader series. We have now reached the sultry summer climes of the south of France and seem reluctant to return to the frozen north. We travel to the western end of the Midi encountering more characters in the shape of an enterprising Belgian hippie and his crazy Dutch girlfriend, a naval officer that goes by the name of Tommy Trinder and a boules-obsessed English country vicar. In the cosmopolitan city of Toulouse, a city of contrasts we find amongst the hubbub a real Irish bar and suffer once again at the hands of the kleptomaniac. There is solace on the Canal Garonne and an expensive and nearly disastrous repair job at Castets en Dorthe. Pretty towns come and go as we pass through the peaceful settlements of the Garonne - Moissac, Meilhan and Mas d'Agenais with its secret treasure. There are more characters, some good and some not so - a gift from the skipper of a hotel barge for being 'nice', a careless French mechanic who drives his van into my car, and Serge, a wonderfully helpful and proficient repairer of all things boat. We retrace steps back to the Rhone, crossing the large inland sea, the Étang de Thau, and are held up by more breakdowns resulting in parts having to be sent from England, and our guests bravely enduring 100° heat for hours on end to sort out problems with, of all things, overheating!

We finally return to the lovely welcoming port of Moissac where we find a permanent year- round mooring, something that we have never had before in the 20 years we have owned Saul Trader.

All the books are available in digital or printed form from:
www.keithharrisauthor.com

Genuine Reviews

This is a joy to read and given the cliff edge ending I can't wait for volume three. Compulsive reading for those minded to venture to European waterways......Gareth

Bloomin' good read ..... Poshratz

Great chuckle - can't wait for the next book ..... could not put it down, read in one weekend laughed all the way through......
Barry

Loved reading and enjoyed it greatly. Quite informative. Look forward to your next book.
M Railey

The author gives us a wonderful travelogue, complete with background information, humorous anecdotes, and the occasional self-induced near-disaster. His viewpoint of a Brit on the mainland is very entertaining to those of us on the west side of the Atlantic.
W.D Silvestri

Keith Harris is a funny man who knows how to use his words, and his sense of humour is something to experience. Reading this book really gave me a good laugh."
Online Book Club Review

Interesting and often humourous reading ......
Self-effacing, inclined to humour and ready to pen an opinion on any subject
Ian Macauley , Editor DBA Magazine. 'Blue Flag'.

Love your books Keith. Essential reading for anyone taking a real boat through the Kennet & Avon - very interesting.
Harry New, nb Warwick, fender maker, musician, singer songwriter par excellence and vintage car restorer .

You have a unique writing style. Loving the stories. When I read the bit about the busybody at Pangbourne I nearly spat out my Chardonnais!

Allen Maslen - Author, wit and raconteur, singer-songwriter, guitarist and during dinner speaker who co-founded the iconic folk rock band Meet on the Ledge.

'Very entertaining, great chuckle, can't wait for the next book'.......... B Withers

.... and maybe not !

'This chap hasn't a clue about barging. He doesn't crash into another boat in the entire book'...... T. West

'The best barge book I have ever read'.... ....Marjorie Tingwall, "Algebra for Beginners"

'Definitely not for the faint-hearted' ....A. Schwarzenegger

'Humourous ! That's a laugh' ....Anon

'I wish my dear husband had read this book years ago'..............P.Scales (Mrs)

'You couldn't make it up'....................Lars Björk, Technical Director, Ikea

THE END- or is it?

Printed in Great Britain
by Amazon

27240599R00152